T0173196

DAVID STEVENS
KIERON O'HARA

The Devil's Long Tail

*Religious and Other Radicals
in the Internet Marketplace*

HURST & COMPANY, LONDON

First published in the United Kingdom in 2015 by
C. Hurst & Co. (Publishers) Ltd.,
41 Great Russell Street, London, WC1B 3PL
© David Stevens and Kieron O'Hara, 2015
All rights reserved.
Printed in India

A Cataloguing-in-Publication data record for this book is available from the British Library.

ISBN: 978-1849043434

www.hurstpublishers.com

DS: For my father, Eric Stevens, whose fascination with both religion and technology, and his liberal outlook, sowed the seeds for my ideas in this book a long time ago. I hope he would approve of the end result.

CONTENTS

ACKNOWLEDGEMENTS

During part of the writing of this book, Kieron O'Hara was supported by the project SOCIAM: The Theory and Practice of Social Machines. SOCIAM is funded by the UK Engineering and Physical Sciences Research Council (EPSRC) under grant number EP/J017728/1.

Parts of this work have been adapted from existing publications: Kieron O'Hara and David Stevens, 'The Devil's Long Tail: Religious Moderation and Extremism on the Web', *IEEE Intelligent Systems*, 24, 6 (2009), pp. 37–43; David Stevens, '*In Extremis*: A Self-Defeating Element in the "Preventing Violent Extremism" Strategy', *Political Quarterly*, 80, 4 (2009), pp. 517–25; David Stevens, 'Reasons to be Fearful, One, Two, Three: The "Preventing Violent Extremism" Agenda', *British Journal of Politics and International Relations*, 13, 2 (2011), pp. 165–88; Kieron O'Hara, Noshir S. Contractor, Wendy Hall, James A. Hendler and Nigel Shadbolt, 'Web Science: Understanding the Emergence of Macro-Level Features on the World Wide Web', *Foundations and Trends in Web Science*, 4, 2/3 (2013), pp. 103–267.

Figure 3 in Chapter Eight is available from Wikimedia Commons (http://en.wikipedia.org/wiki/File:Long_tail.svg), and was created by Hay Kranen (http://www.haykranen.nl/).

The authors would also like to thank the anonymous reviewers of an earlier draft of this book for several perceptive and helpful suggestions for improvement. The authors take full responsibility for any further errors or omissions.

INTRODUCTION

On 31 October 1517 Martin Luther nailed his *Ninety-Five Theses* to the church door in Wittenberg, thereby setting in motion a series of events that culminated in the Protestant Reformation and changed the face of Christianity forever. The story of Luther nailing his *Theses* protesting the sale of papal indulgences to the door is in fact historically dubious—he was something of a stickler for the rules and was thus unlikely to be involved in defacing church property. Yet whatever the exact account of this event, what is certain is that Luther's challenge to Catholic doctrine gained the momentum necessary to cause a schism in the Church, in large part because of his exploitation of the newly founded technology of the Gutenberg printing press. For the first time in history, books could now be produced en masse in order to provide widespread access to information. Without the creation of the press it is unlikely the flames kindled in Wittenberg would have taken hold at all, let alone that they would have spread across the entire continent of Europe, engulfing entire populations in religious fervour and often bloody doctrinal conflict in their wake.[1]

Today, another technology is being written about as the modern version of the printing press,[2] which raises the question as to whether the religious conflict of the sixteenth and seventeenth century will be repeated as 'dangerous' messages are spread throughout the world. The evidence, much of which will be reviewed in this book, clearly indicates that the Internet has a massive potential for reshaping religious views and interactions.

1

This book is concerned with the links or relationships between religious radicalism, violent extremism and the Internet. This relationship, or its absence, poses two distinct challenges:

1. How should we understand the relationship between religious radicalism and violent extremism, if one exists, and how (if at all) one spills over into the other?
2. What functional role does the Internet play in altering the religious environment, particularly in terms of promoting radicalism and fomenting violent extremism?

These challenges are closely intertwined. The power of the Internet and its most important application, the Web, may be sufficient to alter religious views fundamentally, to influence believers, and to fan religious zeal or even violence. This raises questions about what, if anything, governments should do to control or limit such activity. There is no doubt that governments are doing a great deal in this area, as the astounding scale of Edward Snowden's revelations of the extent of government surveillance suggests.[3] It is therefore essential that the adequacy of these measures is evaluated, something which will require separating and disaggregating the two challenges and exploring their core features in some detail. Figure 1 sets out some of the questions the book seeks to address.

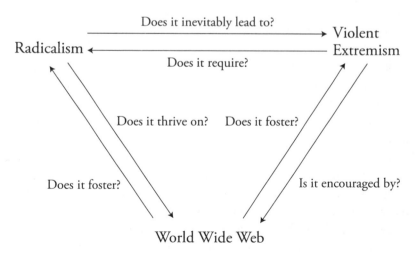

Figure 1: Questions about links between the Web and religious phenomena

INTRODUCTION

Our examination of online religious radicalism proceeds with the two challenges as its focus. We aim to develop a view and recommendations consistent with the liberal foundations of democratic society and the Internet and World Wide Web in order to frame the issues pertaining to violence in the cause of extremist philosophy. The book offers an explanation for why religious radicalism occurs. Unlike many accounts that see radical religious views as aberrations, we argue that radicalism is an inexorable aspect of any flourishing religious environment. Such an environment is itself a necessary feature of any properly functioning civil society with democratic institutions. In democratic societies the religious environment functions much like any other context in which individual choice reigns: some people will—for myriad reasons—prefer different shades of religious views. Sometimes these will be quite radical; outliers are inevitable. Yet their effects need not be negative, and when they are, it is important not to amplify them by overreaction. Our theoretical argument consequently has policy implications, and these will be discussed in the book's conclusion.

We will explain and adopt the 'club model' of religious affiliation, initiated by Adam Smith,[4] and developed by several modern academics since, especially Laurence Iannaccone and Eli Berman.[5] When the uses, affordances and benefits of the Internet are factored into the equation, the model has important explanatory power. The online world radically transforms or even removes many of the constraining features of the environment in which religious groups operate. The transaction costs that groups typically incur often disappear when they migrate online. This has wide-ranging implications for the number and longevity of radical groups.

There are two possible foci for theories of this nature—the group and the individual. This book looks at the issues from the individual's point of view. What benefits does an individual gain from being a member of a religious group? What costs do religious groups impose upon their members? What might tempt them into violence? What might lead individuals to renounce their membership? Given our focus on the individual, the book will also explore how a group's persistence and policies (together with external variables) are affected by different answers to these questions.[6]

The Internet may play a role in reducing the pressures on religious groups to change and reorient—to moderate—in order to gain adherents in the offline world. As Chris Anderson argues, in economic terms the Internet allows a longer tail of consumer demand to be met.[7] Niche interests for products that only a small number of people want, such as a rare book or a little-known film, which would not be catered for by the high street shop with its limited shelf space, can easily be provided for online. Supply can more easily meet demand. In religious terms, those espousing eccentric or unusual religious views can more easily find like-minded individuals and associate with them than in an environment requiring face-to-face interaction and geographical colocation.[8]

There is therefore a *prima facie* case that radical religious doctrines and groups have greater potential to flourish when using the new technologies, though there is no guarantee that they will do so. If true, the social and political consequences of this are manifold, and we will spend a considerable amount of time exploring them.

In particular, if it can be established that (a) the Internet and the Web foster or encourage radical religious groups to form and grow, and (b) that radical groups in this permissive environment are more likely to become violent, then there is clearly a case for policy intervention to disrupt the relationship between the Internet and religious groups. Such an intervention might include the industrial-scale surveillance that Snowden has revealed routinely takes place, or may go further and involve the regulation of the Internet or the Web itself, trying to slow down, manage and even censor the free flow of information.

Through the course of this book, we will work to undermine both propositions (a) and (b), neither of which is supported by the evidence. We argue that in many instances technological regulation or intervention is unfeasible. Even when it is feasible, direct government intervention within the religious environment for the purposes of attempting to limit or prevent radical views proliferating is highly inefficient in that it can provoke the radicalism it seeks to prevent, and it is also beyond the bounds of permissible state action because it violates the central tenets of political legitimacy. Despite much political sentiment to the contrary, we argue that religious radicalism is the wrong place to look for the causes of violent extremism and that contesting religious ideas will do little to prevent violent acts. More plausible drivers of extremism exist, and we will offer arguments about what these are and why they occur, and why attempting to remove or limit radical religious views is unlikely to have much effect. Better policies exist for preventing, deterring and catching violent extremists.

INTRODUCTION

Hence our nine recommendations in Chapter Ten do not include any proposals with regard to strong government intervention because the evidence shows that interventions are likely to be ineffective at best and counterproductive at worst. But the book is not a counsel of despair. Our argument is that a democratic civil society, and the new networked technologies to which many civil society functions have migrated, are sufficiently robust to deal with dangerous and antisocial tendencies, and more effective counters than top-down preventive policies.

Structure and argument

In order to address the two challenges outlined above, the argument of the book is presented in three parts.

Part I considers exactly how the association between the Web, radicalism and violent extremism has manifested itself in political discourse and policy. Chapter One sketches the background to online religion, provides some examples and introduces important concepts that are used throughout the book. Chapter Two assesses Cass Sunstein's argument with regard to online radicalism, which emphasises the Internet's role in confirming people in their radical views by isolating them from competing messages. The processes that might alienate people in the first place will also be looked at through the work of Sherry Turkle. Chapter Three reviews some real-world policies which have been implemented in order to undermine the assumed links between radicalism, extremism and technology.

In Part II the book explores the first challenge—how to understand the links between radicalism and violent extremism—by reviewing an important line of research in the politics and sociology of religion. Chapter Four examines the dynamics and roots of radicalism and considers some of the arguments from Part I in greater depth. Chapter Five takes another view of the creation or construction of radicalism, looking at ways in which religious extremists and governments of the major democracies have conspired to frame the terms of description for radicalism and extremism. Chapter Six takes a more fundamental look at the formation of preferences about religion and religious goods, and Chapter Seven goes on to consider violence and social disruption.

The final part of the book considers how best to pursue the twin, and not incompatible, goals of religious freedom and security in a liberal democracy. We will do this by addressing the second challenge of understanding the effect of the Internet and related communications technologies including the Web on religious radicalism. Accordingly, and building upon Part II's discussion of the relevance of markets to the spread of religious ideas, Chapter Eight considers the long-tail argument about how the Internet has affected markets in general, and applies the theory to the marketplace of ideas. Chapter Nine then evaluates the three main theses that have driven the arguments in this book: Chris Anderson's long-tails thesis, Cass Sunstein's echo-chambers thesis and Sherry Turkle's alienation thesis. To conclude, Chapter Ten looks at the legitimacy of large-scale targeted interventions by the authorities, and considers how the limits of intervention should dictate policy. It argues that freedom of religious belief and personal freedom from terrorist threats are not only compatible, but also essential to preserve liberal values, institutions and practices, which are ultimately the most powerful prophylaxis against radical views. We make nine recommendations based on the arguments in this book on how to restrict extremism, how not to restrict it, and how to preserve the Internet while doing so.

PART I

1

RELIGION AND THE INTERNET

SOME INITIAL CONCEPTS

Double-click on paradise

Religion has been an important driver of technology. Many religious organisations—often those that are small and growing—are enthusiastic, quick and inventive early adopters, especially of communications technologies. The examples are not limited to the early printing press which Luther exploited so successfully. From the use of the physical properties of churches and cathedrals (such as stained glass windows) to tell stories to illiterate peasants, to the nineteenth-century chapel cars (railway carriages decked out as mini-chapels) of the American West,[1] to the TV channels of the televangelists, new methods of spreading the word have been enthusiastically welcomed. Religion and technology are closely intertwined.

Digital networking technologies, especially via the World Wide Web, represent a new era—a leap forward—and religion has not been slow on the uptake. In the United Kingdom, the archbishop of Canterbury,[2] the chief rabbi[3] and the Catholic archbishop of Westminster[4] have their own Twitter feeds, although it is harder to find Islamic tweeting from well-known institutions.[5] Old and new co-exist. Pope Francis I (aka @Pontifex_ln) tweets in Latin,[6] while the Bible has been translated into

SMS texting language ('In da Bginnin God cre8d da heavens & da earth', it begins).[7] Not quite Luther's *Ninety-Five Theses*, admittedly, but an example of how moving online allows religions to modify their communications with new generations.

The benefits of the Internet increase exponentially when those with a common interest are small in number and are thinly distributed geographically. It allows the virtual gathering of people who would otherwise never interact, dramatically increasing the scope for collective action. Brasher describes the experience of Neo-pagan Julia, interested in 'revising old rituals and designing new ones for cyberspace', who discovered that although '[i]t was impossible to gather enough [Neo-pagans] together to do a proper ritual in some parts of the world … on the Web, a gathering was only a few keystrokes away'.[8]

The Web is of course a perfect medium for spreading messages. But because it has no centralised editing, it is disproportionately good, when compared to the mass media, at spreading messages which may appear bizarre, unfounded, conspiratorial or unscientific. In 2011, for instance, a Christian radio host called Harold Camping predicted that the end of the world (the Rapture) would begin on 21 May. The Web played an important role in disseminating the word—the search terms 'end of the world may 21st', 'may 21 doomsday', 'may 21 rapture' and 'harold camping' were all in the top ten Google trends on 19 May.[9]

These benefits are not of course limited to religious groups, as a plethora of examples, including the use of social networking sites for organising resistance against governments in Northern Africa and the Middle East, and the use of BlackBerry's messaging system to coordinate action by rioters in the UK, clearly show. For this reason, what is an opportunity for some is viewed with suspicion and concern by others. While Neo-pagans are unlikely to engage in a campaign of physical violence, the same cannot be said for all of those who shun mainstream religion. For those radicals who have become violent extremists, the Internet has a distinct charm.

Worryingly, the online world is a boon to extremists, whether religious or not. They can use the Web for: communication both internally and to the outside world—the Web has been an important medium for the dissemination of execution and beheading videos; data mining; networking; recruitment and mobilisation; disseminating instructions and online manuals; planning and coordination; fundraising and money-laundering; and engaging in disputes with rival extremists.[10]

The Internet not only has the benefit of allowing contact to be made across vast geographical distances—websites are also cheap to create and run as there is no need to maintain a physical building, and they are relatively anonymous in that there are no physical structures for the security services to spy on. The example of al-Qaeda is instructive in this regard. After its eviction from Afghanistan, al-Qaeda reconstituted itself to a large extent via the use of the Internet, in particular via one of its webmasters Younis Tsouli, or Irhabi007, a Moroccan student arrested in London in 2005.[11] The degrading of al-Qaeda's operational capabilities pushed it online, where it made a strategic move away from centrally coordinated attacks in favour of inspiring individuals (its online journal is called 'Inspire').[12] Its affiliates have embraced social networking;[13] Facebook pages have been created around particular conflicts, such as the Syrian uprising, and clerics such as Anwar al-Awlaki (who was killed by a drone strike in 2011) have become prominent via social media, microblogging and online video. Its media distribution arm al-Fajr Media seems to prefer the more regulated environment of approved online forums, but that has not stopped it and its affiliates from experimenting in other areas.[14]

Even those violent extremists considered 'lone wolves'—that is, without group affiliations or support networks for planning and perpetrating their actions—use the Internet to make online contacts that would have been impossible offline. Anders Behring Breivik, who murdered over ninety people in a killing spree in Norway in 2011, claims to have been in contact with right-wing groups via Facebook, Twitter and other social media sites.[15] The Finnish pupil Pekka-Eric Auvinen, who shot several members of his school[16] before killing himself in 2007, explained his philosophy of 'godlike atheism' and 'cynical existentialism' on YouTube, and was apparently in contact with another would-be killer from the United States via a MySpace site sympathetic to the schoolboy killers at Columbine High School.[17]

The Web has become a central part of terrorists' post-action media strategy; terrorism is of very little note without the publicity that creates public fear, distrust and perception of risk in the target culture. Islamic terrorists' beheadings of hostages are sometimes captured and disseminated on video.[18] Although we can only speculate as to who the real target of these videos are, the biggest demographic group among those who view such videos is in fact Americans who are under thirty-five years old.

As a percentage, the total number of views in the Middle East and North Africa is not particularly high.[19] This implies that their effect is to intimidate the target culture, even if this is not their intended function.

As well as direct control of posted videos, there has been at least one notable incident exploiting the public's tendency to record events as 'citizen journalists'. In 2013 two Nigerian Muslim converts stabbed a British soldier to death in broad daylight in the centre of London. They did not try to escape the scene, but instead 'performed' for the cameras and mobile phones of bystanders, delivering impromptu justifications and brandishing blood-stained weapons.[20] Shortly afterwards, a Muslim couple was jailed for posting offensive videos that glorified the murder.[21]

However, correlation is not the same as causation. It should already be clear that technology has complex effects on the practice of religion. In order to begin our enquiry we need to consider how to characterise the object of study (i.e. religion), and how to understand its dynamics; we will discuss this in the next section. As well as the object of study, we need to consider the field of play, and we will consequently introduce some basic ideas about the Internet in the second section. Finally, we will conclude our tour through the introductory concepts with a section considering the practice of online religion.

Thinking about religion

There is no slippery slope from radicalism to violence; indeed, the idea of a spectrum from moderation to radicalism to violence is hard to sustain.[22] Few who are radical in their religious views, or are experimenting with their philosophies, think for a second about violence or have any intentions of causing anyone physical or economic harm; the vast majority of even the most radical are peaceable. From the perspective of wider society, suspicion of religious radicalism, experimentation, of the 'loner', can quickly morph into a generalised fear. The religious utterances of violent people become part of the news story,[23] as does their use of the Internet—Auvinen, for instance, was posthumously rechristened the 'YouTube killer'.[24] Yet statistically the chances of someone with these interests being violent are vanishingly small. Conversely, why should someone with violent intent not exploit the available tools to his advantage, be they roads, mobile phones or the Internet? Even those who argue that religious moderation is an oxymoron, such as Sam Harris, agree that not every religious person is necessarily violent, if only because suppressants of violence are available outside the religious sphere: 'the only reason anyone is "moderate" in matters of faith these days is that he has assimilated some of the fruits of the last two thousand years of human thought (democratic politics, scientific advancement on every front, concern for human rights, an end to cultural and geographic isolation, etc.)'.[25]

What is (a) religion?

Druidism as discussed by Julius Caesar and Tacitus probably counts as a religion, at least according to most people's understanding of what a religion is. Although very little hard evidence about the Druids' exact beliefs and practices is known beyond the fragments that we can glean from Roman authors and medieval Irish legends, which may be inaccurate and are certainly unsympathetic, the broad outlines of what they believed and the rituals they undertook probably constitute a religious view. However, there are many modern individuals who claim to be Druids and assert continuity with the Iron Age Celtic originals. Arthur Uther Pendragon—né John Timothy Rothwell—is the self-declared reincarnation of the legendary King Arthur and holds the title king of the Druids in Britain. This position was given some legitimacy in English law when Pendragon successfully availed himself of the defence of publically carrying a bladed weapon, his ceremonial sword 'Excalibur', for religious reasons under Section 139 of the Criminal Justice Act (1988).[26] This clause was intended to exempt members of the Sikh community from the general prohibition of carrying bladed weapons because of the central role the traditional Kirpan plays in their religious/cultural identity, but had to be extended to Pendragon once the religious nature of his activities was conceded. Yet are people such as Pendragon religious in any proper sense of the term? Or are they charlatans, as many believe? There are powerful differences of intuitions in cases such as this.[27]

Some religions are invented deliberately for quite specific purposes. Robespierre created a secular religion to bind post-revolutionary French society together as prescribed by Rousseau. Caligula declared himself a god, and was no doubt worshipped by some until his assassination. In the 2001 England and Wales Census, people were allowed to self-report religion: as a result, 0.8 per cent of the country opted to call themselves Jedi Knights (characters from the *Star Wars* films), making the Jedi Order the fourth largest reported religion in the country.[28] By 2011, the Jedi Order in England and Wales had halved, overtaken by Buddhism and Judaism.

Meanwhile, some resolutely secular areas of existence have quasi-religious aspects; followers of football teams show some religious characteristics (intolerance of apostasy and heresy, extreme devotion, inherited devotion, reinterpretation of inconsistent phenomena to make them consistent with a wider narrative of persecution and success, disregard of reasoned humanistic argument). Recondite arguments about such things as computer programming languages or quantitative methods of analysis in the social sciences can become theological. In some parts of China there is a reverence for Mao Zedong, while even in the secular West the utterances of prophets such as Marx, Gramsci or Chomsky are pored over by devoted interpreters in university-cathedrals. Even atheism can be conceived in religious terms—as displaying a 'religious attitude' to the marvel of life and the universe, as claimed by leading political philosopher Ronald Dworkin.[29]

This is an important issue that goes beyond mere definitional stipulation. Many of the claims made in this book in the context of our argument about the religious and the groups they belong to might be thought to apply to many other groups or ways of life; that there is nothing special about religion per se. 'Football is my religion' is a sentiment representative of the importance of different conceptions of the good life to individuals, and many of the benefits of association may be conferred upon groups of football fans and groups of religious adherents alike.[30]

By 'religion' we mean something fairly specific: a religion must include a codified set of beliefs that rest on supernatural factors understood to be independent of the believer's will.[31] From this set of beliefs arises a moral code or set of precepts. The central position of the supernatural element is manifest in a belief in spiritual entities or beings such as a god, gods or other such agents with which adherents engage via various forms of transaction within the moral code. This view has been a staple of the sociology of religion since its earliest days. Sir J.G. Frazer argued that 'religion consists of two elements ... a belief in powers higher than man and an attempt to propitiate or please them'.[32] In a more modern idiom, religion is a set of 'very general explanations of existence, including the terms of exchange with a god or gods'.[33]

Yet these definitional elements miss one of the key points of a religion: the beliefs subtend a group. Moral psychologist Jonathan Haidt argues that 'religions are social facts. Religion cannot be studied in lone individuals any more than hivishness can be studied in lone bees.'[34] Emile Durkheim's definition yokes together the moral and the social. 'A religion is a unified system of beliefs and practices relative to sacred things, that is to say, things set apart and forbidden—beliefs and practices which unite unto one single moral community called a Church, all those who adhere to them.'[35]

This social aspect immediately raises questions about the group's internal dynamic and how it interacts with wider society. This cannot be predicted from the codified beliefs. For instance, it used to be thought that black Protestant churches would keep African Americans at an economic and social disadvantage because of their focus on 'otherworldly' concerns; however, at least since the civil rights movements, black churches are actually more likely to initiate or encourage political activities than other American churches.[36]

This Durkheimian social view is an important corrective to the 'new atheism' set out by such commentators as Richard Dawkins, Sam Harris and Daniel Dennett, which takes a psychological/logical/computational view of the aetiology of religious action.[37] On this account, a deluded individual holds a set of erroneous or even senseless beliefs about supernatural beings or forces from which they deduce how those beings would prefer or require them to act. The individual then carries out those actions. For example, a Muslim might believe that if he were martyred, seventy-two virgins would await him in heaven, which causes him to perform harmful actions such as suicide bombing. According to this view, these supernaturally inspired actions are unlikely to be beneficial to humankind in this life because the interests of the supernatural beings are unlikely to coincide with the interests of natural humans. The new atheists go further by arguing that because the beliefs about the supernatural are demonstrably false, they will almost always cause harmful actions because they do not take into account true descriptions of the world.

This view of religious action is unsustainable because it fails to square with actual religiously inspired behaviour, as will become clear in a number of discussions below (see, for instance, the discussion of suicide bombers in Chapter Seven). Yet the Durkheimian corrective, which sees religion as a this-worldly social phenomenon—even the 'sacred things' are defined only as things hidden from public view—still needs a metaphysical element (which gives religion a different perspective from political belief- and value-systems about the here and now). For instance, Nicholas Wade argues that 'religion is a system of emotionally binding beliefs and practices in which a society implicitly negotiates through prayer and sacrifice with supernatural agents, securing from them commands that compel members, through fear of divine punishment, to subordinate their interests to the common good'.[38] This similarly implies that the supernatural factors are independent of each believer, but via the notion of negotiation allows that a society or social group may be able to provide input into the canon, rather than merely being a passive recipient of the divine message (whether this comes from the priesthood, from holy books or via purported revelations). Wade's view suggests that a religion is suffused through an entire society as a cultural given, yet it could easily be adapted to cover a smaller coherent group within a wider society. It is with such small groups that this book is largely concerned.

This conception has the virtue of applying across both time and space, from historical period to historical period, and from society to society, regardless of how exotic the beliefs. The supernatural element is the central distinction between the religious and the secular. Thus while many systems of thought address moral, existential or metaphysical subjects, those that lack a supernatural element are not a 'religion' in the relevant sense.[39]

Religious organisations and messaging

A number of characteristics follow from this basic definition. First, interactions and exchanges with the supernatural are ordinarily moderated or mediated via a set of agents or institutions, such as clerics and churches. A religious organisation's primary purpose is to create, maintain and supply religious goods to a set of individuals and facilitate their interaction with a god or the gods. The organisation differs, therefore, from the body of believers over which it presides. This is often elided by the use of terms such as 'church' to refer both to the institutional and the congregational aspects of a given religion.

Second, most religious doctrines are both general and comprehensive.[40] A religious conception is general if it covers a wide range of moral subjects, such as individual ethics, relationships, politics and so forth, whereas it is comprehensive when it specifies what is of value in human life, including ideals of personal behaviour and conduct in our lives, within a codified or articulated system. Hence organisations provide a number of distinct religious messages to their adherents about the meaning of existence, salvation and moral community.[41] The message of meaning explains human existence and experience. Often this is an ordering of the physical world or an explanation of causes and events. The message of salvation addresses human emotions and affections, and provides a motivation for adherence by promising to save adherents from, for instance, 'diverse forms of danger and suffering, whether famine, illness, or drought, or feelings of guilt and impurity, loneliness, the anguish of death, tedium, daily routine, or uncertainty about the transience of time'.[42] The moral community provides a specific ordering or relationship between the authors, interpreters, officials and recipients of the religious message; god or gods, clerics and believers.

Third, the definition helps us understand some of the moral characteristics of religious people. As the new atheists argue, religion is an important cause of discrimination (especially racial or sexual discrimination), war, terrorism and genocide, although this is hardly a new insight. In Diderot's words:

Wherever one admits God, there is a cult; wherever there is a cult, the natural order of morals is overturned, morality corrupted. Sooner or later, the moment comes where the notion that hindered people from stealing an *écu* leads to a hundred thousand people having their throats slashed. Some compensation![43]

On the other hand, many ethical theorists, including John Locke, have countered that beliefs about supernatural beings are essential to underpin moral behaviour.

There is thus a debate about the relationship between religion and morality, yet surely both Diderot and Locke could be simultaneously correct. The disputes between Arabs and Israelis, Sunni and Shia, Catholic and Protestant in Northern Ireland, Muslims and Christians in Nigeria and Muslims and Animists in Sudan can no doubt be partially explained in racial or economic terms, but are surely extremely hard to understand without any reference to religion. With regard to domestic behaviour, studies show that religious people tend to be more generous with money, labour or time than non-religious people, especially when their altruism benefits members of their own moral communities.[44]

Those aspects of religion that enhance group selection are likely to improve the lot, all things being equal, of those within the religion, and occasionally to disadvantage those without. Micro-level religious behaviours have unpredictable and incongruous macro-level effects when they occur at scale.

Is religion special?

Although the defining feature of religion is the link with the supernatural, religious groups have structures and incentives that are partly determined by their messaging, and which therefore influence or impinge upon quotidian existence. In particular, the goods that religious belief provides are not limited solely to spiritual ones. Indeed, the non-spiritual rewards of membership in a religious group are considerable, and it is these which are the focus of our argument. Thus in addition to benefits associated with intercession with the deity or deities, social network benefits such as friendship, trust, solidarity, support, identity, healthcare, preferential treatment in employment and political voice are also major factors when considering the attraction of religions.

Such an observation in terms of this-worldly social benefits is likely to face an immediate challenge. Many non-religious groups, which make no supernatural claims, provide tangible and intangible social network benefits such as these. Youth gangs, sports clubs, civic associations and so forth all provide such benefits to a greater or lesser extent. Does this mean that religious groups, qua social networks, are nothing special?

This is not an intuitive view of religion. The religious sphere is usually viewed as in some sense special; as a place where different values, motives and standards apply when compared with the 'ordinary' spheres of daily life. Spiritual beliefs, piety—God, even—may not be thought accessible to the mundane explanations of social science, but rather to inhabit a realm beyond normal categories of analysis. This could not be further from the truth.

As a matter of observable fact, religious preferences are generally treated as qualitatively different from other types of preferences in our societies (they are noted in censuses, while the football teams people support are not), and they often provide grounds for exemptions or differential treatment in certain cases. For example, while Saturday examinations are often rescheduled for certain students due to their religious beliefs, exams are never rescheduled because Arsenal are playing at home. While this might have some deeper justification, our interest is in religious groups' social significance—i.e. their significance for those who design public policy—and the unique combination of spiritual/supernatural and secular/social benefits they provide.

Hence we will not explore precisely where the borderline lies between the sacred and the profane—if indeed there is one. Our concern is the interaction between religious groups and wider society, as mediated in particular by the Internet and the World Wide Web. In this sphere, smaller radical groups, particularly those which are perceived (perhaps erroneously) to be more likely to resort to violent interactions with the embedding society, can have a significant effect on public policy. The USA PATRIOT Act (2001), a piece of legislation that undermined many of the fundamental assumptions that had previously governed American political life, was prompted by a very small number of terrorist acts carried out by members of a group which is only partly religious, and which has an increasingly small number of adherents in the United States.[45] As noted above, the Web is a highly significant aggregator and communication medium for such groups, and its regulation and surveillance are now important policy tools for governments.

Furthermore, because religious groups are aggregations of people who share a common purpose or aim, whether supernatural or otherwise, they inherit the characteristics of such aggregations. Hence studies of social networks in general will also inform our analysis. Our aim is to learn about the effects religious groups have on society, public policy and the Web, not to separate out the effects they have because they are primarily religious from the effects they have because they are social groups.

Hence the challenge is not justified. To the extent that people join religious groups for the network benefits, our claims about religion will apply to these other groups, and we should expect to see similar patterns of behaviour across these different spheres. Indeed, we will draw on research and examples from them as we progress. This is not a failing of the view, but a strength. It is correct that religious groups share this property with other groups, and in that it is instructive to look at other manifestations of the same causal features, but there are important differences between religious groups and others too.

The club model

If we assume that people join religious groups for the network benefits, then that suggests different groups will provide different benefits, and that particular sought-after benefits may be offered by a range of groups. This means that religiously inclined individuals may find themselves with complex choices to make and preferences to trade off, and that groups may find themselves competing for adherents.

We employ a model of analysis and explanation that views the religious environment as relevantly similar to any other competitive environment. Religious groups are not unlike commercial firms competing for customers in a market, and, as such, are subject to all the usual constraints that competing actors face. The more constrained they are, the more innovative they are forced to become in their reinvention of the substance and presentation of religion.[46]

Often termed the 'club' model[47] because religious groups provide goods of a kind found in many other kinds of secondary associations, this explanation (which we will discuss in more detail in Chapter Six) provides a remarkable fit with the various activities, trends and phenomena displayed by religious groups of varying stripes. Moreover, it is a universal model that applies to major and minor religions generally, thus permitting explanations and predictions regardless of creed. We will illustrate our claims with examples drawn from the world's major religions and many of its minor ones. Radicalism and violent extremism are not the preserve of any religion, nor is utilisation of the Internet restricted in this way either. Our argument is premised on a view that is universal in terms of the way religious groups operate, regardless of the specific beliefs they espouse. Islamic, Christian, Jewish, Buddhist and other religious groups operate in sufficiently similar ways—and their adherents too—in order for what we have to say to apply across religious and doctrinal divides.

This is not to denigrate or demean religious belief or the holy. Nothing could be further from our intentions. It is simply to recognise that the people involved in religious activities do not stop being people when they enter their places of worship; they continue to act like people (for example, few religious people indulge in 'the extended reflection on the transcendent that religion requires'[48] to the exclusion of other activities). Furthermore, in their exploration of behaviour (good neighbourliness) that might have religious roots and indeed is found more prominently in religious people, Putnam and Campbell discovered no correlation between any theological belief or statement and good behaviour when they controlled for church attendance.[49] They conclude that 'it is tempting to think that religious people are better neighbors because of their fear of God or their hope of salvation or their reading of the Good Word, but we find no evidence for these conjectures'.[50]

In another example from the work of Putnam and Campbell, the greater intolerance that is found among American churchgoers as compared to secular Americans has little correlation with moral absolutism or a Manichaean moral outlook, but rather seems most strongly correlated with respect for religious authority and obedience.[51] Meanwhile, Hugh Roberts of the International Crisis Group finds that understanding jihadi groups in North Africa is aided by a focus on local, contextual and historical variables, while ideology provides a circular explanation of violence at best.[52] The most significant virtue of the club model is its explanatory power across those divides that are often considered the most basic divisions in human history.

It is important to bear in mind that the fact that religious people's behaviour can be explained by this-worldly considerations does not automatically relegate the spiritual to the status of an epiphenomenon. C.S. Lewis argued that 'because we love something else more than this world we love even this world better than those who know no other'.[53] Michael Oakeshott, who certainly valued religion as a way of understanding the world, wrote:

while religious faith may be recognized as a solace for misfortune and as a release from the fatality of wrong-doing, its central concern is with a less contingent dissonance in the human condition; namely, the hollowness, the futility of that condition, its character of being no more than 'un voyage au bout de la nuit.' What is sought in religious belief is not merely consolation for woe or deliverance from the burden of sin, but a reconciliation to nothingness.[54]

For Oakeshott this reconciliation obviously has a spiritual dimension, but the consolation may surely also be achieved through a social interaction and a powerful bond with fellow believers—in short, with the feeling of belonging and having a place in a world in which otherwise one was nothing. The importance of this-worldly fact, even the routine and apparently irrelevant aspects of existence, has been seen as an important means of 'getting at' or reconciling the believer to his or her minute role in God's existence (a means, for example, central to Montaigne's *Essays*).[55]

Those who focus on beliefs and texts, on prayer and ritual conceived as a means to achieve things in the world or shape the world in various ways, are themselves missing out on a vital aspect of religion—its ability to coordinate human behaviour and to weld human societies and groups together with 'honest signals'.[56] As William Irons writes:

the theory of religion as it applies to commitment emphasizes the vital importance of religion to most human communities and the fundamental [role] that religion plays in the lives of most human beings. The theory also suggests that the core of religion is not belief (which most scientists and intellectuals are prone to criticize), but rather, for the most part, commitment to socially constructive behavior.[57]

This is not to say that such a view captures the 'essence' of a religion or type of religious experience, but rather that this is a key variable for understanding how religion functions in society. The question from the point of view of social science or social policy is not whether religious claims are true, but whether they are adapted to the embedding society.[58]

It is all too easy for a scientist or a philosopher to make sceptical play with the tenets of a particular religion—which might seem utterly implausible to non-believers—but surely the key part of the explanation for a religion's survival and growth is not the truth or falsity of its metaphysics, but the ways in which its prayers and rituals tend to enable the group to retain coherence and to survive.[59] It is a way of fighting off what has been called social entropy—the tendency of cultures to lose their distinctive features when they collide peacefully with other cultures for the purpose of socialisation and trade.[60]

Thinking about the Internet and the Web

Religion is one of our subject matters; now we turn to the other—technology. The Internet is an extraordinary assemblage of software[61] and physical infrastructure,[62] and the Web that sits on top of it is perhaps the world's most complex piece of technology.[63] They have penetrated our lives, societies and economies (and, some have argued, our minds)[64] for what seems like forever but is in fact only a couple of decades or so at the time of writing. They have provided enormous benefits, but of course, like any tools, they are capable of misuse and of causing harm. Despite their apparent ubiquity, they are also capable of destruction, or of having their utility regulated away.

RELIGION AND THE INTERNET

The Internet is a network of computer networks. The key to its success is the general-purpose and universal nature of the links between them. Before the Internet, smaller computer networks could be and were supported by those with sufficient resources—often for military, academic, governmental or commercial applications—and those networks could be connected together. But those connections tended to be special purpose, hand-crafted and individually tailored for the anticipated transfer of specific items of information in a specific form. The often-unappreciated beauty of the Internet is that its protocols make few assumptions about the information that will be passed between networks, making it a uniquely general purpose tool. Information held in a wide variety of electronic representations, most unanticipated by the Internet's developers, can be passed around efficiently.

The software consists of a series of protocols that define how computers talk to each other. There are two levels of protocols. The first is the Internet Protocol (IP) itself. This is the heart of the Internet (a more accurate definition than the one given above is a network of computer networks linked using IP), and defines how a piece of information should be divided into information packets. Above that sits the Transmission Control Protocol (TCP), which defines the routing system to send the packets from start point to end point. In effect, TCP makes a virtual connection, via other computers in the network, between sender and receiver, even if they are not directly connected. It also treats each packet equally—although packets need to indicate their relationship within a message, and to specify their destination, the content of the message need not be read en route, and so the whole system treats the greatest works of philosophy and the least significant pieces of tittle-tattle with equal reverence and respect. This is a good thing from the network point of view because any method of information transfer which required knowing the content would slow the system down and create bottlenecks.

There are alternatives to TCP and IP, but these have been the most successful. The two protocols are often referred to together, as the TCP/IP suite.[65] TCP/IP provides a basic platform upon which further applications can be defined to use the Internet, exploiting the very clean method of transferring information across a network. The lack of information friction means that TCP/IP is an extremely versatile platform which can be used by a wide variety of applications. The World Wide Web is one of these.[66]

The Web is the main application that brings people to the Internet, so that recent users come to other applications, such as email, afterwards. Its essence is to link hypertext documents using the Internet. A browser is used to access material that may be in any one of a number of media—text, pictures, video, sound—and can then follow hyperlinks from document to document. Key technologies include the Hypertext Transfer Protocol (http, and its secure variant https), which tells computers how to access and retrieve hypertext pages, and the Hypertext Markup Language (HTML), which enables the structure of a document to be apparent online (e.g. in terms of headings, lists and so on), and enables it to be supplemented with other objects, such as embedded images, interactive forms or hyperlinks. There are other protocols, languages and technical requirements (in particular, more flexible markup languages such as XML), but http and HTML are the basics.

The Web sits on top of the TCP/IP suite of protocols, facilitated by the latter's neutrality and careful design; if TCP/IP were less elegant in terms of making more assumptions about the information it could be used to transfer, then it would not be so straightforward to design something to sit on top of the platform. And, similarly, the Web is designed to be as neutral as possible about applications that sit on top of it. The end result is the huge hypermedia/multimedia space that is the Web, which in effect allows individuals to treat every webpage as a file on their own computer.

Its decentralised linking structure is essential for it to scale up. If a communication system links n people, then it may have to facilitate a number of links of the order of n^2. As the system grows, then the number of links grows at a much faster rate, so if there are $10n$ people, there will be of the order of $100n^2$ potential links, and so on. If the system is engineered so that, for example, there is centralised scrutiny of communications (e.g. if every website had to be passed by a censor), then the centralisation, which might work very effectively with n members, would create a bottleneck when the number of members is an order of magnitude higher, as the number of potential links would be several orders of magnitude greater. The beauty of the Web is that the main communicational and navigational tool—the hyperlink—is inserted by a page author without the need to consult anyone else. Anyone can link to anything. The result is that the size and, crucially, the complexity of the network can increase without imposing any impossible costs on anyone; no one needs to keep an index or a map of the Web,[67] and so its complexity has no serious fundamental upper bound. This is important, as the complexity of the link structure is a rich source of information.

As well as this radical decentralisation, the packets of data that pass through the wires are all treated equally, with little or no discrimination between them. This is why they function so smoothly, and why, for example, many scientists and engineers[68] join political idealists[69] to argue that so-called net neutrality is an essential principle. It may be that some deviations from core neutrality are essential, for example to provide a given standard of quality of service[70] (e.g. for voice communications it is essential not only that each packet of information is received, but that the packets come in at a steady rate and in the right order), but major centralised editing and over-regulation will slow them down to an intolerable degree. It will also threaten the Balkanisation of the Internet or Web, by splitting them into disconnected chunks as different jurisdictions impose different standards. Yet if a particular type of behaviour or attitude is seen by policy-makers as depending on the Internet or the Web for its existence, then a view may develop that the technology needs to be adjusted to prevent that behaviour from occurring.

We can see this sort of push, for example, in the regular attempts the International Telecommunication Union (the ITU, a regulatory body run by the United Nations) has made to take over management of the Internet from the loose coalition of engineering-driven US bodies which have responsibility for the technology. The ITU has been used for some time now as a Trojan Horse for states which want either to (a) track Internet usage more closely, (b) tax Internet usage or allow large firms to discriminate between particular uses, (c) censor content, to insert damaging chokepoints into the infrastructure, or (d) express a visceral anti-Americanism.[71] It is unlikely that a bureaucratic body like the ITU could administer a lightweight, open system like the Internet. Although the wider issue of net neutrality is beyond the scope of this book, we do have an interest in the function of the Internet and the threats that surveillance, monitoring and censorship pose to its open spirit.

Properties of the Web

This architecture means that the Web has certain important properties, which need to be invariant across all Web experience. If they were subverted, then the Web would lose its uniqueness and universality and it would ultimately connect far fewer people.

These desirable properties include:

- Decentralisation. As a webpage author, you can link to any other page, resource or repository of data that has been published online, and indeed the creator of any other Web resource can link to you. There is no central hub to monitor linking, which helps efficiency, and also promotes the freedom to cite or reproduce the content of whomsoever you feel significant. Similarly, as it is a decentralised network with no hierarchical information structure, information can be taken direct from the appropriate source. The lack of a hierarchy rules out direct and pervasive censorship.

- Anonymity. A user of the Web does not need to 'sign in' to establish an identity before he or she can read or write material. Individual applications or sites might demand that the user shows some credentials, whether to prove that she or he has paid a subscription, that she or he is the owner of the resources within the site (e.g. a banking site), that she or he can pay for resources they are receiving access to, or merely that they have not been excluded for trolling. The level of identity security will of course vary across all these sites, and the user is not obliged to present a single identity across all the applications.

- Open standards. The growth of the Web can be attributed to the fact that several heterogeneous representation formats, languages and file types can peacefully coexist on it. This is because it is defined by standards for the formalisms that make it up, using open standards that can be accessed, for free, by anyone. The Web is not a restricted piece of intellectual property. Someone writing an application can easily connect it to the Web using these openly available standards. No one has to write in a particular computer language, or to pay a licence fee, dramatically reducing the barriers to entry.

- Living texts. HTML is designed to allow texts to be commented on, added to, included in other texts, referred to and linked to. Digital technology keeps texts alive and open in a way that paper does not. Think, for instance, of the comments that follow an article in an online newspaper, compared to the closure in the paper version. On paper, commenting would follow in subsequent editions, perhaps on the letters page, and the newspaper would retain editorial control.

- Non-linearity. Web texts can exploit the hypertextual aspects of the Web and adopt a non-linear structure, allowing the reader to navigate through a site as they interest him or her. So, for instance, a highly allusive text such as Eliot's *The Waste Land* can be rendered in such a way that one can follow the allusions around the Web, or through the poem.[72]
- Serendipitous reuse. Because linking is democratic, material can end up being reused serendipitously in contexts undreamt of by the author. In the paper era, the value of knowledge was created by scarcity—the methods for allowing the collection of rents on intellectual property, such as copyright or patents, meant that knowledge was valuable by virtue of the restrictions placed on it. A user would have to pay (buy a book, or pay royalties or licence fees) to receive it. In the digital age, knowledge adds value through abundance—knowledge of little intrinsic value in an isolated context can have value added to it because it can easily be placed in a new context. So, for example, the diary of someone from the seventeenth century might be, in isolation, of interest mainly to the specialist historian. But in the context of a large number of such documents, it could be of great value for a range of social historians, philosophers and scientists—for instance, meteorologists could gain useful evidence about weather patterns.[73]

Principles underlying the Web

These invariants have meant that the Web is a system governed, explicitly or implicitly, on a series of principles or norms.

- Liberalism. The Web is a space engineered on liberal principles, where freedom of speech is a privileged value. This works on two levels. It is a liberal space, where interactions are understood as a free conversation in the liberal mode. But its success as a piece of engineering, able to scale in terms of both users and information, also depends on a liberal attitude to all the information packets moving around it.
- Freedom of entry. The Web is not an exclusive space. No one is forbidden access,[74] and no one has to prove who he is.
- Conversation and dialogue. The Web is intended to promote free, uninhibited self-expression, dialogue and compromise where possible.
- The free flow of information. Issues such as intellectual property and copyright intrude, but basically the more information flowing around the Web, the better.

- Adding value through abundance and reuse. If the Web had a single purpose, it would be to add value to information through its serendipitous reuse in novel situations.
- Promotion of science and human progress. In all this, the Web embodies the Enlightenment principle that society can progress, and does so through the development of intellectual capacities, among other things.[75] A Web which promoted pseudo-science, conspiracy theories and pornography while failing to serve science would be seen as a failure.
- A platform upon which undreamt of applications can be built. As with TCP/IP, the Web is intended to be a clean technological platform, making as few assumptions as possible about how it will be developed, upon which new applications can be built even though they are as yet unplanned. In this way, new technologies can appear on the Web almost overnight, because once they are developed and made available, nothing impedes the rapid development of a user base. Examples of some of the technologies which have grown up on top of the Web include: social networking sites such as Facebook; the Semantic Web; Web services; Web 2.0 and social software; peer-to-peer systems; software agents; pervasive or ubiquitous computing; the mobile Web; grid computing; personalised computing services; e-commerce systems; revolutionary search engines such as Google; and massive multiplayer online role-playing games. All of these have high numbers of users, and none of them could work if it were not for the clean infrastructure they rest on.

Many of these principles, though commonly accepted in the West and Western-style democracies, are not universally accepted across the globe. Nevertheless, they are so deeply entangled with the infrastructure and engineering of the Web that it would be next to impossible to unpick them while preserving the Web's role as an effective global information management system.

We take it as an important premise for our enquiry that whatever policies are formulated to address the threat of violent extremism as promulgated by the Web, its invariants need to be preserved and its underlying principles protected.

Security, encryption and surveillance

But this is not a priority for many authorities. As a social and political matter, it is not immediately obvious that the policy response revealed by Edward Snowden in 2013, of massive surveillance by the US National Security Agency (NSA), the UK General Communications Headquarters (GCHQ) and others, is consistent with enlightened, liberal democratic principles, yet this debate is beyond the scope of our book. Within scope, it behoves us to look at how the security agencies have exploited another property of the Internet—that it leaves traces of its use.

The Internet has become a key communications technology in many areas of life, including those where privacy and security are important considerations. It is used to transfer money between banks and bank accounts, store medical records and carry confidential messages. In order for users to have confidence in the system, a key technology is encryption—the encoding of electronic data in such a way as to prevent it being understood by unauthorised people.[76] Powerful computers can create codes that are very hard to crack. Encryption brings privacy, confidentiality and security to the Web, but like all tools of concealment it also defines a space in which antisocial, criminal and violent activities can take place or be planned. As such, they have come to the attention of the authorities.

The United States has long classified cryptography as a weapon, and demanded that tools exported from companies in Silicon Valley be weakened to give American intelligence agencies easier access to foreign communications. For a long time, many people in the security industry suspected, without proof, that a great deal of software included so-called 'backdoors', or secret methods for decoding encrypted data, despite the NSA having lost a legal battle in the 1990s to make the presence of US-designed backdoors compulsory for all encryption software. Snowden's revelations show that the NSA has worked hard since then to insert backdoors into encryption systems clandestinely.[77] The United States has suspicions that China may be trying to do similar things—Huawei, the world's second-largest network technology supplier, whose roots are in the People's Liberation Army, has fallen under political pressure as it tries to export its technology to America.[78] A backdoor in a piece of hardware, a military chip, was discovered by researchers at Cambridge—the problem was that the chip was designed by a US firm,

Actel, but manufactured in China, thereby making it hard to determine responsibility.[79] However, what matters is that someone is trying to subvert digital systems.

There is also some evidence that the United States has been trying to influence international standards (a much more far-reaching and insidious measure). Cryptography depends on the generation of random numbers, but the NSA, which sits on standards-setting bodies, has supported relatively slow (and therefore less effective) random number generators. It promotes a particular type of mathematics based on elliptic curves, rather than the usual method of finding prime factors of large numbers, to support cryptography—this is respectable mathematics, but it has led to suspicions that it has some insights into how to undo the resulting encryption functions.[80] All these worries have been given powerful support by Snowden's leaks.

For the purposes of this book, it is not necessary to evaluate the likelihood of the NSA or the Chinese government deliberately and secretly inserting vulnerabilities into parts of the Internet.[81] The point is that agencies of each government have previously argued that these vulnerabilities are essential to their policing missions,[82] and so the policy option is already on the table. Of course, intelligence agencies will quite naturally and, to the extent that they are legitimate agents, quite properly expend energy on uncovering messages from foreigners, suspected criminals and so on. It would be naïve in the extreme to think otherwise.

However, there are two reasons why any policy solution that goes so far should be resisted. The first is that the success of the Internet stems largely from the success of Silicon Valley companies and the US-led governance bodies of the Internet and Web in creating the standards, software and hardware that have created what we rightly think of as a technological miracle. Chinese companies are also becoming increasingly important in developing low-cost hardware which will be important as the Internet continues to grow, particularly as an entertainment medium. Undermining trust in their own companies—which governmental actions have done—will not only hurt those companies, but more importantly will hobble the smooth development of the Internet. The second reason is more obvious: inserting vulnerabilities will weaken security in the Internet. Vulnerabilities exploitable by one government will ultimately be exploitable by others, or by criminals, if news of their existence leaks or the backdoors are discovered.

RELIGION AND THE INTERNET

The Internet's social aspect; online markets

The Internet and the Web are important pieces of technology—but more than that they connect people. They are not used by people, in the way that, say, a revolver or a television set are used. They are co-created by the people who use them. A new link from one website to another alters the Web's structure, and is created by a person for a human purpose. Even performing a Web search changes the Web by producing a new webpage with immediate links to the target pages, such that the distances between the target pages, in terms of clicks, are suddenly altered.

One of the most important uses of the Web is e-commerce, using it as a medium to buy and sell goods and services, which has transformed trade. A free market online has a number of desirable properties when compared with a physically situated one because the cost of seeking information is drastically reduced. Searching for goods, finding the lowest prices and matching a wide range of buyers and sellers are all relatively cheaper online. One need not shoulder the costs of looking from shop to shop (either physically walking to examine goods, or using another important communication technology, the telephone, which if not expensive in shoe leather still consumes time) for the goods one wants. One is not restricted to the buyers and sellers who happen to live or work in the immediate vicinity; one has access to anyone across the world. Put another way, the Web amalgamates markets which would be fragmented if they required co-location in physical space. Finally, financial transactions can happen at the speed of light, with automatic transfers of resources from one bank account to another. Offline, the analogous transaction costs can be quite significant.

Moving to e-commerce increases both supply and demand, resulting in more goods sold for lower prices and higher profits. This is not to say that every firm or consumer benefits—the Web is disruptive of business models that thrive on scarcity, and many companies have gone bankrupt and whole industries, such as print media and the music industry, have had to adapt. But the global effects are widely beneficial.

In short, the Web removes much if not all information asymmetry. Economic theories of markets, which claim to show that they are in some sense optimal allocation mechanisms for resources, are usually premised on an ideal called 'perfect competition', defined by a number of characteristics including the following.[83]

- There are infinite numbers of buyers and sellers.
- All relevant information is available to everyone.
- Entry and exit from the market are costless.
- Transactions are costless.

Each of these axioms is affected by the move online. The first axiom naturally remains false; there are not and never will be infinitely many people in the world, but as the Internet allows markets to be globalised, the number of buyers and sellers brought together increases dramatically. Geography is no longer a limiting factor. Furthermore, the Web allows the human buyers and sellers to be supplemented by artificial agents ('shopbots' as they are called), already widely used and theorised.[84] Hence numbers of market participants (human and artificial) are not limited to the number of people in the world.

The second axiom is specifically about information. Again, it is unrealistic to expect all information to be available, but search engines enable buyers and sellers to find each other much more quickly and effectively. A buyer can search for as many sellers for the good they are interested in, worldwide, until diminishing returns set in. Furthermore, price comparison sites can leverage economies of scale by doing the search once for many clients, and such is their influence that they can often affect markets by promoting discounts.

The third and fourth axioms concern transaction costs. Again, these are never zero, but the specific costs of retailing are drastically reduced online. Transactions are virtually costless, apart from the fixed cost of the Internet connection. In the case of information goods such as software or music downloads, the costs of delivery are also minuscule. Purpose-designed markets such as eBay or Alibaba have revolutionised small-scale commerce in this way. This has increased trust across markets by reducing the transaction costs specifically associated with enforcing payments and deliveries.

E-commerce therefore brings competitive bidding markets closer to the asymptote of perfect competition, and hence closer to the allocative and productive efficiency that economic theories predict. This result can also be expected to affect the marketplace of religious ideas.

The Internet's social aspect; social machines

Trust has featured strongly in the last two subsections, and this is key to the Internet and the Web being used. Their value comes from the size of the network of people they connect—the accuracy of many apparently routine functions, taken for granted by most of us, depends on crunching lots of data about the previous use of the Web. Google searches and Amazon recommendations take into account what people have searched for in the past. More searches and purchases improve future performance.

It goes without saying that the use of the Web depends on users trusting that any data they volunteer, or that is created about their visit, will not be misused. A person searching for information about a disease, or a mental state, or about sexuality is likely to want their interests kept private. When GCHQ intercepted still images from 1.8 million Yahoo! webcam users using a program called Optic Nerve in 2008–12 it was experimenting with automatic face-recognition methods (so not, strictly speaking, spying on the webcammers). It only grabbed one screenshot every five minutes, in order to protect the webcammers' human rights. Furthermore, it worried about protecting the extremely large number (between 3 and 11 per cent of the total) of sexually explicit images from prying eyes.[85] So GCHQ was arguably operating within the law, and seems, according to the documents released, to have been properly mindful of privacy and human rights concerns.

However, it is unlikely that anyone caught in the act of using a webcam, even if they were not doing anything sexually compromising, will be overjoyed about the prospect. Trust in the Web is eroding. The result could be problematic in three ways. First, people may use the technology less. At the time of writing, this does not seem to be happening, but there may come a tipping point. This is important for governments, which have seen e-government as a means of reducing the costs of bureaucracy by putting services and information-gathering exercises online. This is only possible because so many people use the Internet; drive people away, and the costs of government will begin to rise once more. Secondly, and perhaps more likely, it may be that legislators hinder the free flow of information by imposing stronger data protection on Internet traffic. Thirdly, people may turn inward, to their own groups, trusting only those people they know offline and being very careful about what they do online.

This last point matters. Of course, people tend to work or socialise online with more or less the same people they know offline, but one of the great qualities of the Web is the fact that people can get to know others virtually. The massive Internet dating industry, for example, is based on that possibility, and several types of game (e.g. World of Warcraft, or online poker) depend on it too. These are major industries which provide innocent or not-so-innocent pleasure for millions. Various more serious projects are made possible by social interaction with strangers, particularly networked thinking[86] and crowdsourcing information (we discuss crowdsourcing in more detail in Chapter Nine). Mechanical Turk[87] is a marketplace to crowdsource workers to perform small tasks that computers cannot do. Galaxy Zoo[88] is an online citizen science project that recruits non-experts to help classify galaxies, which has resulted in many published astronomy papers.[89] Ushahidi[90] is a platform that has allowed the crowdsourcing of interactive maps and visualisations of complex situations, for example the pattern of violence after the disputed Kenyan election in 2007.[91]

Such networked problem-solving has been theorised as a type of machine, as described by Tim Berners-Lee. 'Real life is and must be full of all kinds of social constraint—the very processes from which society arises. Computers can help if we use them to create abstract *social machines* on the Web: processes in which people do the creative work and the machine does the administration.'[92] The concept of social machines holds out the prospect of people using their networks and network technologies to solve their own problems, leveraging their own expertise and local knowledge, without having to commission or submit to top-down solutions.

Yet for them to do this, they need to trust the systems with which they are interacting. If ordinary people do not, then the social machine concept will only benefit tight, inward-looking groups where trust is at a premium and which are very hard to infiltrate. Such groups are much more likely to live at odds with the wider community and may include the very religious extremists that worry the authorities. Such groups are likely to invest more time and resource into discovering technologies to subvert their surveillance, including technologies such as Tor, which conceals a user's Internet activity, and Bitcoin, a hard-to-trace online currency. It may be that by monitoring and disrupting the soft ties that harmless users create online, the surveillance programmes of the authorities actually leave the benefits of the Internet for radicals and extremists. We discuss trust in more detail in Chapter Four. The worry which we will explore in this book is that groups who feel isolated from their geographical communities will make extremely effective social machines once they have the technological capability, especially if policy turns them in on themselves.

Our conclusion from this brief discussion of the Internet is that there are policy options that could disrupt it, and which could only have a serious effect on violent extremists' use of the Internet by undermining its many positive uses. We have listed some of the Web's invariant properties, and some of its underlying principles. It is our contention that these need to be preserved unless religious or political violence becomes genuinely intolerable. In the unlikely event of this threshold being reached, a decision to degrade the Internet's or the Web's capabilities should not be made in secret.

Religion and the Internet

Having discussed religion and the Internet in separate sections, our final introductory task is to think about how religion manifests itself online, and put the challenges presented in the Introduction in context, in light of what we have learned.

What does a religious website look like?

Online religion can assume a large number of different forms. Many Christian churches have a coordinating website aimed specifically at their congregations. The Church of St Michael and All Angels near South Shields, England, for example, uses http://www.stmichaelschurch.info/[93] to publicise its services and events, to invite requests for baptisms and weddings, and to provide a history of the church and its parish; http://www.cirenparish.co.uk/ represents a parish in the English town of Cirencester with three churches, and performs similar functions for the congregation, together with extra information for tourists.

Somewhat more hi-tech is the site of Hillvue Heights Church, Bowling Green, Kentucky (http://www.hillvue.com/index.html). As well as links to pages about its history, beliefs and so on, it also has its own Internet TV channel (http://www.hillvue.com/tv/tv-index.html), with a downloadable archive of videoed sermons and music. It is concerned with the religious experience of the site visitor rather than the supply of factual information—it is very hard to find any reference to its denomination (Baptist) on the site.

The Green Lane Mosque in Birmingham, England, was accused of extremism in the mid-2000s, although it also came second in a 'model mosque' competition.[94] Its website (http://www.greenlanemasjid.org/), which has since been redeveloped, provides links to online TV and radio channels, timetables for prayers and mosque activities, and a page to donate online.

Not all sites are focused on a physical location; there are online religious experiences that take place in cyberspace. There is a Facebook church (https://www.facebook.com/the.fb.church), whose *raison d'être* is 'Church is not a building, your clothes, the music … It's the people gathered in HIS name!' This is not to be confused with the Church of Facebook (http://churchoffacebook.com/), which is a blog run by a Christian promoting a book of the same name which describes the Higher Power behind social networks. There is also a Facebook Cyberspace Ashram (http://www.facebook.com/cyberspace.ashram?sk=info), where visitors can 'Learn to apply Solutions of Love for all Situations of Life. Here you find the complete Initiation to the holy science of Kriya Yoga and God Yoga online.'

Shrines there are aplenty,[95] such as that to St Anthony (http://www.stanthony.org/), which, although it pertains to an actual shrine in Cincinnati, allows the worshipper to post requests for prayers. The prayers themselves are presumably similar to offline offerings reflecting people's myriad desires and fears both sacred and profane—some selfish, some odd, many moving. On a day chosen at random in June 2011, prayers posted included (all typos, grammatical innovations and abbreviations in the originals):

Please pray for me & my Husband to get a visa for Australia & to Help us to Process our Documents, guide us and protect us in all our Problems, Bless us and all our family members. Thanks

[X] fell in the canal about a month ago and the doctors are giving up on him but with the power of prayer he is off the breathing machines and has opened his eyes so please help our family and pray for a full recovery. Thank you

please pray that my husband will stop drinking and we will become closer as a family.

Please let [Y] have a good day at work.please let his pay heck be good and me get 300 dollars and no problem to cash it. Let me sell motorhome this week.

Dear St. Anthony, I pray that you would finally unite [Z] and me in heart, mind and sould for the unity of our family. I pray that you would also protect

[Z] and our family from all temptations and evil attacks, keep us strong and healthy. Keep us safe and continue to shower and bless our family with abundance and work. Bind us St. Anthony forever and ever.

He's awaiting his MRI results and his family are praying it isn't a tumor causing his headaches. He's just a child.

In thanksgiving for having been selected for a promotion; please pray that I may be exonerated from my pending investigation.

There were over 400 prayer requests sent in on that single day, many from other states in the United States besides Ohio, and several from South Asia. Via the site, visitors can also send e-cards, light a candle at the physical shrine for a donation of $5 or donate money for alms for the poor.

Religious believers can even go on a virtual pilgrimage. For instance, in 2009, a number of British Christians organised a virtual pilgrimage to the Holy Land, and in a photo opportunity leaders from several denominations dressed in hiking gear to be photographed with their laptops at Westminster Abbey, under a sign pointing the way to Jerusalem. According to a report in *Christian Today*:

The online pilgrimage gives people the chance to watch short videos, photo galleries, read stories and pray in the places where Jesus preached. They also meet local Christians, Jews and Muslims living there today, hear their personal stories and hear how the conflict touches the lives of both Israelis and Palestinians, and learn how hard many people are working for peace.[96]

A group of Benedictine nuns from Oxfordshire, England, ran an online retreat service (http://www.onlineretreats.org/):

A retreat, whether made online or at a monastery or retreat centre, is essentially a time when we draw back a little from everyday activities in order to seek God. Usually it helps to have someone else acting as a guide and supporting us with prayer. ... A virtual retreat is no substitute for spending a few days away in a monastic atmosphere, concentrating wholly on God; but our online retreats are meant for people who, for one reason or another, can't do that. Making a retreat online still makes demands on the individual. We can provide the material, but it is you, and the Holy Spirit, who must make the retreat.

Retreats came in three forms: a Five Minute Focus, for those who are pressed for time, consisting of a series of podcasts and texts delivered over a few days; Shared Retreats, with twenty people at a time considering forty minutes-worth of material per day for five days, with a dedicated chatroom, for £85 per person; and Companion Retreats, restricted to three people at a time, with an hour's material per day for five days, and a twenty-minute one-to-one phone call or Skype call daily with one of the nuns at £150 per person. At the time of writing (2014), this service had apparently been in abeyance since 2012 as the order had moved location, and updated websites were being prepared.

There are a number of religious apps for iPhone and Android. In early 2014, http://www.christianiphoneapps.com/ listed apps for: receiving uplifting religious texts at a preset time on an iPhone; teaching very young children the Christmas story; showing the user how his or her life and daily choices match up with the word of God; downloading wallpaper and lockscreens with a religious theme; receiving a short personalised letter from Jesus every day; sharing inspiring photos and images; and exploring biblical archaeology.

For non-established religions, the Web is a godsend. Phaedra Bonewits hosts a Neo-pagan site (http://www.neopagan.net/) described as a cybernetic grove and a virtual stone circle, as well as a tribute to her late husband Isaac. It contains a blog, 'View from the Cyberhenge', with detailed discussions of various aspects of Neo-paganism, including vexed questions of how to define it without being prescriptive or exclusive. The blog but not the site was being updated since the death of Isaac. There are many lively Neo-pagan forums across the Web, such as http://www.paganforum.com/activity.php. This sort of enterprise has many advantages over offline sites in that they can bring people together to explore their own, perhaps idiosyncratic, spiritual ideas in anonymous or pseudonymous guise. Such forums ask for usernames, for instance, but do not insist on real names.

Oliver Krüger has argued that religious sites are generally intended to do one or more of four things. Some present religious principles, doctrines or institutions. Some facilitate discussion, communication and interaction in chatrooms and similar media. Some support religious activities, such as retreats, shrines and rituals. Finally, others distribute materials such as podcasts, CDs, DVDs or books, sometimes for money, sometimes not.[97] To these four functions we can add fundraising as a fifth.

What can we draw from the above examples? We argue that such Web presences are competing to cater to the demand of the religious adherent for religious goods. Religious websites are analogous to e-commerce, bringing products to the market in the hope that enough people will find them attractive and consume them. It should be clear that we will not be concerned with the distinction, mooted by some, between mainstream religion on cyberspace, and religion that only exists in cyberspace.[98] But first we have to consider the objection that religion does not belong online at all.

Symbol and symbolised

It has been argued that online existence has a cheapening effect—that the immersive effects of rituals, congregations or sacred buildings cannot be replicated via a digital device and that these virtual experiences are therefore inauthentic when compared to the 'real' thing.[99] Brasher makes the point that 'the numinous, or holy, experience that cyberspace makes possible by way of Digital Avatar is almost entirely an affair of the mind. This stands in huge contrast to the immersion of mind and body in the numinous of an actual visit to the Kali temple.'[100]

While an iPad is certainly not a cathedral,[101] it is fairly obvious that life and reality are being transformed by digital technologies—more information more easily available, more access to people, more traces of our activities left behind. Reality, for many, has its digital side, and the venerable online/offline distinction appears increasingly old hat.[102] It seems clear that a good many people can feel as warmly for, and interact as deeply with, digital artefacts and digitally mediated traces of friends, colleagues and family as with the analogue versions.

That should not come as a surprise, however, when we consider how easily people have always moved between the symbolic realm and the symbolised. From the medieval days of minstrelsy, people have fallen in love with images of famous people they have never met (and nowadays people will pay good money to see a Robbie Williams imitator aping Robbie Williams' on-stage persona, which is presumably very different from the man himself).[103] People used to hoard things, then gold, then paper money, and now are excited when a number which represents a stock market index or a growing bank balance increases on their computer screen; each stage in that progression symbolises the previous one. Sexual fetishism is the transfer of desire from a person to a representative, be it an article of clothing or the acting out of a type of scene. Art was one of the earliest human impulses—we do not know the significance of cave paintings, but even if they were just Neanderthal wallpaper it is remarkable that our ancestors were able to create and relate to arrangements of pigment that represented the animals they hunted (and remarkable that they look like animals to us, too).

Even some of the deepest, most treasured and valued religious feelings irrevocably involve symbols. The Host, when consecrated in the Eucharist, becomes something that people of many religions can relate to very powerfully—though it is 'only' a piece of bread. Symbols live, and they die when the social conditions that made them possible disappear. The Greek gods were meaningful at one time, yet now they have become myths, stories—culturally important but no longer moving or persuasive.

So it should not be surprising that people can form or conduct relationships with remote people, live in Second Life, or make a virtual pilgrimage. Humans are meaning-makers—we create significance in our environment, and in the objects we engineer.

Meeting the challenges

With regard to the first of our two challenges, the relation between radicalism and violent extremism, the history of religious thought tells us that original thinking has a tendency to result in novel positions very different from the mainstream. Such ideas usually disappear very quickly; sometimes they retain a small influence, even if only in the penumbra; sometimes they survive as cults; and sometimes they become mainstream themselves. Hence it is not unusual for someone questing after religious truth to be radical. Furthermore, whether someone is radical or not depends not only on their own ideas, but on those of the people around them. For instance, when criticised for interviewing religious extremists and ignoring moderates in a television programme, atheist Richard Dawkins replied that 'In neo-con America [Pastor Ted Haggard] is mainstream. President of the 30 million-strong National Association of Evangelicals, he has a weekly phone conversation with Bush.'[104]

With regard to the second challenge of the role of the Internet, we should always remember that technology does not cause violence or terrorism; it may facilitate it, like roads, telephones or Hallowe'en masks, all of which can be and have been used with profit by terrorist groups. Of course, if there are ways in which the Internet does aid violent extremism, these need to be examined while remembering that violent extremists are a tiny proportion of religious radicals or Internet users. It does provide benefits to groups and individuals that use it, removing traditional barriers or costs to interaction and providing access to identity signifiers that can increase solidarity and cohesion within a group, while simultaneously setting up invisible boundaries between the group and its embedding society.[105] It makes coordination and agreement easier within a group. This is crucial for understanding how religious groups and their doctrines—irrespective of any claims or concerns about violence—behave, evolve and mutate in the modern, technologically enhanced, world.

To borrow a concept from sociologist Anthony Giddens, it also has the effect of 'disembedding' religion (both religious thought, and the worldly cycles of ritual and interaction) from temporal and spatial constraints.[106] Interactions are, or can be, quasi-anonymous. Many of the stage props of authority, such as uniforms, spatial positioning (e.g. at the altar), insignia, a band of servants and/or helpers, a cowed audience, access to imposing buildings and works of art, are absent or denuded of significance. Commonalities of experience and language that can usually be assumed in real-world interactions may not exist, for example where groups span large geographical areas. Hence the Internet decontextualises many hitherto well-understood aspects of religion. This makes it harder for those in traditionally authoritative positions to assert authority, and easier for those without formal training or qualifications to be heard. This is particularly an issue for Islam, where there has never been an institutionalised notion of a privileged group of scholars having a monopoly over, or special access to, wisdom,[107] and can be even more pressing for newer religious movements.[108]

This crisis of authority is exacerbated by a parallel crisis of authenticity. As Dawson and Cowan ask:

has the meaning of the concept not been irretrievably compromised if in the online world a 'coven' can be created by anyone regardless of experience, can include as many people as wish to join, regardless of the interpersonal dynamics that emerge in covens offline, and can exist (in many cases) as little more than chatty discussion lists rather than serious religious working groups? If a coven can mean anything its online users want it to mean, has it not ceased to mean anything at all?[109]

If, as Harris argues, religious moderation is imposed from outside and rarely driven from within,[110] then the reduction of constraint is a cause for concern.

Nevertheless, we should always bear in mind that the Internet is rarely the only method for communication, either within a group or to the outside world. Harold Camping's over-enthusiastic predictions of the end of the world certainly spread online, but the Web is not the only source of news even about non-mainstream events like this (and some of Camping's target audience would not have been terribly Web-savvy). In fact the message of the forthcoming Rapture was also disseminated with more conventional technologies such as billboards and the $100 million that Family Radio spent on promotion,[111] while volunteers and believers were reported to have given up their jobs in order to preach (one retired man spent $140,000 to publicise the non-event).[112]

Hence the relation between the Internet and religious groups is not as simple as it appears. In the rest of Part I, we will state the *prima facie* case that has been built up with respect to the need for public policy on this point before looking at some of the arguments in Chapter Two and some of the resulting policies in Chapter Three.

2

THE POLARISATION OF ONLINE DEBATE

One answer to the two challenges set out in the Introduction has been to postulate strong connections between radicalism, violent extremism and the Internet. The Web and other communications technologies have been on the radar of those concerned with security for many years. Yet it is not enough merely to claim these links—can we show that there are mechanisms in place which rely on the Web for at least some of their efficacy, and which increase the likelihood that a radical person will become violent, and/or that a person subjected to those mechanisms will be radicalised? If such mechanisms for both transitions are in place then, all other things being equal, the probability of violence has been increased by the Internet.

This chapter examines two sets of ideas about how these mechanisms, which include psychosocial mechanisms as well as technology, might have been implemented. These ideas have proven influential for policy, partly no doubt because of their intuitive plausibility. In this book we argue that their influence is misplaced, and their effects unfortunate. But our first task is to set them out, and to show what policies have been developed to reduce the probability of extremist violence spreading through the mature democracies.

Villagey globalism

In the programme notes for the 2011 world premiere of Nico Muhly's opera about the multiplicity of identity on the Web and Internet, *Two*

Boys, cultural commentator and pessimist Will Self argued that 'the web represents a further evolution of a pre-existing negative tendency in human affairs ... the progressive withering away of our capacity to feel'. It 'makes monsters of us all':

[T]he politics that the web most obviously promotes is identity-based, as people globally choose to 'be with' others who they view as self-similar—and is it any coincidence that such people-groupings are ideal from the marketing point of view? ...

[T]he tragedy depicted in *Two Boys* ... could only happen in a society that has become subject to a villagey globalism, a level of physical alienation and moral anomie whereby it's possible for young people who live within minutes of each other to not only not meet in the flesh by chance—but to avoid it also by design.[1]

Jonathan Kay, a researcher of conspiracy theories, concurs. 'The Internet actually has exacerbated the human instinct toward parochialism, tribalism, and conspiracism.'[2]

Yet is this particularly a Webby problem? A century and a half before the dramatic acceleration of the Web's growth, Friedrich Engels wrote:

The town [Manchester] itself is peculiarly built, so that someone can live in it for years and travel into and out of it daily without ever coming into contact with a working-class quarter or even with workers—so long, that is to say, as one confines himself to his business affairs or to strolling about for pleasure. This comes about mainly in the circumstances that through an unconscious, tacit agreement as much through conscious, explicit intention, the working-class districts are most sharply separated from the parts of the city reserved for the middle class. ...

I have never elsewhere seen a concealment of such fine sensibility of everything that might offend the eyes and nerves of the middle classes. And yet it is precisely Manchester that has been built less according to a plan and less within the limitations of official regulations—and indeed more through accident—than any other town.[3]

Division and exclusion was clearly possible in communities of more than moderate complexity without the benefit of filtering technology. The tendency of individuals to select their neighbours (e.g. of immigrants to seek out their own compatriots, of tradesmen to seek out those in the same and related business) has left many cities with quarters, barrios and ghettos, for good or ill, even though the geography of these quarters is unplanned. Is this phenomenon exacerbated by the Internet?

This chapter explores some of the political and sociological arguments about how those who hold radical religious views can be affected by the functionality afforded by digital communications, in particular the ways in which they can insulate themselves from outside influence. Given their basic condition of existence is antagonism and opposition, there is a *prima facie* argument that such insulation would be an important tool for radicalism, radicalisation and perpetuation of the radical ethos. In particular, we explore the views of political theorist/scientist Cass Sunstein about how democracy and free speech themselves are threatened by the ways that digital technology are supportive of intolerant, anti-democratic radicalism, and of sociologist Sherry Turkle, who has argued that our increasingly ubiquitous reliance on computers has correspondingly reduced the emotional support that we desire or expect from our friends and family. If their descriptions of current socio-political circumstances are persuasive, then we must admit the possibility that the long tail of the religious marketplace plays a disproportionately large role in our political life.

Alone together with digital anomie

The notion of *anomie* was introduced by Durkheim to describe the feeling of an individual that social norms did not apply to, or were inappropriate for, him or her. The anomic individual feels purposeless, uninvolved in wider society. Durkheim went on to postulate that one of religion's functional roles was to provide the basis for shared values and norms which could help support the anomic individual.

This was an important area for sociological and political research in the previous century, and while we will not delve deeply into the nature or causes of *anomie*, we will consider some of the arguments that have developed out of a growing sense that it is an important psychosocial phenomenon in today's rich democracies, nurtured not only by globalisation and capitalism, but also by the proliferation of technologies which lack or suppress human warmth and society.[4]

In one prominent recent instance, sociologist and psychologist Sherry Turkle examines our relations both with technological artefacts and with each other mediated technologically, and finds the future bleak.[5] The burden of her argument is that many of the intricate and intimate nuances of human relationships are being lost as technology is incorporated into our emotional and social lives.

In Turkle's view, technologies start off being 'good enough' to support a particular type of human emotion or relationship. So, for example, the care of elderly people can be hived off to appealing and efficient robots. Unlike relatives, they have the advantages of always being available to help, having infinite time (unlike hard-pressed nurses) and being immune to feelings of guilt. And since they are admittedly incapable of caring, the fact that they do not 'really' care about the elderly person in their care is not as humiliating and dispiriting as a lack of interest on the part of a human nurse or relative would be. So the caring robot is good enough.

But eventually, the elderly person might come to prefer the efficient and always-on 'care' of a robot, even if 'care' is encased in inverted commas. Some robots are deliberately made to be cute, and people quickly come to treat them as sentient, and as autonomous as pets; this can be very therapeutic.[6] They read emotions and motives into the robot's behaviour, particularly via facial expression, that are simply not there. The robot, which always has time, never answers back and always has a kind word, goes from being good enough to being better than a relative or a nurse. There is some evidence, for example, that in Japan (where the humanoid robot industry is the most advanced in the world), many elderly people prefer a robot carer to an immigrant from, say, the Philippines, because the robot has a keener eye for the nuances of Japanese etiquette, and is much less likely than the human to make a terrible faux pas.[7] In her work on robots,[8] Turkle claims to have seen this trajectory over and over again, particularly with children, who, for instance, preferred animatronic animals in an exhibition to real animals, which do not move, often hide and are much less interesting ('aliveness seemed [to the children] to have no intrinsic value').[9] The view also surfaces in more adult contexts, such as David Levy's manifesto on sex with robots; the artificial robot is initially conceived to be 'good enough' for a decent sexual experience, but when considered more deeply, the robot has distinct advantages over a human lover. No caprices, unreasonable demands, headaches, premature ejaculations, unexplained absences, infidelities, mothers-in-law, complexities.[10] In each case, the human interlocutor eliminates a number of the difficulties of navigating the world of autonomous humans, at the cost of a radical simplification and demystifying of his or her emotional and social life.

Turkle identifies a similar if less dramatic process with respect to virtual relations in the digital world, mediated via a PC, a mobile phone or other type of portable computational device. Facebook created the 'friend' function, with the result that our ideas about the complex phenomenon of friendship are being coarsened. People can 'friend' someone quite casually, and 'unfriend' them just as easily. All Facebook friends are equivalents in our online social network. People can just as easily friend their next door neighbour as Barack Obama or Sarah Palin. Yet our relationships with real-world friends are highly heterogeneous. People share different confidences, and do different things, with different friends. Friendship inspires loyalty, but to different degrees with different friends and in different spheres of life. Friendship's borderlines with love on the one hand, and acquaintance on the other, are intricate. All these factors are glossed over in the Facebook world. Digital immersion means that anything not appearing in the digital record is either trivial, or non-existent.[11]

For Turkle, this is evidence that we live in a culture of simulation, where authenticity is a problem and a challenge in much the same way as sex was to the Victorians.[12] A holiday or gap year is spent ignoring our surroundings and texting and chatting with friends from home (who may of course also be away from home),[13] echoing Susan Sontag's complaint that in an age of photography 'travel has become a strategy for accumulating photographs'.[14] For many years, the philosophy of mind entertained questions about whether a sufficiently lifelike robot could mimic humans perfectly,[15] yet this now seems to put things the wrong way round. We are adapting our behaviour to resemble the behaviour of robots.

Hence Turkle describes a situation in which people whose relationships are substantially mediated by technology will adapt them, simplifying and coarsening them to fit the demands on the permanently present network. '[T]he culture in which [the selves formed in the cacophony of online spaces] develop tempts them into narcissistic ways of relating to the world',[16] in other words 'getting on with others by dealing only with their made-to-measure representations'.[17] The wired modern crafts his or her appearance to a specification. The technology allows even the most trivial communication to be edited and tailored, eliminating the immediate and the potentially over-revealing instant reaction which we might expect face to face or on a telephone.[18] We can create ourselves to ease our anxieties, but this only works temporarily. One tries to design one's profile so that it reveals the 'real me', but this merely shifts the agony of the question: who is the 'real me'?

When a man who, in his real life social contacts, is quiet and bashful, adopts an angry, aggressive persona in virtual reality, one can say that he thereby expresses the repressed side of himself, a publicly non-acknowledged aspect of his 'true personality'—that his 'electronic id is here given wing'; however, one can also claim that he is a weak subject fantasizing about more aggressive behaviour in order to avoid confronting his real life weakness and cowardice.[19]

The echo chamber of positive feedback

Turkle abhors this inauthentic life. But for our purposes the value of this new mindset is less important than whether we adapt our relationships to the technology that facilitates them. In that case, the Internet, to quote Turkle once more, 'is more than old wine in new bottles'.[20] In a world where people are searching for their own identity and have ready access to a wide and heterogeneous network of friends, acquaintances and friends of friends, a key factor in the development of a confident position will be the feedback they receive from others.

A number of thinkers have developed this thought. In this section, and throughout this book, we will focus on the argument about online influences put forward by Cass Sunstein, who argued from the early days of the Web's popularity that there was a risk that people would seek out feedback from favoured sources, which would threaten to distort their psychosocial lives even more than the base condition of isolation and *anomie*. This chimed in with some arguments about newly formed religions with uncompromising messages, which claimed that 'as such a polarized worldview could be endangered by qualifications or questioning, any middle-way option or ambiguity is likely to be demonized as part of the bad, the false and/or the satanic alternative'.[21] Sunstein's argument, which first appeared in 2001,[22] and was revisited and updated in 2007,[23] is simply stated and has intuitive force. Between the publication of the first and second editions, political events such as the terrorist attack on the Twin Towers, and sociotechnical developments such as the appearance and growth of the blogosphere conspired to add *prima facie* evidence that Sunstein was correct.

He was not a lone voice. Jaron Lanier, a pioneer of virtual reality and commentator on matters digital, believes the link between online feedback loops and dangerously antisocial, even violent, behaviour is stronger and even more explicit. For him, only the Web as it is currently constituted could have produced such behaviour due to its support of 'anonymous, fragmented communication':

New patterns of social connection that are unique to online culture have played a role in the spread of modern networked terrorism. If you look at an online chat about anything, from guitars to poodles to aerobics, you'll see a consistent pattern: jihadi chat looks just like poodle chat. A pack emerges, and either you are with it or against it. If you join the pack, then you join the collective ritual hatred.[24]

The technological change that particularly concerned Sunstein was the development of personalisation techniques for the delivery of Web content. One of the many boons of the Web is that people can filter out material that is of no interest. News feeds can be tailored to someone's individual interests, or even their particular political views. Shopping sites can point people to the items they are likely to prefer.

This can all be done without conscious input, reasoning or self-knowledge from the individual. Your purchases, downloads and even searches are highly suggestive of your interests. Furthermore, others' choices and searches can illuminate a model of your preferences. If you have enjoyed goods X, Y and Z, and if it can be shown, using Bayesian statistical techniques, that those who enjoyed X, Y and Z also enjoyed A, then the system can recommend A to you.[25] And similarly, you provide important data to an e-commerce site for free merely by buying some things and not buying others. You can also add value to the site for free by reviewing, ranking or rating those purchases (as tens of millions of people have done on amazon.com, for example). Indeed, you can add even more value for free by voting on whether you found others' reviews helpful or not. The amount of data collected and often traded by commercial websites is colossal, allowing very precise calculations based on fairly solid statistics. The power of data and number crunching is awesome;[26] recommender algorithms using techniques based on collaborative filtering are extraordinarily potent ways of selling goods to willing consumers. E-commerce companies quickly realised that automatic recommendations dramatically outperform recommendations made by informed humans (in terms of purchases made in response to recommendations).[27]

Public forums and deliberative democracy

Sunstein is particularly concerned with our ability to filter news. While our new-found ability to focus on the goods we want to buy is not a problem, if all our information comes wrapped in a specific viewpoint, or is about specific topics, we will find ourselves with an attenuated understanding of the world around us. Recommendation and filtering software creates a 'filter bubble', 'a unique universe of information for each of us'.[28] One could easily create a personalised journal focused around one's idiosyncratic interests, an idea that Nicholas Negroponte called the *Daily Me*.[29] This could result in what Eli Pariser has called 'invisible autopropaganda, indoctrinating us with our own ideas'.[30] In contrast, a newspaper aggregates material that an editorial team deems essential and topical and presents it to the reader as 'the state of the world'. It is not complete, and will of course be biased, but the bias is different from the reader's, and the gaps will not conform to the gaps in the reader's knowledge. This paper artefact serves alternative and important functions, as memorably described by right-wing politician and journalist Boris Johnson when arguing the importance of left-wing newspapers such as the UK's *Guardian*:

It's no use telling us that the content would all be there 'online'. Everything is online, a great charnel-house of porn and piffle. We need the *Guardian* lowering at us from the news-stands in all its highmindedness … Take it online and you lose all political impact; you lose the vital editorial marshalling of the often excellent journalists and cartoonists and photographers into a single daily statement, a single product—and everything gets lost in the morass of Google news.[31]

Sunstein insists that a functioning democracy must have two important counterweights to this image of 'the morass of Google news'. A well-functioning system of free expression must expose people to materials they would not have chosen in advance, and most citizens must have a range of common experiences which will aid mutual understanding and sympathy.[32] If these two requirements are not fulfilled in a free society, there will be three major and unfortunate unintended consequences.[33] First, there will be social fragmentation, as diverse groups polarise. Second, people will use the filtering power of the Web to create bespoke information goods for themselves, rather than creating goods that are valuable for many people. Third, satisfaction of people's preferences will be taken as definitive of their well-being, ruling out a conception of well-being that takes into account not only the content of their preferences, but also the condition of their development. Citizens cannot be autonomous if their preferences are formed under coercive conditions, however much they acquiesce in them, as Aldous Huxley's *Brave New World* reminds us.[34]

Sunstein lays great weight on the constitutional right of citizens to appear in public forums, where they can make contact with other citizens in an accessible and public space, in order to address them freely.[35] This right serves five functions. First, those with a point of view or a grievance, however marginalised they are, can draw attention to it. Second, citizens can also contextualise their arguments to particular institutions. Those who wish to complain to legislators can demonstrate outside parliament or council buildings, while those who wish to complain about fracking can peacefully picket a responsible company's offices. Third, other citizens will thereby be exposed to arguments or points of view they would not otherwise have chosen to consider. Fourth, public spaces are subsidised by the government, giving democratic authority to the promotion of free speech. Finally, such forums will tend to increase everyone's exposure to points of view about which people feel strongly, and so will tend to increase the homogeneity of citizens' common experiences.

Sunstein argues that the pre-Internet mass media had settled into the role of public forums of this nature. One can, of course, filter one's experience with mass media, as they are supported by a market. For instance, a neo-liberal might only read *The Economist*; a Tea Partier might only watch Fox News, a left-leaning liberal might restrict himself to PBS, *The Guardian*, *Le Monde* or *El Pais*. Even so, they are all likely to be exposed to ideas, opinions or events of which they would otherwise have been ignorant because they will inevitably see news stories other than those they would have chosen to read, and programmes or news items other than those they would have chosen to watch. However censored, however ridiculed, these ideas and events get an airing by virtue of being presented to people who would not have been interested in them, and would not have sought them out. The Tea Partier, for example, might catch an item on urban poverty that challenges his strong views on government spending. The point is not that the item will change his mind, but he will be better informed, and better able to address contrary arguments to his own ideas. He will have a more nuanced view of the world, and be a more effective debater as a result.

Such forums make most sense within a system of deliberative democracy, in which an engaged citizenry collaborates and debates with its representatives and agrees to respect the outcome—the type of democracy upon which the US Constitution was premised. Deliberative democracy contrasts with direct democracy, the gauging, aggregating, counting and acting upon votes or opinions without mediation, and Sunstein assumes that the former produces superior outcomes to the latter[36] (an assumption which the current authors share). A snapshot of opinion will not necessarily produce coherent policy (as, for example, in California, where, until Governor Jerry Brown and Proposition 30 reversed the trend, citizens' initiatives regularly endorsed spending measures, such as longer prison sentences and generous pensions, and just as regularly rejected tax-raising measures, resulting in near-bankruptcy for the state), and is subject to change and undue influence. In a direct democracy, people's opinions are simply aggregated, so the way they are formed and influenced can have a powerful effect on outcomes. A deliberative democracy, on the other hand, is set up to create opinion through debate and negotiation, so that all sides of an argument are tested. In a direct democracy there is no need to compromise or avoid partisanship as long as there is some kind of decision mechanism (e.g. the ability to command a majority vote); dialogue is inessential.

In each type of democracy the citizen is sovereign, but a deliberative democracy produces political sovereignty, whereas direct democracy produces something more like consumer sovereignty.[37] The latter involves the satisfaction, where possible, of the consumer's preferences. The former denotes the ability of the citizen to demand reasons for policy, as opposed to arbitrary rule, in the public domain, and to hold governments to account on the basis of their reasoning.

Cyberpolarisation

According to Sunstein, the Internet is not a deliberative public forum. Ideological sites tend to link to each other, rather than to sites containing opposing points of view. Sunstein has analysed some small samples,[38] but the tendency of groups to focus inwardly on like-minded Web resources is reasonably well known. For example, a pioneering study of political blogs in the 2004 US election showed different patterns of behaviour characteristic of liberal and conservative political commentators; the two sides found different news items significant, and linked more readily to ideologically congenial sites, although conservative bloggers linked more densely both to each other and to the liberal opposition. Over 90 per cent of links between political blogs which self-identified as liberal or conservative were to like-minded blogs and resources, creating a pair of insulated communities.[39] Hate groups, unsurprisingly, are even less tolerant and cosmopolitan.[40] Conspiracy theories flourish, sheltered from objective criticism, and supported by carefully selected evidence.[41] As Sunstein writes, 'the blogosphere, like the Internet more generally, is certainly good for democracy because it increases information. But if linking behaviour on blogs can be taken as a proxy for information filtering, it is reasonable to think that many readers are obtaining one-sided views on political issues.'[42]

Although Sunstein does not press this point, it may also be the case that messages are simplified in order to facilitate their communication and spread in this ecosystem. In what has been called the 'attention economy',[43] getting the attention of 'customers' in the middle of a crowded marketplace is the *sine qua non* of success. This of itself renders traditional 'guardians of the faith', whose job it is to protect and promote a particular detailed position with complex, subtle or inconclusive arguments, redundant. One commentator has argued that simple messages, and the certainty that accompanies them, are increasingly prevalent in the modern world,[44] while another worries about new media creating a 'soundbite Islam'.[45] Soundbites militate against the informed interaction with embedding societies that some commentators argue is the root of religious moderation, and which serves as a brake against radicalism.[46]

Sunstein is especially concerned with group polarisation. Individual groups' members who primarily communicate with each other will tend to become less diverse over time, and so each group becomes more coherent.[47] There will be greater diversity between groups, which is probably a good thing, but at the cost of rigidity of outlook within groups. The net result may easily be polarisation and partisanship across society as a whole. Furthermore, each group, while becoming more coherent and homogeneous, is also likely to occupy more extreme positions. There are three reasons for this.[48] First, group members are disproportionately exposed to persuasive arguments coming from one side only. Second, they adopt positions to appear in a favourable light to their peers in the group. Third, increased solidarity leads to greater confidence, which is in turn associated with more extreme positions. People are in 'echo chambers of their own design'.

In such chambers the result may well be an effective and coherent social machine, to use a concept introduced earlier, that may make the 'machine' more effective in terms of decisive action. However, the degree of integration with the embedding society will be smaller, and so the routes to effective cooperation and collaborative action will be closed down, leaving the inevitable temptation of refusal to compromise and the valorisation of conflict.

For Sunstein, this is an especial danger for the Internet, and he warns against cyberpolarisation:

> Group polarization is unquestionably occurring on the Internet. From the evidence thus far, it seems plain that the Internet is serving, for many, as a breeding ground for extremism, precisely because like-minded people are deliberating with greater ease and frequency with one another, and often without hearing contrary views.[49]

The Internet as a public forum

The idea that the Internet is not a public forum is a remarkably strong claim, although he is careful to hedge most of his ideas with caveats. There is certainly a tension between his thesis and the ideas of Jürgen Habermas, to take one influential commentator who has theorised at length about the ethics governing discourse and debate in order to foster publicity, inclusiveness, equality, solidarity and justice.[50] Following an analysis of the eighteenth-century salons of the Parisian Enlightenment,[51] Habermas developed a theory of 'ideal speech situations' which function as goals for communicative discourse to facilitate self-correcting learning.[52] These speech situations are characterised by four important properties: (1) no one capable of making a relevant contribution is excluded, (2) participants have equal voice, (3) they are internally free to speak their honest opinion without deception or self-deception, and (4) there are no sources of coercion built into the process and procedures of discourse.[53]

Sunstein explicitly rejects the claim that the blogosphere is 'a vast public meeting of the kind that Jürgen Habermas describes',[54] on the grounds that group polarisation makes that impossible. 'The challenge to the Habermasian understanding is that because of self-sorting, people are often reading like-minded points of view, in a way that can breed greater confidence, more uniformity within groups and more extremism. From the Habermasian point of view, this is nothing to celebrate.'[55]

It must surely be conceded even by those who are least enthusiastic about the blogosphere that characteristics (1)–(4) apply to it in some degree. Both (1) and (4) seem plausible, and (3), if it is true of anything, is surely true of the blogosphere, but Matthew Hindman has argued *contra* (2), and on the basis of a survey of the most often-read bloggers, that participants do not have equal voice. 'Overwhelmingly, they are well-educated white male professionals. Nearly all the bloggers in our census were either educational elites, business elites, technical elites, or traditional journalists.'[56]

The scale-free link structure of the Web, in which a few well-connected sites tend to dominate any particular corner of it, produces a winner-takes-all culture where success reinforces success.[57] Since the political portion of the Web in most languages or cultures is too large to be accurately surveyed, readers are reliant on search engines which rank the pages they retrieve according to the number and quality of the links to them. The result is that a well-linked-to page is more likely to be discovered by someone searching for political or religious information, and will therefore become even more likely to be linked to. To that extent, voices in the blogosphere are not equal.

Nevertheless, it is important to note that these four characteristics do apply to some degree to the blogosphere and so—even assuming that ideal speech situations cannot guarantee ethical discourse—it is reasonable to hope that blogging is an important activity which might in the aggregate approximate the ideal of the disinterested pursuit of truth. Individual blogs might of course be extremely partisan, even written in bad faith, but when taken as a whole, debate in the blogosphere would approach the important standard of ideal speech situations. Consensus will never be reached; as el-Nawawy and Khamis point out, much of the consensus in the Islamist websites they study happens not because of deliberation and debate, but rather because of 'a collective endorsement of shared interest' by a group of people who share a relatively homogeneous outlook.[58] Gary Bunt's detailed treatment of Islam online seems consistent with the Habermasian ideal, and implies that in the aggregate a wide range of positions and attitudes are expounded:

The impact of blogs reaches from the cybercafé in the *souq* to governmental offices and international media. They can be a point of protest and/or a propagation of Islamic beliefs and values. For blogging iMuslims, there can be little separation between online and offline worlds. Blogs have become a significant adjunct to, if not the primary thrust of, conversation, intellectual stimulus, and Muslim networking. They reach down into the Long Tail of segmentation and nuanced content delivery, with highly specialized content emerging throughout sectors of the Islamic blogosphere.[59]

The blogosphere appears to meet many demands that one might make upon an ideal forum for debate and discourse; Habermas's four conditions appear at first blush to be highly positive things to say about a discussion space. Yet Sunstein rejects the whole idea that blogging or online discussion is ideal in this sense. Although he has no problem with blogging as such, and admits that it adds to the variety, diversity and colour of our discourse, he ultimately concludes that 'blunders, confusion, and extremism are highly likely, not in spite of the blogosphere but because of it'.[60] 'The world of blogs is pervaded by the propagation of errors, hidden profiles, cascades, and group polarization.'[61]

The Internet as a tool for collaboration

Sunstein is implicitly less sanguine than the many positive accounts of online collaboration which have appeared, which argue that phenomena such as Wikipedia, the decoding of the Human Genome, mashups and the Grameen Bank showed how mass collaboration was tending to outperform hierarchically driven mass production.[62] To take one example, Charles Leadbeater writes that:

we will not make sense of the mass of information generated by the web on our own; our only hope is to employ our shared intelligence. The more people contribute, the more we need to collaborate. ... [For instance] the best way to find out which blogs are good is to rely on the judgements of other web users whom you trust.[63]

There are many interesting examples of crowdsourcing systems that aggregate input to create an interesting product or service. The citizen science initiative Galaxy Zoo[64] allows amateurs to collaborate to classify galaxies from astronomical data, a highly labour-intensive operation. Several peer-reviewed scientific papers have resulted from the initiative, which has been copied in other areas of science and social science where a relatively routine task cannot be automated. Following the violence after the disputed election in Kenya in 2007, the Ushahidi platform was created to allow people to upload geotagged and timestamped photos of the violence, to create an emergent map of the troubles.[65] The platform was reused by relief workers to create a digital map of Port-au-Prince following the 2010 earthquake (incredibly, there was not one in existence beforehand).[66]

Commentators on crowdsourcing argue that the aggregation of opinions of a diverse enough group of people will in all likelihood be more accurate than those of a single person, even an expert on the topic. Genuine collaboration (a) avoids groupthink, (b) internalises critical analysis and (c) brings local perspectives and a range of interests into play. Sunstein would certainly agree with that, while raising the bar for 'genuine' collaboration very high. He would, for instance, be suspicious of Leadbeater's statement quoted above about relying on the judgements of others one trusts. It is important from Sunstein's view that one is also exposed to the judgements of others whom one does not trust. Furthermore, on the polarisation thesis, one's opinion (if not actually degraded) is likely to be rendered more extreme if one relies solely on those one trusts. That is likely to make the effects of the opinion worse, while also making the holder of that opinion impervious to reasoned argument. Furthermore, someone wishing to establish or spread his opinions is motivated to isolate himself from alternate views and is technologically enabled to do so.

We-Think or group collaborations discussed by Leadbeater and others are often impressive, and those authors are right to draw attention to the phenomenon.[67] However, we need to consider what we might call the Wikipedia problem. Wikipedia qua encyclopaedia is an impressive and counterintuitive achievement. It is fairly accurate, has impressive coverage (certainly in areas such as computing, mathematics and popular culture), is up-to-date even, or especially, in fast-developing areas, and provides access to whole tranches of people who would otherwise be too poor or geographically isolated to access a 'respectable' encyclopaedia. There is a heated if not terribly illuminating debate as to whether it is more or less accurate than expensively edited and curated competitors such as *Encyclopædia Britannica*, but there is no doubt that it has earned its place as the first port of call for anyone who wishes to know when Diderot was born or why people write 'Gouranga' on road bridges. Wikipedia had some 270,000 regularly active contributors as of 2011 and 31,000 editors in 2013 (although these numbers are on a declining trend),[68] all unpaid—although after a few scandals their efforts are filtered and monitored by a tighter group of dedicated editors—and many millions of readers. This community (or social machine) keeps everyone honest.

On the other hand, any individual article in Wikipedia will of necessity be written by a smaller number of people than the total number of

Wikipedians, and so if the reader's interest is specifically in a particular area she may be unwittingly exposed to a biased account.[69] Naturally one might expect this in a topic such as climate change, nuclear power or the merits of George Bush Jr or Barack Obama as these topics will attract several authors and may become small theatres of war, but at least these will be well-known flashpoints and the editors can probably handle the resulting dialogues of the deaf. The problem may be more acute in more arcane areas, where the number of interested authors and commentators is very small.

In other words, Sunstein would make very strong demands on the diversity required for online collaborations at scale. So even if the blogosphere itself is an impressive human construct where every opinion is monitored and countered by others, any individual blog or tightly linked group of blogs may still be subject to strong bias which is only countered externally.[70] Such a group of blogs may work as a social machine disseminating a particular point of view, or even pushing its members to extremes, and functionally inclined to resist or reject moderating influences. A neophyte coming fresh to a coherent group of interlinked blogs may come to believe that, with its strong internal links, it is sufficiently diverse to subject strong claims to relevant scrutiny, but the appearance of debate and diversity would be misleading. We have a classic J-shaped curve, where the information quality of a Web 2.0 collaboration may initially fall as the number of collaborators increases, only rising once the collaborative group exceeds a threshold for quantity and diversity.

The advocates of crowd wisdom are also aware of the delicate balance to be struck. Leadbeater acknowledges that blogging 'is high on participation, low on collaboration',[71] which raises a subtle dilemma. Leadbeater writes about the importance of a creative core of workers or thinkers in a crowdsourcing application: '[s]omebody has to be willing to work harder than everyone else or nothing ends up being done'.[72] But it is not simply a question of harder work—the core to some extent defines and drives the mission of the group (Leadbeater cites people such as Jimmy Wales of Wikipedia or Linus Torvalds of Linux). The connection between the core and the mission exemplifies the dilemma that Sunstein wants to highlight: if the core is sufficiently well defined to drive a successful crowd-based collaboration, it may also be such a powerful idea in the relevant community to ensure that only like-minded people participate. On the Internet, it is unlikely to be problematic if someone like Wales sets himself up as a benevolent dictator of a virtual realm; in the religious world, a core built around, say, David Koresh of the Branch Davidians (which we will discuss in Chapter Four), may define the mission too successfully.

Sunstein's later exposition of his view in 2007 is less prescriptive than the 2001 edition, and he is alive to the problems that many of his remedies would have produced. In the end, he discusses six types of remedy, although he does not endorse them all.[73] At this stage in our argument, we are more concerned with his general description of the problem, although we will be discussing some of his concrete ideas later in this book—in particular, the ideas of creating deliberative domains that 'ensur[e] opportunities for discussion among people with diverse views',[74] and subsidies 'to assist high-quality efforts in non-profit, non-governmental spaces on the Internet'.[75] Most of his other suggestions either involve a level of interference with online content that would be unfeasible given the ease with which sites move around the world (think of how difficult it has been to censor WikiLeaks, for example), or a level of self-regulation that is unlikely to interest the hate sites and extremist sites which concern him. In common with other academic writers from the United States, he also often appears unwittingly to assume that the Internet is an American infrastructure for Americans to read American content sited on American servers. The First Amendment, for instance, is certainly an important piece of law, but appeal to it is not sufficient to establish anything about the Internet as a whole.

Non-violent and violent engagement

It is of course true, as Sunstein accepts, that the Internet can actually expose us to a much wider range of influences than was formerly the case, which is partly why small cults gain from the long tail of the Web.[76] For our part, let us accept most of Sunstein's assumptions, at least for the sake of argument. The idea that the Internet or the Web could be regulated is often criticised from cyberspace, most famously by John Perry Barlow of the Electronic Frontier Foundation in his 'Declaration of Independence of Cyberspace' in 1996.[77] Whether or not one considers this exciting and idealistic, or so much unrealistic claptrap, its claim that governments are illegitimately jumping on to a newly created/discovered space, in the same way that British colonists claimed Virginia or Tasmania under the blinkered assumption that no one had right or title to the land, is hardly a tenable position.[78] The Web is a very open technology, one developed with public money, and one of the reasons why websites are not hacked very often or that viruses are not as prevalent as they might be is that certain types of behaviour are against the law even online, and that denizens of cyberspace have some property rights.

There is no doubt that regulation of the Internet would be problematic in terms of the engineering, as noted in Chapter One, and could impose serious costs.[79] This is quite possibly one of the reasons underlying Sunstein's adaptation of his position between the first and second editions of his book, although the main reason seems to be a close reading and consideration of the free speech amendment to the US Constitution. However that may be, we would argue that the Internet's success depends on its decentralised engineering, and that of the Web embodied not only in standards administered by the World Wide Web Consortium (W3C), but also in the values of liberty, communication and openness for which it stands. In that case, attempts to impede the flow of information could potentially damage the infrastructure itself. As Sunstein clearly accepts that the Internet as a whole is a good, then its health should obviously be a factor in political considerations about it.

We will conclude that, as the Internet is a good, one should be cautious about the unintended consequences of trying to make it inhospitable to paedophiles, political and religious extremists, organised crime gangs and so on. That is not to say that one should not use the law to prosecute abuses of free speech, whether they be by spreading spam, viruses, hate speech or pictures of abused children, in the same way as one would use the law to prosecute analogous abuses using other media. It is not to say—Sunstein reminds us forcefully and correctly of this point—that the Internet should (or even can) be unregulated. It is to say that one should not take advantage of the fact that the Internet is a totally engineered environment to try to engineer abuses of free speech out of the system.

How, then, should we react to Sunstein's argument about the tight feedback loops within very closed groups, the echo chambers, the *Daily Me*s which threaten to undermine public debate? The first question to ask is whether radicals and extremists will go away. Robert Nozick has hypothesised that extremists are attracted to extreme positions independently of their content (so a communist might become a fascist, a radical evangelist might become a radical Muslim);[80] that is consistent with the observation that a religious organisation that moves toward doctrinal orthodoxy may gain adherents while losing radicals alienated by the change (as with the splittist tendencies of the People's Front of Judea in *The Life of Brian*). We will elaborate on these questions in Chapter Four.

It will be difficult to engineer such people out of the system; radicals, like the poor, are always with us. Sunstein is worried that echo chambers on the Web will tend to increase intra-group solidarity and inter-group polarisation, thereby allowing radicals to cut out moderating influences and dissenting voices, and work each other up into more foaming at the mouth. The evidence is that not many people, at least by their own self-reporting, filter out unwanted views (well under 10 per cent in the United States),[81] but if these small percentages happen to include the radicals then it is not inconsistent with Sunstein's hypothesis.

But the obvious question follows: so what? Radicalism per se is hardly a problem. If radical groups are to become a serious threat to a society, then they will need to engage with others. In a democracy, if they are to become influential in policy terms they will have to engage with voters, administrators and policy-makers in debate; their messages will have to be scrutinised. Ultimately, they will be held to account for their policies in areas where they have achieved power. In a dictatorship, the radicals will have to engage with apparatchiks and administrators.

These are difficult enough hurdles. To clear them, radicals have to leave the echo chambers into which by hypothesis they have put themselves. They have to try to persuade, which means debate, which in turn means conversation, argument and inevitable exposure to dissenting views. The very process of trying to influence brings with it the risk of being influenced. By ring-fencing themselves and their views away from scrutiny, they deprive themselves of wider influence. Solidarity in an isolated position and lack of influence in the embedding society are two sides of the same coin.

Hence when radicals disappear into their own circles, and deliberately cut themselves off, they insulate society from their influence. Their views will spread, if at all, at a glacial pace. Even if they are distasteful, dangerous or even evil, there seems little danger that wider society might be undermined. Conversely, if there is a danger that radical or extreme views could infect society, then there will simultaneously be a (quite probably greater) risk to the purity of the radicalism. Even if it was not overly paternalistic to try to persuade insulated radicals to renounce their extreme views, there seems little gain compared to the large costs of undermining free speech and personal autonomy that it would entail.

Let us take an example from US politics where the Web provided the wherewithal to expose extremism and dissipate its effects. One of the most memorable incidents of the 2012 elections in the United States had roots in an echo chamber of sorts (how far it relied on the Internet for its creation is a moot point). Todd Akin, Republican senatorial candidate for Missouri, remarked that women who were victims of 'legitimate rape' were usually if not always able to prevent themselves from becoming pregnant, as fear-induced hormonal changes have a contraceptive effect. This is clearly ludicrous—there are 30,000 unwanted pregnancies from rape annually in the United States alone—but the pseudoscientific trope is as old as the culture wars.[82] It is a view that is only tenable in the absence of significant interaction with anyone who has any knowledge of basic science.

There is no evidence that Akin's absurd views were fostered by the Internet, but there is a wider lesson about the Internet's role in this affair. Strict ideas about abortion were not themselves barriers to election in 2012—plenty of people were elected who believe abortion to be wrong even in cases of rape and incest. Akin's offensive assumption was that these strict ideas did not involve a tough trade-off against compassion for the victim, and this was relentlessly exposed by online discussion. Although Missouri should have been a Republican gain (Mitt Romney beat Barack Obama in the presidential election there by ten percentage points), the voters rejected Akin. His view, so plausible in the echo chamber, did not survive contact with the wider political process—and the Internet had a part to play. One commentator has identified the Internet as a specific problem for new religions, on the basis of its tendency to 'undermine the plausibility structure'.[83]

On the back of this observation, we may find comfort in a sociological theory called the contact hypothesis, which states that the best way to reduce conflict between groups is to foster contact between them.[84] After all, the members of the extremist group can hardly avoid meeting people who accept mainstream society. However, the contact hypothesis requires four conditions to be met for intergroup conflict to be reduced: the groups must be of equal status, share common goals in dealing with a task together, must work together without competition and have authoritative support, for example from law or custom. It is unlikely that these conditions will be met in the special case of an extremist group.

Anyway, this cannot be the whole story about engagement, as the attacks on the World Trade Center, on the underground train systems of Madrid and London, on the citizens of Mumbai and on the students of Columbine School show. When radicalism becomes extreme and violent, then the engagement envisaged by the extremists can short-circuit legitimate and two-sided forums of debate, and become the asymmetric application of lethal violence. In those cases, the political calculation has to change.

A strategy of violence, though, brings with it serious costs. Without wishing to descend to the relativism of 'one man's terrorist is another's freedom fighter', it is perfectly true that many terrorist groups do have political ends. Although they find it hard to compromise, and therefore have difficulty in planning a move toward their desired state through legitimate methods of persuasion, at least there is a realistic endpoint which can be the subject of painstaking negotiation, as the ending of a number of points of conflict (as for instance in Northern Ireland, Rhodesia and South Africa) demonstrates. Indeed, even one of the world's most entrenched and apparently hopeless conflicts, between Israel and the Palestinians, has seen the broad outlines of a two-state solution gradually evolve, although of course it is a long way from implementation.

Yet the problem of self-referential political violence refuses to go away. Even though they are a small minority of a small minority, some extremists' refusal to contemplate compromise in pursuit of manifestly unrealistic ends (Osama bin Laden was prone to call for the restoration of Islamic rule in Spain, for example) means that serious negotiation is virtually unthinkable. There are no intermediate goals which might act as the basis for a potential compromise.

Similarly, those guilty of school shootings appear to be driven by feelings of revenge and hatred. The problems of killers such as those at Columbine School are too trivial to appear on the radar of any organisation until the individuals in question take drastic action. The quasi-religious ideas that such people often have (the Columbine killers were supposedly immersed in goth subculture, for example, and still have admirers) are tangential at best to their ideas of inadequacy and indiscriminate hatred. With rare exceptions (Seung-Hui Cho, for example, who was responsible for the massacre at Virginia Tech in 2007, fell into a deplorable gap between mental healthcare and firearms regulation), there is nothing to negotiate with, no reasonable step that can be taken prior to the murderous action.

In such cases, rare though they be, where extremists engage directly through violence, there may be a case for addressing the dangers of self-reinforcing feedback loops and echo chambers. Perhaps technology is alienating in this particular way. In that case, we need to consider how technologically enabled networks behave, and how people within them function, both with respect to their colleagues, and with the wider embedding society.

In this chapter, we have argued that there is a *prima facie* case for the Turkle/Sunstein thesis about *anomie* and echo chambers, even if we might doubt its detail. In Part II we will examine some of the assumptions about religious radicalism, online markets and online behaviour in more detail—an examination which will increase our doubts. However, these assumptions continue to inform the work of policy-makers, who have been busy developing schemes to deprive radicals of their influence. These policies are the concrete expression of the Turkle/Sunstein intuition, and are the subject of the next chapter.

3

INTERVENTIONIST POLICY STRATEGIES

The notions of 'radicalisation' and 'de-radicalisation' are now firmly part of the political discourse. Governments throughout the world are embroiled in attempts to identify the types of individuals at risk of being radicalised, the processes that radicalise them and to discover antidotes. Attention has inevitably turned to the role of the Internet. The worries we encountered in Chapter Two are reflected in government departments and policy-making bodies. Radicalism is assumed to have a greater potential to take hold and turn the youthful mind to thoughts of extreme actions where alternative viewpoints are weak or absent, or where personalisation of the Internet is at its strongest. Much of the focus in the post-2001 world has fallen on Muslim communities and Islamic radicalism. Governments have only recently begun to recognise the risk posed by other, perhaps more common, forms of extreme thought and action—from neo-Nazi and right-wing groups to violent animal rights campaigners. Counterterrorist policies have been developed and reinvigorated with this newly constructed opponent in mind, and feature a strand that seeks to understand and combat the dissemination of the very ideas that apparently cause individuals from diverse cultural, geographical, educational, economic and familial backgrounds to seek violent revenge on the societies they view as harming them. There is remarkable overlap and many striking similarities in these policies. From the UK to the United States, from the countries of the EU to

Australia, governments have sought to contest, and ultimately to win, the battle for the hearts and minds of their Muslim populations—to prevent 'radicalisation'.

In this chapter we will take a brief tour through some of these government policies, concentrating on efforts to understand how individuals can be persuaded or indoctrinated by ideas in such a way that they are moved to undertake indiscriminate killings in pursuit of their beliefs, and on the efforts by—largely Western—governments to contest these ideas and to rescue individuals from them. Millions of dollars, pounds and euros have been invested in attempting to repel people from pernicious doctrines and religious teachings, and to promote a moderate alternative that fills the doctrinal vacuum and prevents radicalisation. We will see significant overlaps with the theories of Chapter Two in these real-world attempts to get to grips with them.

Most importantly, for our purposes, we will begin to expose the assumption that guides these policies and brings them into being, according to which it is the actual ideas themselves (whether religious or otherwise) that do the work. 'Radicalisation', as it has come to be used, is assumed to be intimately tied to the motivation to join radical groups and, ultimately, undertake extreme actions. On one level this assumption seems perfectly logical, particularly as extremists themselves make much of their faith as the motivation for their actions. Radical doctrines feed upon various disaffections and present themselves to the vulnerable as the explanation and solution. If only it were possible, reasons the policy-maker (unconsciously adopting the extremists' own characterisations of their situation),[1] to provide alternative information, better reasoning powers or more moderate doctrinal interpretations, then we might prevent people from being seduced by radical groups and thoughts, and ultimately from harming others in the name of their cause.

CONTEST and Prevent

The September 11 attacks prompted a re-evaluation of security policies against terrorism in the United States and in much of the rest of the world—whether they were implicated in anti-Islamic actions (such as the UK), or not (such as Finland). Further attacks in Spain, the UK and elsewhere gave the policy development process further impetus—at the cost of producing policies that are arguably event-driven improvisations rather than a strategic engagement with a potential enemy.[2]

In many ways the UK has been at the vanguard of this development; its own strategy was honed while it held the rotating presidency of the EU and adopted across EU institutions.[3] Crafted after the July bombings of 2005 in London, and the attempted bombing of Glasgow Airport in 2007, the CONTEST anti-terrorism framework is a four-pronged approach comprised of the elements Prevent, Pursue, Protect and Prepare.[4] Much of the strategy focuses on areas such as intelligence gathering and monitoring, the apprehension of suspects, the discovery of terrorist plots and preparations for terrorist attacks on infrastructure. The 'Prevent' arm of CONTEST—or 'Preventing Violent Extremism' (PVE)—seeks to tackle support for and promotion of extremist Islamist ideologies within British society. Prevent has concentrated almost exclusively on the perceived threat posed by Islamist radicals. The attacks of 2005 undoubtedly played a role in the government's decision to adopt this focus on Islamic radicalism, along with other events such as the presence of British Muslims in jihadist training camps, and the failed attempts of individuals such as Richard Reid the shoe-bomber; as noted, policy has been reactive and event-driven. The occurrence of terrorist acts perpetrated by 'home-grown' Muslims (which directly contradicted post-2001 assumptions that this was a primarily external threat)[5] has indicated the existence of a disaffected, alienated and disenfranchised section of young British Muslims, some of whom are susceptible to radicalisation and extremist violence.[6]

Prevent was launched in 2006 with an initial budget of £6 million, rising to £45 million in 2008, and has concentrated on the battle for 'hearts and minds'. According to government guidelines, 'Prevent includes: work to challenge the ideology behind extremism', including supporting the voices of a 'moderate' Islam in this struggle.[7] As the then Home Secretary Jacqui Smith said in 2008: 'That means challenging the sort of ideology that supports terrorism, it means working in our communities to make sure that those mainstream voices are stronger, it means identifying people who might be at risk of being drawn into terrorism and violent extremism.'[8]

The UK is not alone. France has long been fearful of radical imams within its towns and cities and has undertaken efforts to construct what it perceives as a Euro-friendly Islam via various methods, including imam training programmes.[9] Like the French, whose training competes with private Islamic education institutions for students, and which encourages them to teach the Qur'an in a manner consistent with the values of the *laïcité*, Prevent includes a 'range of programmes to build civic leadership and strengthen the role of faith leaders and institutions'.[10] The oxymoronic 'Radical Middle Way' spin-off programme seeks to create a grass-roots movement within Muslim communities 'aimed at articulating a relevant mainstream understanding of Islam that is dynamic, proactive and relevant to young British Muslims'.[11]

Britain already has public universities that certify programmes of imam education and provide the necessary credibility for such organisations to confer degrees through a loose affiliation with many of the twenty-five or more Islamic educational organisations in the UK. The New Labour government considered exercising more influence directly over the content of these training programmes and of sponsoring imams to train on accredited courses.[12] It poured resources into local activities such as funding and charitable status for mosques, Muslim community and youth groups and initiatives, forums against extremism and anti-extremism 'road shows', as well as aligning itself with various moderate Islamic groups and associations. The Department for Communities and Local Government (DCLG) has also weighed in with an estimated £85 million for these local initiatives, making the sum total spent on PVE initiatives in the period 2008–11 £140 million.[13]

Take up of government funding and support has not been lacking. According to the Prime Minister's Office an estimated 44,000 people have had some contact with the various local initiatives.[14] The town of Dudley, for example, was one of the first local authorities to hold anti-extremism forums and to support Muslim groups in dispelling the extremist interpretations of their faith as part of the Prevent Pathfinder initiative, leading it to be selected to run the first Winning Hearts and Minds Pathfinder, which included a 'learning academy', an imam capacity-building programme and a series of conferences for tackling radicalisation and bolstering a moderate version of Islam.[15] Similarly, moderate Muslim groups and clerics have aligned themselves with the initiative, and have taken up the challenge of contesting the ideological basis of Islamist radicalism to prevent potential recruitment. The Quilliam Foundation, an advisory organisation formed by a former Hizb ut-Tahrir activist, and funded by the government to the tune of £1 million, is a case in point. The Foundation consistently urges governments on both sides of the Atlantic to channel resources into supporting moderate Islamic individuals and groups as an antidote to violent Islamic extremism.[16] One critic of Prevent has listed—not without irony—some of the recipients of anti-radicalisation funding intended to drive young Muslims away from violent extremism:

Barking Mosque received more than £5,000 to provide rap 'workshops' and lunches. Something called 'Bedford: Faith in Queens Park' received £9,000 for its basketball club, another £10,000 for its cricket club and £11,000 for 'fusion youth singing'. It received £1,350 for a talk on 'prophetic medicine.' The Cherwell 'Banbury Fair Trade Society' was paid by Prevent to deliver a 'multicultural food festival.' Across the country Prevent money went to boxing, karate, judo and five-a-side football clubs, while the 1st Bristol Muslim Scout Group bafflingly received £3,180 of Prevent money for camping equipment.[17]

Like the UK, the Netherlands—despite not facing a terrorist threat of the same magnitude as the UK—has designed and implemented a complex and ambitious counterterrorism strategy. This development was largely event-driven too, born out of the shock of Dutch filmmaker Theo van Gogh's assassination by Mohammad Bouyeri on 2 November 2004, an act carried out in response to a film he had made that was critical of Islam. The resulting framework, 'Polarisation and Radicalisation Action Plan 2007–2011', provided a multi-pronged approach to countering the potential terrorist threat by seeking to increase social cohesion, target at-risk individuals or groups and increase law-enforcement measures.[18] Like Prevent, the Dutch action plan focuses on tackling extremism at the level of ideas:

The model argues that there is a potential demand for ideology among young Dutch Muslims concerned about their identity, as they seek answers and guidance over 'the meaning of what it is to be Muslim in today's world.' At the same time, there is a supply of jihadist ideology coming from preachers, mosques, and the internet 'which intends to appeal to these young people as they search for answers relating to their identity.'[19]

Again, the response is to take an interventionist stance at several levels, taking down websites, deporting radical preachers and—most relevant to our inquiry—censoring radical ideas. The 2011 'National Counterterrorism Strategy' states: 'Undermining the supply [of violent extremism] means tackling the content of the terrorists' narrative.' 'The government is taking steps to analyse this "narrative" and, where possible, provide counterarguments or a "counter narrative".' This alternative message will vary depending upon context, but will include political, moral and theological aspects.[20] In concrete terms, this has translated into general activities such as a 'Day of Dialogue' and a series of 'Islamic Debates', interfaith meetings and various self-esteem/self-control workshops and events, all aimed at younger Muslims with the aim of making them more resilient to extremist messages by strengthening their interpersonal skills, pride in their identities and critical thinking skills.

While there is some emphasis on 'moderate' Islamic theology in the Dutch approach—as a counterbalance to more radical messages—the main emphasis has been on individual abilities, vulnerabilities and empowerment. The target has been radical views in general, not just violent extremist ones, with the underlying assumption that radical variants of faith challenge social cohesion and lead to the adoption of violent means.[21]

This preventative model is not restricted solely to European countries. Where the UK has taken the lead, others have followed. Interestingly, Australia and the United States are adopting Prevent-like measures at a time when Prevent is undergoing serious criticism and re-evaluation at governmental, community and academic levels in the UK. Australian efforts are still relatively embryonic, but a 2010 White Paper mirrored the British CONTEST strategy, and included a 'Resilience' strand that proposed various counter-radicalisation methods analogous to Prevent, such as spreading anti-radical messages and building social cohesion and inter-community harmony, as well as other trust-building exercises at the grass-roots level, and co-opting local communities to help in the de-radicalisation process. Like the Dutch, the Australian counter-radicalisation efforts focus on individual interventions—identifying individuals at risk of becoming radicalised or those already arrested for or convicted of terrorist activities—and seeking to de-programme them or rescue them from the grip of radical beliefs while replacing those beliefs with more moderate ones. Teams of professionals, presumably including a large contingent of psychologists, are enlisted for these purposes.[22]

In recent years the United States has emulated the UK's counter-radicalisation programme, particularly with regard to countering the message of radical doctrinal messages, and attempting, in effect, to create or sponsor a 'moderate' and therefore more acceptable Islamic message as an antidote. Indeed, it has had to, as the Bush administration's concept of terrorism as fundamentally evil precluded any search for other 'roots'.[23] This proselytising turn has sought to encourage engagement at all levels, both at home and abroad. Samuel Rascoff summarises some of these activities:

The FBI, the Department of Homeland Security, the National Counterterrorism Center, the Department of Justice, and numerous state and local agencies have each engaged with members of the Muslim community inside the United States for the purpose of counter-radicalization. For example, the officials from the Department of Homeland Security and the National Counterterrorism Center recently participated in a community awareness briefing for Muslim leaders in Hartford, Connecticut, devoted to 'Understanding Radicalization and De-Radicalization Strategies.' Among the panel discussions was a session devoted to 'Seeking a Counter-Reformation in Islam.' The U.S. Attorney in Oregon created his own 'network of Muslim community leaders' motivated by the desire to 'educate Muslim partners and give them resources and support so they can counter radicalization on their own.' And Ohio's counter-radicalization efforts have included the creation of an imam council.[24]

Those who meet the criteria for partnership under this 'official' version of Islam are co-opted into developing and spreading the message, such as the Islamic hip-hop group Native Deen, from Washington, DC, and Khaled Latif, the Islamic chaplain of the New York City Police Department, who were sponsored on various overseas visits.[25] Similarly, state and government officials have entered the arena of Islamic theological clarification. For instance, John Brenna—a senior White House official—opined at an official gathering that the correct meaning of jihad is about the individual's struggle for purity rather than the murdering of the innocent, and the Ohio Division of Homeland Security has issued its own 'Guide to Arab and Islamic Culture' which offers similar clarifications on doctrinal interpretation.[26] Such official pronouncements are underpinned by a plethora of outreach programmes at the community level to fund and promote moderate versions of Islam, particularly within the arena of younger Muslims. Meanwhile, a number of US states have banned or have considered banning Sharia law; although there seems little danger of Sharia being imposed in the United States, warnings continue to emerge from think tanks.[27]

Nevertheless, it is worth pointing out that the United States lacks an overall strategic umbrella for understanding and trying to deal with home-grown radicalisation, and most of the responses have been relatively ad hoc. Awareness of the problem was late in coming, and US officialdom has been slow to respond.[28] However, as we will see, this may not be such a bad thing after all.

The online component of radicalisation

According to this model, in which vulnerable individuals are swayed by unorthodox or extreme ideas where they lack alternatives, the Internet has the potential to play a dangerous role in enabling disaffected or otherwise disenfranchised people to engage with radical views. Worse, while impressionable youths may have to bump along in the real world with others who do not share radical religious views, the increasing amounts of time such individuals spend online is likely to mean that they can almost completely isolate themselves from differing views. Cole and Cole have a measured view of the value of the Internet in promoting 'Islamic' terrorism, emphasising that its importance should not be overstated because important and significant ties to offline entities (mosques, individuals, student societies, etc.) also existed in the cases they studied. Nevertheless, it does have some specific roles:

The role of the internet in globalising Islamism is central to this relationship [between self-radicalising cells and transnational terror networks] as it allows the widespread transnational community of Islamists to maintain contact with each other. ... [T]he internet also provides access to violent media, propaganda and technical 'know how' to conduct acts of terrorism.[29]

Consequently, governments have long been looking at strategies for understanding and countering radicalisation online. The authors of the Bipartisan Policy Center's 'Homeland Security Project', for example, directly endorsed the echo chamber view in December 2012.[30] Much of this governmental attention may have been kept below the radar if it has been undertaken largely by security-related personnel, but gradually official policy suggestions and initiatives emerged with the outline of a coherent approach which advocated two types of action: negative measures, such as the taking down of websites and prosecuting those who break laws such as incitement to religious or racial hatred to show that online activity has consequences; and positive measures, such as fostering moderate counter-messages and enthusiasm among Muslim 'thought leaders' in their host countries. For instance, a 2013 event hosted by the New America Foundation[31] was intended to 'empower' thought leaders to make more effective use of information technology, especially 'social media, search engine optimization, application for free advertising and grants, and multimedia design'.[32]

Counter-messaging is also evolving as part of this strategy of bringing an alternative set of moderate beliefs into the online arena, challenging extremists' ideology. Tactics such as mockery and ridicule are intended to undermine the credibility of extremists. More factual engagement contrasts the aims of terrorists with likely outcomes—and it is important to note that Osama bin Laden's stated aims were wholly unrealistic[33]—or states the reality of terrorists' activities (e.g. that the majority of those killed by their actions are Muslims, and that they disadvantage Muslim communities in the Middle East and elsewhere).

There is also growing recognition that governments sound less than sincere when they articulate these doctrinal or ideological messages themselves, and that the co-option of 'friendly' members of the target community is a better option. Grass-roots initiatives, sponsored by government money but with enough distance to remove the taint of bias, is a common suggestion.[34] The Bipartisan Policy Center's 'Countering Online Radicalization in America' makes several such suggestions:

- Bringing together community groups with public relations, advertising and media-production companies, who can help craft better, more powerful messages and turn them into attractive media products;
- Setting up prizes and competitions for online projects that promote civic participation and alternatives to violence;
- Encouraging foundations, philanthropists and private business to launch a grass-roots start-up fund for initiatives seeking to counter extremism and terrorism on the Internet.[35]

Hence the 'echo chamber' hypothesis discussed in Chapter Two, exemplified by Sunstein's argument, is taken as a key component of the analysis.

Problems with Prevent

Although new counterterrorism structures have given a more coherent framework for cooperation, for instance between countries, or between the judiciary and the police, it is fair to say that they have not shown themselves to be silver bullets. Within the EU, for instance, there is some scepticism about the value of cross-border institutions such as Europol (a law enforcement agency) and Eurojust (a body of magistrates aiming to improve cooperation between investigators and prosecutors). Europol is unable even to produce Europe-wide statistics on terrorism, while Eurojust is hampered by lack of mutual confidence in its member countries and the inability to locate its 'value-added'.[36] It looks like the most important area is the battle for 'hearts and minds' as encapsulated in the Prevent strand of the CONTEST framework.

Sadly—and ironically, in the wake of Prevent's widespread adoption as best practice—the strategy of countering radical views is itself undergoing considerable reconceptualization in its home country after much public condemnation. There is clearly an inherent tension about such approaches to radicalism. The specific nature of the 2001 attacks, and subsequent suicide attacks, appeared to mean that deterrence and other preventative strategies that assume the relative rationality and willingness to compromise of the terrorist were rendered inoperative by jihadis' unrealistic demands and their welcoming death. Prevention, then, could only happen if the main causal drivers of jihadi terror were undermined. The main driver was taken to be ideology (as opposed to, say, contested US/UK Middle East policy, or illiberal measures such as extraordinary rendition or the abuse of prisoners),[37] and so government concluded that the most effective way to meet its security aims of preventing terrorist activity was to nullify the ideology. Yet terrorism is a crime, which of course makes it a legitimate target for law enforcement, but discussions of radical ideology may be protected as free speech, and as such are arguably not part of the government's security remit.[38]

Beyond that inherent tension, however, more specific criticisms have emerged. The emphasis on 'Muslim communities' is starkly at odds with the UK government's more general approach to community cohesion, which seeks to avoid the entrenchment of physical and cultural ethnic segregation that were viewed to have resulted from previous policies of anti-racism and 'political multiculturalism'.[39] These latter policies caused a backlash against ethnic groups' perceived receipt of a disproportionately large share of resources. Current policy neglects ethnic-specific agencies in favour of funding more general cohesive projects that cut across cultural lines. As Thomas points out, given its direct emphasis on Muslims and Islam this puts Prevent at odds with current policy and is dangerously reminiscent of previous counterproductive efforts.[40]

The second criticism is that counterterrorist strategies of this type lead to a general depoliticisation, especially among Asian groups and within Muslim areas of the UK.[41] A rising level of suspicion 'may well have stymied or depressed political engagement', Jarvis and Lister conclude on the basis of focus group studies throughout the UK.[42] Legislation was widely seen as leading to targeting, alienation and a prism through which existing racism could be focused, and within such communities the intimidation felt by many under Prevent is viewed as a potential contributor to extremism.[43]

Thirdly, the UK government's Preventing Violent Extremism strategy assumed that all radical groups are suspect, and refused engagement with any of them, even those who had been constructive community partners with the Metropolitan Police's Muslim Contact Unit. As well as undermining some potentially useful police–community links, in the words of the Unit's former head, 'Muslim groups who had no legitimacy in the field of combating violent extremism so far as the MCU was concerned were embraced as DCLG's key partners.'[44]

A fourth line of criticism is that the emphasis on Muslim communities has labelled an entire community as vulnerable to violent extremism, and that this has been exacerbated by the government's tendency to concentrate on what Birt terms a 'value-based' rather than a 'means-based' approach to distributing resources.[45] Instead of offering support at the practical level to groups that work with the particular target section—vulnerable, disenfranchised young men—in an effort to prevent a slide to extremism (means-based), the government has targeted its funding toward the influencing of religious practice itself, of bolstering particular doctrinal understandings of Islam, and of attempting to create a dominant moderate voice and leadership to contest more radical variations.[46] This has led to resentment because it implies that the Muslim community previously possessed an erroneous understanding of its own religion.[47]

One of the problems facing such an approach is that it depends upon the assumption that responsibility for doing something about the radicalisation process rests with the Muslim community. Much emphasis is placed on the wider community providing an alternative doctrinal message, with the help of government funding, to fill the vacuum or to provide education, training and other social skills to help young members find an alternative identity. Yet this misunderstands the very nature of the membership of radical and extremist religious groups, which is anything but under the control of the community. If we set aside radicals of all religious and non-religious types for the moment, and concentrate on Islamic extremists in particular, the groups that have been apprehended are rarely ethnically homogenous, as Olivier Roy has painstakingly pointed out. The Hofstad Network in the Netherlands, whose member Mohhamed Bouyeri was convicted of the murder of Theo van Gogh, for example, was comprised of second-generation Moroccans (including Bouyeri), the 'white' former police officer Martine van der Oeven and two 'black' Dutch citizens—brothers Jason and Jermaine Walters.[48] Traditional Islamic communities are unlikely to have much sway over such individuals at the best of times because many do not hail from those communities, and those that do are explicitly rejecting traditional ties:

They do not represent an Islamic tradition; on the contrary they break with the religion of their parents. When they convert or become born-again, they always adopt some sort of Salafism, which is a scripturalist version of Islam that discards traditional Muslim culture. They do not revert to traditions: for instance when they marry, it is with the sisters of their friends or with converts, and not with a bride from the country of origin chosen by their parents.[49]

Sociological explanations are little more helpful or precise. The often-assumed profile of terrorists as ill-educated, juvenile loners driven by economic deprivation is completely inaccurate.[50] The so-called 7/7 bombings in the United Kingdom in 2005 are a reminder of that: one of the bombers (Mohammad Sidique Khan) was thirty years of age, worked in primary schools with special needs children and had a family of his own. 'Explanations based on poverty, exclusion, racism, acculturation, etc., are simply not specific enough.'[51] Diego Gambetta brands the 7 July bombings as perhaps the most extreme case (in an already extreme set):

What makes it so is both the nature of the target [public transport] and the characteristics of the attackers, which compared with the rest of suicide attacks reveal a mystifyingly weak set of motivations to kill *and* to die—both in the sense of being unrelated to any clear benefit for the attackers and of lacking features that seem to be required to produce and sustain the state of mind necessary to die in that way.[52]

Talk of inferior minds, lack of education, brainwashing and the like is largely misplaced. Khan and other contemporary suicide bombers, including those who attacked the World Trade Center, share a notable feature with groups such as converts to the New Age cults of the 1960s and 1970s: namely their relatively affluent, educated backgrounds. There is something to be learned from this. Unfortunately, the dominant Prevent-type policy model largely ignores this evidence with regard to the reasons why people join such groups, and instead operates on the outmoded assumption that there is a need to 'rescue' the brainwashed—a tactic that did not work in the 1970s and is not likely to work now.

Roy's analysis is far-reaching and well made:

> There is clearly a generational dimension: Islamic radicalism is a youth movement. Frustration is obviously a key element in their radicalisation, but has more to do with a psychological than a social or economic dimension. They tend to become radical within the framework of a small local group of friends, who either met on a destitute estate (as the Farid Benyettou group in France in 2006), a university campus, a gang of petty delinquents and drug addicts or … in jail.[53]

Joining radical groups and sects has little to do with cultural traditions, wider communities or sociological explanations, and more to do with friendship and the search for solidarity, belonging, identity and self-worth, as well as political grievances. As Cole and Cole report of one young man, his decision to join a radical Islamic group in the UK took him 'from being very confused and ashamed of my colour and religion, I was told that I was a lion—a warrior, with an identity of my own that I could claim if only I accept Allah into my heart'.[54] Doctrinal interpretation and theological debate misses the mark by a considerable distance. Creating a theological reformation in Islam or a 'moderate' Islam is a red herring; it has no bearing on the motivations of such individuals, even if it were possible. Religious pluralism, we will argue at length, is the only way of managing radicalism and violent extremism. It will not eradicate it—nothing can—but it can make it more manageable.

An aggressive takedown policy on sites that promote violent extremism or incite hatred and violence, or which provide information on such things as bomb-making, coupled with the use of the law to prosecute such individuals where possible, should be part of any sensible counterterrorist policy. However, online counter-messaging and 'empowering' Muslim clerics and community leaders (i.e. bribing them to make their messages more congenial to the embedding society), is likely to hit the nail squarely on the thumb. Such interventions will lack credibility—anything that has the whiff of government responsibility or support will drive the targeted individuals away from it—and the moderated voices will not appear upon the radar of those attracted to stricter or more radical versions of their religion. As Vidino concludes in a survey of US counter-radicalisation measures, 'considering the potential for stigmatization and backlash that programs like Prevent inevitably possess, it might be wise for American authorities to find a middle ground between the European programs and the admittedly insufficient counter-radicalization measure they have been implementing'.[55]

Legitimacy

We might also consider the threat to political legitimacy that attempts on the part of government to create a 'moderate' Islamic doctrine represent. It is a cornerstone of democracies that the state's exercise of political power should be based upon the broader consent of its citizens. Even when citizens differ on politics and in their interests, there must be a widespread, deeper commitment to the legitimacy of the democratic framework. Even the losers in the political process must have support for the process itself. What counts as such support or consent is of course less than clear. Realistically, getting (even if it could be measured) unanimous consent would be impossible. Some people, such as the insane, cannot be expected to give their consent. Others might reject the democratic process entirely, or hold views that are radically inconsistent with the foundational principles upon which the system is premised, such as those who reject any moral worth (and hence any rights as citizens) of some because of the colour of their skin. Such people are free-riding on those committed to democracy, whose political and non-political activity creates a tolerant civil society.

These issues aside, when it is apparent that the consent of a significant proportion of citizens may be ebbing away, then the charge of illegitimacy can arise. The complaint that the state lacks the requisite level of legitimacy is one of the most serious that can be levelled against it. We might wonder, therefore, whether the state taking a stand on matters internal to religious views—such as the 'correct' doctrinal understanding of Islam—will test that legitimacy. Given the plethora of different religious and non-religious doctrines that citizens affirm within contemporary democratic societies, the state's endorsement of the truth of one such doctrine and privileging it above others will cause concern for some who will begin to question whether the state truly respects their religious or other commitments. This has been a perennial issue in the UK, with its centuries-old church and constitutional strictures against Catholic monarchs, although over time tensions have cooled (even though the settlement is consistently revisited, even today). But the relation between the state and its citizens, when the state is effectively telling perfectly peaceful people who adhere to a brand of Islam which has not received the official stamp of approval that they are dangerous to it, will be rendered more fraught by exercises such as this.

In such cases the state seemingly takes on the mantle of religious authority, and many citizens might reasonably reject not only the particular conception it supports, but also its authority to do so.[56] Consequently, those who provide theoretical and philosophical support for liberal democratic institutions often endorse a particular stance of state neutrality on questions of the truth or superiority of religious views or doctrines.[57] By remaining neutral—in the sense of not basing policies or positions on the perceived truth or falsity of comprehensive beliefs—the state will find it easier to navigate the tricky waters of pluralism and remain legitimate. Backing, and even more so creating, a moderate version of Islam might be thought to violate such neutrality.

However, it is important to be clear as to what exactly would constitute a violation of neutrality. Once we understand this, we will have a more nuanced position that does not necessarily rule out such state intervention, at least in principle. The legitimacy of the state solely depends, as we have seen, on those who might be said to 'buy-in' to the fundamental principles of the democratic political project. These principles include a respect for all fellow citizens as in some sense equal and deserving of respect, and an acknowledgement that citizens are reasonable in affirming a plurality of religious and non-religious doctrines or ways of life. Those who endorse or engage in violent extremism typically reject one or more of these fundamental ideas. They often view the only legitimate state as one formed along religious lines where religious dissent is unreasonable, and where such a state does not exist they believe it is permissible to punish those who reject the word of God, or to change the state by violence. Clearly, the democratic state does not need to garner the consent of such individuals—this would be impossible. The stance of neutrality in such circumstances is not therefore a requirement, and the state might seek to argue that those who believe their version of faith requires violent disobedience are wrong, and that their view is false on religious grounds.

Such a stance, however, might sound disingenuous or deceitful, or at least lack credibility. Those who hold a moderate version of that faith compatible with democratic values may deeply resent government pronouncements on doctrinal interpretations, regardless of stripe, undermining its legitimacy in a wider community. The solution found to this dilemma in the Prevent strategy is to co-opt moderates to lead the debate against extremists. If this can be done without compromising legitimacy, then we still have to address the empirical question of whether such actions are workable in practice, or whether, as we will argue in Part II, that they are counterproductive because of the way the market in religion works, and miss the mark because they are based on the erroneous assumption that what matters in terms of attracting individuals is the religious ideas themselves.

Although Prevent has been subject to widespread criticism in the UK by, among others, the coalition government of David Cameron—which inherited it from the previous Labour government—its underlying rationale has been retained. One of the sustained criticisms of its earlier (pre-2010) guise was that it lacked clear direction or criteria regarding what it should be doing or whom it should be funding. It was criticised for actually funding the types of groups it was supposed to be discouraging.[58] A revamped Prevent strategy outlines three areas of concentration: (1) to 'respond to the ideological challenge of terrorism and the threat we face from those who promote it'; (2) 'to prevent people from being drawn into terrorism and ensure they are given appropriate advice and support'; and (3) 'to work with a wide range of sectors and institutions (including education, faith, health and criminal justice) where there are risks of radicalisation which we need to address'.[59] The new commitment is to meet Prevent's aims in a more efficient, targeted manner, but the aims remain essentially the same. There is little that has changed from Jacqui Smith's statement of 2008.

Conclusion to Part I

Counterterrorist thinking rests on two foundations. First, the main causal driver of terrorism is assumed to be radical ideology, which motivates certain disaffected individuals. The antidote is therefore to focus on the ideas, to provide a moderate version of a particular religious faith—one that is congenial to peaceful participation in liberal democratic societies—to compete for popularity and adherents. According to the prevailing thinking with regard to counterterrorism, the Internet plays a dangerous role in making it easier for people to come into contact with antisocial ideology, and hence increases the pool of potential terrorist dupes.

Second, government intervention in the religious market is the best way to promote a moderate version of a particular faith. Even where governments do not intervene directly but instead support or finance particular sets of adherents, they are able to skew the marketplace of ideas in a particular direction.

Thus far we have raised a number of doubts about these foundations. However, in Part II we will scrutinise these assumptions critically. We will argue that individuals join radical religious groups—even participate in violent extremism—because of the tangible social and personal benefits that membership brings. Members make a calculation of the costs and benefits of membership, and act accordingly; they are not brainwashed to act against their 'authentic' instincts. We will argue that direct or indirect government intervention in the religious market unbalances a comfortable equilibrium where moderation is dominant, and creates an environment that is more conducive to radical versions of particular faiths. Government subsidy, ironically, actually has the effect of assisting the very positions it seeks to undermine. An anti-radicalisation policy of challenging doctrinal messages with government intervention rests upon very shaky foundations indeed.

PART II

4

RELIGION AS A MARKETPLACE

From fleeing the lynch mob to running for president

There are many extraordinary stories in the history of the United States, but few are more extraordinary, or indeed so quintessentially American, as that of the Church of Jesus Christ of Latter-Day Saints, more popularly known as the Mormons. It is a story that features the mob murder of its founder in 1844, and a prominent member very nearly being elected president in 2012. How could a motley crew of outcasts, driven to the very frontiers of America, become so mainstream that it is now one of the fastest-growing churches in the world?

Joseph Smith was a poorly educated farmer. In 1827, at the age of twenty-one, he received a visitation from the angel Moroni telling him where to find the story, engraved on metal plates, of Jesus's visit to the New World. Divine inspiration guided Smith's translation of the mysterious text from Reformed Egyptian into English. Sitting behind a curtain, he dictated The Book of Mormon to his scribes, and returned the plates to Moroni upon completion in 1830.

Their doctrine was eccentric even by the Christian standards of the Midwest, and the Mormons were loathed. Smith taught that matter came before God (He had merely assembled the world), and that the dead could be baptised. The Book of Mormon contains certain anachronisms, including references to wheat and horses, which are not native to North America. Most importantly, Smith received a revelation of the legitimacy of plural marriage, and is understood to have had more than two dozen wives. In 1844 he ordered the destruction of an anti-Mormon printing press, which was run by a disgruntled former Mormon whose wife Smith had attempted to marry. While Smith and his brother were in jail awaiting trial, a lynch mob broke in and killed them.

It is an extraordinary story. But what is most remarkable is that it is only the beginning. In the years that followed the Mormons relocated en masse to Utah; renounced polygamy in the face of legal sanctions; and eventually allowed the ordination of black members after growing tensions over civil rights. Mormonism ceased to advocate practices at odds with its wider society. In the 1960s, George W. Romney became the forty-third governor of Michigan, and made an ill-starred run for the Republican Presidential nomination. In the following decade, the wholesome features of teenage pop star Donny Osmond adorned millions of girls' bedroom walls without notable complaint from their non-Mormon families, and in 2008 George's son Mitt Romney made his first, far more credible, run for the Republican presidential candidacy, having already served as the seventieth governor of Massachusetts.[1] During the campaign he was even relaxed enough to joke that he was the only Republican candidate to have restricted himself to one wife.[2] A Gallup poll just before the Iowa Caucus showed that 80 per cent of Americans would vote for a Mormon if they thought he was the best candidate.[3]

There is a similar pattern in business. Romney was a founder of private equity investors Bain Capital, while his father was president of American Motors Corporation. One of his unsuccessful (though more cerebral) rivals for the 2012 nomination was the son and namesake of Jon Huntsman who created the Huntsman Corporation, a multi-billion dollar chemicals behemoth. One finds Mormon founders of companies across sectors, from cut-price airlines (JetBlue, Azul and SkyWest Airlines) to hotels (Marriott). A number of successful management gurus are Mormons, including Clayton Christensen and Stephen Covey, and the Marriott School of Management at Brigham Young University in Provo, Utah, has an excellent reputation.

The Church is now the fourth largest in the United States and one of the fastest growing worldwide; from under 2 million adherents in 1960, almost all of whom lived in America, to 12.7 million by 2005, over half of whom live outside the United States (1 million each in Mexico and

Brazil, where the Mormons compete fiercely for lapsed Catholic souls with the Pentecostal Churches).[4] This is a remarkable turnaround. Now comfortably in the mainstream, Mormons attract attention because of their neat, polite, sober image. They have made the transformation from outsiders to being the ideal embodiments of a particular clean-living booze-free conservative lifestyle, neatly dressed with stable marriages and large families.[5] A recent Broadway send-up, *The Book of Mormon*, was even used by the Church to promote itself.

Existing alongside this journey to respectability, however, is a darker side. Not all Latter-Day Saints are paragons of virtue. Fundamentalist versions of the creed have periodically surfaced to reassert the original teachings of Smith, and the wider movement has had its fair share of megalomaniac leaders who have been successfully accused of being paedophiles, rapists, bigamists and murderers. Many Mormons (including some who refused to be hounded out of their original home of Missouri) refused to give up on plural marriages or the need for bloodletting to atone for sins.

Ervil LeBaron is probably the most notable personality in this line of descendants from Smith. Ervil was booted out of the Church of the Firstborn of the Fulness of Times after leadership disputes with his brothers Joel, Ross and Floren. The Church of the Firstborn was itself an offshoot of the Apostolic United Brethren—a small Mormon fundamentalist sect presided over by Rulon C. Allred. Ervil formed his own church—the Church of the Lamb of God—in 1972 and immediately launched a quest for domination by claiming to be the rightful successor of Smith—as well as the Messiah—while embarking on a murder spree (with the help of relatives) eliminating his brother Joel, one of his daughters, a brother-in-law, plus many others including Rulon Allred. Ervil's reign of terror continued from behind bars and even after his own death thanks to a hit-list compiled as part of his theological work *The Book of the New Covenants*. His disciples, including a number of his fifty-four children, worked through the list. Seven of his relatives killed three former followers and an eight-year-old girl simultaneously at three different locations in 1988 (the final culprit was only captured in 2010). Thanks to the complex intertwined and polygamous nature of the LeBaron family, siblings and relatives have been both murderers and murdered.

We have an extraordinary set of linkages. If we trace back from Donny Osmond and Mitt Romney, we reach Joseph Smith. Yet moving forward from Smith we find a direct link to Ervil LeBaron. Romney and the Osmonds are upstanding citizens and pillars of the community, yet it is the fundamentalists who preserve, in however warped a way, Joseph Smith's innovations of plural marriage and blood atonement. How is it possible for a single tradition to encompass important public servants such as Romney on the one hand, and murderers such as LeBaron on the other? Millions of highly respectable Mormons who make an important contribution to their host societies are the heirs of Smith when viewed in terms of the continuity of the institutions, but if we select Smith's heirs on continuity of ideology, then authenticity has the American Gothic flavour of the Church of the Lamb of God.[6]

This is a deep issue in both religious sociology and theological history. What are we to make of the conduct of a church? The founders may be in extreme tension with the embedding society, wilfully ignoring its norms—indeed, sometimes gaining adherents precisely because they point out the contradictions and immorality of current norms. Yet as a church grows, it becomes, or at least influences, the norm. It would not grow if it did not do so—it is impossible for everyone to be a rebel. But then what are we to make of fundamentalists or radicals? Are they wrong to adhere to the founder's precepts? Are they mad? Are they evil? How can we make a conceptual distinction between a transgressive figure who provides a genuine and important moral challenge (it should be obvious that Jesus was precisely such a figure)[7] and the wholly vile Ervil LeBaron? Is such a distinction possible, or are we merely articulating our own prejudices?

The trajectory of religious radicalism is the theme of this chapter—and to explain this we will rewind the story a further 100 years or so before the arrival of the angel Moroni, to the Enlightenment.

What good is religion?

The eighteenth-century Enlightenment was a period of opposition to religious irrationalism, or what was known as 'enthusiasm'. Newtonian physics had pushed the boundaries of science and understanding; God and reason were destined to collide, and collide they did. The schism in Christianity brought about by the Reformation was deepened and complicated by the further rift over the new science. Some found reason enticing and argument seductive, others wholly rejected it in favour of revelation. A bewildering variety of Christian sects began to emerge—and in many places managed to co-exist without fatal social fracture—each with their own reconciliation of God and reason.

The reasonable, balanced and moderate Enlightenment figures were deeply suspicious of the antics of the enthusiasts. The loud, excited religiosity that included speaking in tongues, evangelical joy and other unseemly outbursts appeared hysterical. When prejudice and superstition were taken as grounds for certainty and intolerance, the result was deeply distasteful, primitive and open to ridicule. As Shaftesbury argued in *Characteristicks of Men, Manners, Opinions, Times, Etc.* 'there are many panics in mankind besides merely that of fear. And thus is religion also panic; when enthusiasm of any kind gets up, as oft, on melancholy occasions, it will.'[8] Religious enthusiasm was especially difficult to damp down or laugh out of polite society in America. The frontier and the large distances made it possible for enthusiastic groups such as the Separate Baptists to thrive away from the straitlaced New England establishment. Charismatic thinkers like Jonathan Edwards led a religious 'awakening', a backlash against versions of Christianity seduced by reason, in the 1740s and 1750s.

Like many at the time, philosopher David Hume believed that a moderate religion, ideally subsidised by a government interested in social harmony, would be the best means for damping down this unseemliness. A 'ghostly practitioner', in Hume's phrase, who relied on the number and enthusiasm of his adherents for resources would have to move to extreme positions 'to excite the languid devotion of his audience', while the government-backed salaries of clergymen of established churches would make it 'superfluous for them to be farther active than merely to prevent their flock from straying in quest of new pastures'.[9] If religion would not wither away under the force of reason and science, then its more irrational manifestations and excesses could at least be controlled by careful official management and intervention.

Hume's practical view is underpinned by the view of religion we discovered in Part I, as the product of simple minds and irrational choices. He equated religious belief with a primitive, pre-scientific thinking process that would fade away when ignorance was replaced by the light of reason. To put the point bluntly, the demand for religion would decline when people wised up to its silliness. Thus began a venerable tradition of commentators on the sociology, psychology and anthropology of religion, including Comte, Spencer, Freud, Ostow and more recently Dawkins, which identifies the drivers of religion (particularly in its fundamentalist varieties) as irrationality, brainwashing, authoritarian personality dispositions, poor education, ignorance, lack of maturity, low self-esteem, mental illness (to name just a few). Stories of religious practices and conversion, particularly the rise of sects and cults (think of the Hare Krishnas and the Moonies) are often told in terms of mass brainwashings, and charismatic leaders preying on the emotionally and mentally vulnerable. The Prevent strategy, as we have seen, is effectively based on the same assumption. Let's call it the Dumb-and-Malleable (DAM) thesis.

However, there is a feature about religious belief that causes a significant problem for the DAM thesis: namely, the facts. In particular, religion and religious belief have not faded away as many had predicted, but are very much alive and well despite the progress of modernity. If DAM was correct, we should expect to see moderate, state-established churches thriving, and virtually no radical (enthusiastic) sects, within a broad context of declining religious adherence. The reverse is in fact true. Religious adherence is in anything but decline throughout the modern world, and demand remains high. Moreover, in many if not all countries with government-sponsored churches, the more radical sects flourish while the churches of the state stand empty. Higher levels of education, and scientific research and knowledge, have done little to dent levels of religious belief, with those professionals at the sharp end of hard science showing little sign of jettisoning their religious beliefs en masse.[10] The preferences, intelligence, education and mental health of the religious do not differ from those of the non-religious, as studies have shown time and again.

The goods of religion

The DAM thesis lacks an adequate understanding of the human side of religion and the goods it provides for individuals. In particular, it ignores the fact that religion provides important messages of meaning.[11] Religious views provide a particular schema or mental order for understanding the world that explains causes and purposes, a guide to making sense of that world and living correctly in it. This is in marked contrast to the apparent chaos of reality and the paucity of the irreligious scientific worldview in terms of support and guidance on how to live our lives. As Ronald Dworkin argues, religion (in which he includes the possibility of a religious atheism), is comprised of a science part (albeit not a science that adopts the methods or standards of enquiry of modern science), and a value part:

> The science part offers answers to important factual questions about the birth and history of the universe, the origin of human life, and whether or not people survive their own death. ... The value part of a conventional theistic religion offers a variety of convictions about how people should live and what they should value.[12]

Messages of salvation provide emotional comfort and a sense of purpose in suffering and danger, while the existence of a moral community provides a sense of belonging and role. Religious adherence has not declined in the way predicted and hoped for by the Enlightenment rationalists, but continues to fill a deep psychological need in human beings. Even in the most troubled periods for religion of recent times— the 1960s—where institutional religion appeared, finally, to be on the wane, the result was merely a shift to alternative forms of the religious message. As Karen Armstrong writes: 'Instead of going to church, the young went to Kathmandu or sought solace in the meditative techniques of the Orient.' The demand remained constant; it merely shifted its attention to new forms of religious product. The so-called New Age sects and the rise of individual religiosity took the place of formal religions for many, sating, in their own way, 'a hunger for *mythos* and a rejection of the scientific rationalism that had become the new Western orthodoxy'.[13] Although these are very important goods, their significance is largely denied or ignored by the DAM theorists.

There are other goods that religion can supply. It may also become an expression of political ideas. Some have argued that the Bible was a post hoc justification for Israelite nationalism, promoting the centralisation of worship in Jerusalem and uniting the two kingdoms of Israel and Judah.[14] The theology of the Promised Land was also useful in promoting exploration and colonisation, particularly of the new continent of America.

Finally, religion supplies group cohesion.[15] A religious community provides the adherent with a ready-made community or social network where members have plenty in common.[16] Humans as social beings benefit enormously from such community. For instance, although there is a cost in that an individual has to be prepared to make certain sacrifices for the common good, they no longer have to rely solely on their own resources for problem-solving. Others are likely to take one's part. Early small communities might easily be kept together as they wandered by the resulting solidarity. In later static communities, religion would be a powerful means of mobilising and uniting individuals in warfare, while simultaneously making them confident in victory (this of course is hardly an unalloyed good, but those societies that did this most successfully would tend to survive, along with their religions, in a warlike world). In more recent settings, people who might find themselves lost and alone in a city of millions can find a community with more in common than mere geographic proximity.

This sense of belonging and membership is extremely important,[17] and will be a central theme for the rest of Part II; for instance, it helps to explain God's deep and some might think prurient interest in His followers' sex lives, as '[r]eligion also solemnizes marriages, dedicates parents to children, and binds generation to generation in a web of indestructible vows'.[18] The continuity of the group is often, if not always, assured by regulation of sexual relations.[19] And the harder it is to keep up with the behavioural requirements of a group, the easier it is to deter free-riders; anyone wanting the benefits of the group must make the sacrifices.

All ways of binding a religious group together depend on mutual trust between its members—and, in the case of some groups, mistrust of non-members.[20] For that reason, it is worth making a brief excursus into the issue of trust.

Religion, trust and antitrust

Trust is a complex problem. It is often naïvely posited as a general social good—the more trust in society, the better that society is.[21] It is also sometimes confused with trustworthiness, where what is described as a problem of trust is really a failure to show honesty and loyalty.[22] The way to make sense of the issue is to note that the concept of trust makes little or no sense without reference to the prior concept of trustworthiness.[23]

We can roughly define trustworthiness as the property of an agent that she will do what she says she will do—specifically, she will suppress or augment her own interests in the interests of a delimited set of others.[24] Trust is then an attitude taken by one agent to another—the trustor trusts a would-be trustee if and only if he believes that she is trust-worthy.[25] Trustworthiness is relative to a particular context, task and audience. A trustworthy brain surgeon is not necessarily a trustworthy car mechanic. Someone who is trustworthy with her friends' cash will not necessarily be trustworthy with her friends' husbands. Someone might only be a trustworthy lawyer during office hours, and only for the benefit of paying clients. A spy might be trustworthy with respect to the foreign power that employs her as a double agent, but not her home nation which is her 'official' employer.

It is clear from this brief description that the problem of trust is not how to increase it, but rather how to coordinate trust and trustworthiness so that we trust all and only trustworthy people. To trust the untrustworthy is to leave oneself open to fraud or worse. Failure to trust the trustworthy produces opportunity costs. The latter also gives precisely the wrong incentives; trustworthiness imposes costs, and if people come to learn that there is no point in being trustworthy (because they are not trusted), then they will not behave in a trustworthy way.

Against this background, societies and groups have evolved methods of signalling their trustworthiness—such signals are ideally connected with and derived from their trustworthiness, are costly and credible (for instance, 'if you don't like our product, you get double your money back') and are difficult to forge (the best signals are often based on personal acquaintance).[26] One of the most important relations of trust are within-group relations, where a small group—which could be a kin group, or an interest group, an ideological party or a group of co-religionists—are bound together by relations of trust.[27] Members of the group are particularly trustworthy in their dealings with each other, and trusting of each other. The group's effectiveness, in the sense of it being a social machine, will be enhanced by the resulting coherence.

If the group exists in important respects in opposition to social values, then membership of the group will indeed be costly and hard to forge, which makes it an ideal signal of trustworthiness and a particularly reliable sign for group members that they should trust each other. Of course, if we also see group cohesion as a religious good, it follows that what makes membership of a radical religious group attractive and valuable for its members will also help increase the bonds of trust within it. Hardin makes the point that 'extremist and fundamentalist groups are often able to block such corrective devices as come from interactions in the larger society' because they are able to use their dense networks of trust to block out non-members with demands for very costly signals.[28] Sociological surveys bear this out with empirical evidence. 'Fundamentalist religious convictions are associated with low trust, but adjusting for that theological effect, active participation in a religious community, even a fundamentalist one, is associated with high trust.'[29]

Given two churchgoers, the one with fundamentalist views is likely to be less trusting, while given two fundamentalists, the one who goes to church more often is likely to be more trusting. It seems to follow that the more closed the community, the worse the outlook for trust in and of wider society. Hardin calls the state that results from isolation from alternative influences a 'crippled epistemology'[30]—an echo chamber by another name.

Recall that someone is trustworthy if they will reliably subordinate their interests to the interests of a specified set of others. If this set of others is a small radical or extreme group, then trust and trustworthiness, far from being helpful contributors to social capital, can have dramatic social costs. The trustee will work in the interests of members of the group—but if it is defined in opposition to the norms and mores of the wider embedding society, then the group members' interests may be in outright opposition to the interests of everyone else. Trust and trustworthiness become weapons for the extreme, and burdens on wider society.[31]

The market for religious ideas

Fourteen million moderate Mormons live in a state of minimal tension with their host societies, creating a stable centre of gravity that could never be achieved by the thousands of heretical (from the point of view of the main church) polygamists, or the dozens that are prepared to live with murder and institutionalised child abuse. When we think about the way that churches evolve, the whole situation seems extraordinary. How could a successful and conservative group such as the mainstream Mormons have become so socially integrative despite never having been subsidised by a government? It is perhaps even more surprising that the appalling offshoots like the LeBarons never seem to go away, as more recent examples such as Warren Jeffs (president of the Fundamentalist Church of Jesus Christ of Latter-Day Saints, at the time of writing in prison for serious sexual offences) show. Abhorrent though their ideas may be, they do seem to attract a tenacious rump of people who are prepared to commit crimes in order to follow their own strange moral codes.

It is consequently possible that the DAM thesis still produces sensible policy. Those who are willing to live in extreme tension within their host society may take that as the price for sticking to their beliefs, yet on the part of the host community there will be a desire (and given the prevalence of terrorism, possibly a need) to rid itself of what from its point of view will be dangerous sociopaths. In such a context, it would seem to make sense for the majority community to reward the religious behaviour it is able to tolerate, to give incentives to leave behind intolerable practices, and to provide alternative practices to follow, as Hume suggested.

The flaw in the argument is that there are already many incentives for the heterodox minority to live in harmony with the host community. Harmonious living is itself an incentive, and for most of us the supreme one. A strong heterodoxy already commits the believer to discounting the benefits that integration into mainstream society provides.

In his great theory of market societies *The Wealth of Nations*, the economist and philosopher Adam Smith denied the intuitive doctrine of his friend Hume, and instead argued that state sponsorship of religion would merely aid extremism by disincentivising moderates and increasing the vigour of religious enthusiasts. Smith was no less suspicious of the claims of religious enthusiasts or of their potential for social disharmony than his friend, and recommended the teaching of science and philosophy and the public provision of entertainment as 'antidotes' to excessive religious zeal and enthusiasm.[32] Yet despite his reservations about the more radical variants and his moral scepticism more generally, Smith held no similar conviction that religion would expire; instead, he understood that people would continue to seek the goods that religious affirmation provided for them. Rather, his concern was the correct mechanism for tempering the advance of socially disruptive movements of any kind. A free marketplace in religious ideas was the way, *pace* Hume, to promote moderation. With total freedom of conscience—rather than state sponsorship or prohibitions—'a great multitude of religious sects' would be forced to compete for the centre ground:

The teachers of each sect, seeing themselves surrounded on all sides with more adversaries than friends, would be obliged to learn that candour and moderation which is so seldom to be found among the teachers of those great sects whose tenets, being supported by the civil magistrate, are held in veneration by almost all the inhabitants of extensive kingdoms and empires ... The teachers of each little sect, finding themselves almost alone, would be obliged to respect those of almost every other sect, and the concessions which they would mutually find it both convenient and agreeable to make to one another, might in time probably reduce the doctrine of the greater part of them to that pure and rational religion, free from every mixture of absurdity, imposture, or fanaticism, such as wise men have in all ages of the world wished to see established.[33]

In other words, churches, sects and other religious groups are constrained by the forces of the market as much as firms are in other sectors of the economy.[34] Forced, in the absence of government funding, to compete to survive, the clergy depend for their financial existence on the donations of their flock. 'It is with them as with the hussars and light infantry of some armies; no plunder, no pay.'[35] Because of this, Smith conjectured, they would seek to maximise membership.

Although the model is of Western derivation, the market or *souk* metaphor has also been used specifically to apply to competition between Islamic ideas; for instance, one commentator has written that Islamic websites constitute 'a bustling marketplace in which diverse "goods"—in the form of ideas and concepts about Islam and Muslims—are exchanged; bought and sold',[36] and that jihadi cyberspace has taken on the paradigm of viral marketing.[37] Indeed, some historical interpretations suggest that the idea predates theories of the market altogether; Robert Graves put the following speech into the mouth of the Emperor Claudius:

This was the time that I began going closely into the question of new religions and cults. Some new foreign god came to Rome every year to serve the needs of immigrants and in general I had no objection to this. For example, a colony of 400 Arabian merchants and their families from Yemen, which has settled at Ostia, built a temple there to their tribal gods; it was orderly worship involving no human sacrifices or other scandals. But what I objected to was disorderly competition between religious cults, their priests and missioners going from house to house in search of converts and modelling their persuasive vocabulary on that of the auctioneer or the brothel-pimp or the vagabond Greek astrologer. The discovery that religion is a marketable commodity like oil, figs or slaves was first made at Rome in the late Republican times, and steps had been taken to check such marketing, but without great success.[38]

Of course the historical Claudius might well not have reasoned, or have been able to reason, like this. Yet Graves's description of cosmopolitan Rome is accurate, and the fictional Claudius's attitude is representative of the views of some in authority, at least until the coming of Christianity.

This market-driven incentive to innovate does not mean a total free-for-all. In the first place, innovation is generally produced incrementally within the context of an existing tradition with which continuity is broadly maintained.[39] Furthermore, as a consequence of competition to recruit, most groups will gravitate towards the moderate centre-ground where most potential adherents actually reside. Many people will of course simply inherit their parents' religion, but where there is competition there is also a great deal of churn. Around a quarter of people in the United States do not follow their parents' religious traditions, but if we include those who have switched denominations (e.g. within Protestantism) and those who have rejoined their parents' religion after leaving, the figure rises to over one in three.[40] Putnam and Campbell set out the import of these figures, and describe what looks very like a market-driven structure of demand and supply:

Many Americans—at least one third and rising—nowadays choose their religion rather than simply inheriting it. And a significant fraction of those who remain in the religion of their parents must surely have contemplated leaving it, and they too may be reasonably said to have chosen and not simply inherited that religious affiliation. Religion in America is increasingly a domain of choice, churn, and surprisingly low brand loyalty. That is the demand side of the religious marketplace. On the supply side, we would expect successful 'firms' (denominations and congregations) in such a fickle market to be especially entrepreneurial in 'marketing' their product, a prominent feature of American religious life on which historians have recently commented.[41]

What does this mean for religious groups? Small, extreme groups are tightly knit, but only a very small number of people are prepared to undergo dramatic tensions with the embedding society. It follows that groups can grow only by decreasing those tensions. Hence there is a feedback loop—less rigid doctrine puts off fewer people, while a desire to increase congregational size will engender the aim of compromising with non-believers and maximising consensus.[42] Those churches which do not take practical steps to move towards a more consensual position will fail to create economies of scale and tend to stagnate or wither. The actual doctrinal or institutional compromises which allow such nifty footwork need to be justified in such a way as to appear consistent with founding texts, principles or ceremonies. Fortunately, religious revelation—exposure to a truth that comes direct from God and is therefore both undeniable and is based on a fixed interpretation—is a useful mechanism for justifying what may otherwise seem tergiversation.

The spatial metaphor for understanding competition is a familiar one that has been used for explanations of party competition in democratic polities, as well as economics more broadly. Groups—whether religious sects, businesses or political parties competing for votes—will converge on the centre-point (the median voter in party political terms) of their target audience, analogous to two profit-maximising retail outlets looking to locate on a busy high street where potential customers are evenly spread. Each outlet would do best to locate as close to the middle of the street as possible. The optimal position will be for them to locate next to one another at the centre-point. This is a counterintuitive point that Smith, unlike Hume, grasped well.

To see why any other location would be sub-optimal we need only imagine one of the businesses relocating a few doors to the left of the centre-point. If, in response, the other outlet were also to relocate, again to the immediate right of its competitor, then it would put itself in a better position to acquire the business of the majority of those customers who are located on the right of the street because it has control of more of the spatial territory of the street. This is a general tendency that goes far beyond economics.[43] If potential religious adherents tend to prefer a low-cost version of their faith because it is in greater harmony with their daily existence (an assumption that will be explored in the next section), then religious groups will quickly converge on the moderate centre-ground inhabited by the median adherent in order to maximise membership.

This is not to say that religions can easily abandon what have been regarded as keystones of their traditions. It was a struggle for the Mormons to give up polygamy, for instance, though a necessary one given their need to bring Utah into the United States. When traditions are relatively low-cost, the benefits of rejecting them may be outweighed by the benefits of retaining a key aspect of the religious identity. As an example, the Second Vatican Council of 1962 attempted to adapt the Catholic Church to the modern world with various measures such as replacing the Latin mass with liturgy in the vernacular. These measures sought to boost attendance in the democratic West, but the result was a dramatic decline (by 50 per cent in England and Wales and by 35 per cent in the United States since 1960). Attending a Latin mass hardly put Catholics in very much tension with their embedding societies, while for many the spectacle communicated important aspects of the adherent's relation to God. As a result, there has been a revival in the Latin mass (with a sevenfold increase in its prevalence in the United States between 1991 and 2012, and a sixfold increase in England and Wales between 2007 and 2012), while Pope Benedict XVI felt the need to endorse the Latin mass in 2007 (and, as noted in Chapter One, Pope Francis I tweets in Latin). This is not simply an indulgence of ageing congregations—there is even a movement, Juventutem, for young traditionalists.[44]

Smith's account seems to have been vindicated by experience, such as that, for example of the United States, one of the least regulated religious environments in the world. Unlike societies with state-established religions, it demonstrates both high levels of religious belief and participation, and a large number of religious sects that tend to gravitate towards a moderate theological and normative position (protected, of course, by religion's special constitutional status).[45] Almost 65 per cent of Americans adhere to a religion and claim to attend church regularly on Sundays.[46] The United States also boasts more than 6,000 Christian denominations, the vast majority of which are very small in terms of membership.[47] Moreover, the biggest churches—on the various measures of membership, attendance and participation—are those that would be considered moderate in their teachings and social requirements in Christian terms: the liberal Quakers, the Roman Catholic Church, the Unitarians and so forth, as well as the moderate Mormons. However disconcerting or even horrifying Mormon theology appears to an 'average' Christian American, the behaviour of most Mormons is sober, discreet and conservative—a little boring possibly, but certainly not offensive. And when we look at the factors determining levels of tension between a minority belief and the majority, behaviour looms largest.

The same tendencies are similarly evident within Islamic religious environments. Under conditions of free religious competition, radical and extremist sects, and ultra-liberal groups, have limited success. The most successful are those movements capable of occupying the moderate centre-ground. Turkey is a case in point. It has gradually, but increasingly, moved from a position of religious establishment to one of considerable latitude. According to Introvigne, Turkey's period of de-Islamization under Kemal Ataturk (around 1925) led to the rise of a number of radical and extremist movements resisting state coercion on religious matters, such as the insurrection in South East Turkey in 1925, the conspiracy of the Tarikat-i Salahiya from 1920 to 1925, and the religiously oriented uprisings such as the 'Menemen incident' in 1925. By contrast, from the 1950s onwards the Turkish religious market has become increasingly deregulated to the point at which a vast array of groups exists in relative freedom. As a consequence, the number and predominance of extremist groups has diminished and a preponderance of moderate-conservative movements has emerged. This moderate centre 'has offerings that are both rich and diverse and which have met with a notable degree of success. In this central niche of the religious market, at least three different expressions of Turkish Sunni Islam compete.'[48]

Religion, moderation and socialisation

The opposition to enthusiasm characteristic of such philosophers as Hume or Shaftesbury is of a piece with the Enlightenment prejudice against superstition and uncivilised behaviour. Smith, on the other hand, not only gives reasons why religious enthusiasm is a problem, but also argues the converse, namely that centrist, moderate behaviour is a public good which cannot be produced by the use of public funds to reward it. Again, his conceptualisation of theological debate as a marketplace of religious ideas is central.

Religious groups produce and distribute moral information for individual members. Churches provide a context in which a moral code is learned and its practice internalised, observed and enforced. The rise of industrial capitalism created an urgent need for social groups that could provide this function, as the sprawling urban habitat of the industrial poor had displaced observant, small-scale, pre-industrial, largely rural communities.

Smith argued that support networks for norm compliance were unnecessary for the affluent because they were not sunk in obscurity, as were the poor. The wealth and social status of the affluent kept them, on the whole, sufficiently within the gaze of the public eye. Constant exposure to social scrutiny in this manner compelled them to behave with propriety. Smith was not only troubled by the material deprivation of the poor, but also their social invisibility within the Great Society, which was responsible for the demoralisation of citizens and undermined political and social responsibility:

A man of low condition, on the contrary, is far from being a distinguished member of any great society. While he remains in a country village his conduct may be attended to, and he may be obliged to attend to it himself. In this situation, and in this situation only, he may have what is called a character to lose. But as soon as he comes into the great city, he is sunk in obscurity and darkness. His conduct is observed and attended to by nobody, and he is therefore very likely to neglect it himself, and to abandon himself to every sort of profligacy and vice.[49]

Religious sects provide the face-to-face interaction the poor require in the absence of small and intimate social settings. It is in these settings that we learn to develop the virtues that spill-over to our dealings with others. Hence a member of the labouring classes:

never emerges so effectually from this obscurity, his conduct never excited so much the attention of any respectable society, as his becoming the member of a small religious sect. He from that moment acquires a degree of consideration which he never had before. All his brother sectaries are, for the credit of the sect, interested to observe his conduct, and if he gives occasion to any scandal, if he deviates very much from those austere morals which they almost always require of one another, to punish him by what is always a very severe punishment, even where no civil effects attend it, expulsion or excommunication from the sect. In little religious sects, accordingly, the morals of the common people have been almost always remarkably regular and orderly; generally much more so than in the established church.[50]

Within the wider context of Smith's moral theory these small sects provide the sites of individuals' socialisation. Other people act as the mirror for individuals to observe their own behaviour. The individual then internalises these external responses to his own motives and actions. 'We suppose ourselves spectators of our own behaviour, and endeavour to imagine what effect it would, in this light, produce upon us.'[51] Participation in religion serves both to cultivate virtues conducive to participation in, and support of, modern industrial society, and to provide information about the character and reliability of members to others—a service crucial for the poor in Smith's time in order to gain such things as employment, credit and so forth.

There is anthropological evidence that religion does help socialise its members, facilitating adaptive responses to diverse environments by developing flexible cognitive mechanisms, evoking emotional responses that provide reliable information about individual physical and psychological states, supporting theological ideas that support and endorse the existing social order, and encouraging public displays of support for the social order via rituals, badges and taboos.[52] Furthermore, this sort of information-spreading can help religion flourish even in a society with a large number of non-believers, on the assumption that non-believers are impressed to some extent by the positive contribution believers make to society.[53]

There is some evidence that non-believers are indeed attracted by the contribution that believers make to society. In one type of experimental psychology game, subjects allocate more money to strangers when they have been primed with religious words, even if they are not actually religious.[54] Such constructs about the 'this-world' value of religion abound; in the United Kingdom, for instance, there is stiff competition to get children places in faith schools, which are perceived even by irreligious parents to have a better social ethos and quality of education and discipline than state schools.

As non-believers are attracted to some aspects of religious groups or institutions, can those groups turn this to their advantage? This has been tested via computer simulations of interactions in which two kinds of agents, believers and non-believers, interact. Non-believers pass on verifiable information to their offspring, while believers pass on verifiable and unverifiable information (unverifiable information might include details about an afterlife that can pass on no conceivable advantage in this world to offspring). Under most scenarios, believers gradually became extinct because their beliefs did not help the next generation adapt. But in simulations where non-believers were attracted to belief because of some presumed real-world advantage, believers flourished.[55]

Nancy Rosenblum has termed this the 'logic of congruence'.[56] Participation in groups helps cultivate certain values and virtues in the members. Which ones are cultivated depends somewhat on the nature of the group in question. What has been said so far applies to all religious groups, small or large, moderate or extreme. The important thing is the idea that membership in moderate groups—i.e. groups that exist in little tension with the surrounding social environment—tends to create individuals who are predisposed to internalise, uphold and perpetuate the values and virtues of that environment. Smith believed that this was inherently valuable.

The nature of modern society, with its emphasis on the private pursuit of an individual's ends, undermines the capacity for the type of engagement that the public sphere requires for its own stability and success.[57] Paradoxically, a free society that is not respected by its members is liable to be overthrown by those members, precisely because they have been given the freedom to act; hence such a society can only be sustainable if it is judged favourably by its citizens. On Smith's account, such citizens are the products of moderation, and moderation produces the right kinds of citizens. Hence he provides (as Hume does not) a political imperative to address the issue of extremism, and to try to ensure that the moderate centre remains influential.

The persistence of radicalism and the radicalism of persistence

With this map of the terrain in place we are now able to explain the persistence of radical religious groups. The wearisome, seemingly eternal splintering of religious groups, the rise, decline and fragmentation of denominations, is cyclical and has been dubbed the Church–Sect Cycle (CSC).[58] The CSC is illustrated by Smith's observations that such apparently economic phenomena as the burdens of monopoly, the benefits of competition, the constraints of the market and the hazards of state regulation are as tangible in the case of religion as any other sector of society.[59] This in turn points us towards an explanation for the persistence of small, radical sects such as the Apostolic United Brethren and the Church of the Lamb of God in the face of the great success of mainstream churches such as the Church of Jesus Christ of Latter-Day Saints of which they are offshoots.

The Church–Sect Cycle

The logic of the CSC is a continual process of movement from a position in tension with the surrounding social environment and its cultural norms towards greater harmony with it, until a split occurs with those who are unable or unwilling to adjust their beliefs and religiously inspired behaviour any further and a new sect arises that seeks to assert a fresh high-tension position. As a sect grows and begins to attract increasing numbers of members there is an inevitable moderation of its stance towards this-worldly positions, as Smith observed. Popularity and security come at the price of having to accommodate a wider array of members. The largest potential pool of members occupies the moderate centre ground of the surrounding social environment, so sects gravitate to this pool of potential adherents. Those who resist the move to the centre to preserve the aspects of the faith that cause the tension (e.g. plural marriage, in the case of the Mormons) will become increasingly restless and dissatisfied until a rift occurs and a splinter group moves to reaffirm the old position by splitting with the main group and forming a new sect.[60]

Logically, the radical member of the splinter group does not see himself as the splitter; from his point of view he is providing the meaningful continuity. The continuity of the institution, as perhaps embodied in property, bank accounts, enrolment lists and mailing lists as well as its rituals and texts, is not as important, for the sectary, as the continued fundamentalist and literalist interpretations of the texts and practices that set the group apart.[61] This is an important part of radical thinking; as Scruton put it with regard to violent actions where someone puts their life at risk for perfect strangers (in both religious and secular contexts), 'it is very difficult to contemplate the sacrifice of your life without believing in the durability of the thing for which you die'.[62]

On the other hand, because the new outlook may be more fragile and open to persuasion from outside, 'founders of new religions are likely to feel the need (1) to protect their followers from outside influences and (2) to ensure that, within their movement, the new way of seeing things is being constantly reinforced and, if need be, enforced'.[63]

The moderates

Most people are moderate in religion; for instance, Putnam and Campbell found that despite the extreme religiosity of Americans, most accept that there are basic truths in all religions. The hard core that believes one religion is true and the others false, and that people of other faiths will not reach heaven, only constitutes about 11 per cent of the American population.[64] What explains the predominance of moderate adherents—i.e. their clustering on the centre-ground—is the low cost of participation. Most people are not sufficiently interested in religion to allow it to inconvenience them in other spheres (in the United States, Putnam and Campbell found that when someone's political and religious affiliations are perceived as out of line, they are more likely to resolve the issue by changing their religious affiliation rather than their politics).[65] As the sceptic philosopher Sextus Empiricus pointed out two millennia ago, if your beliefs are mild or even absent, it makes sense to go along with the general thrust of local behaviour:

Thus, attending to what is apparent, we live in accordance with everyday observances, without holding opinions—for we are not able to be utterly inactive. … By the handing down of customs and laws, we accept, from an everyday point of view, that piety is good and impiety bad.[66]

Such passivity no doubt caricatures the apathy of the average moderate believer. Yet Sextus links this basic disinterest with contentedness (*ataraxia*), while insisting that those with strong opinions on religion or indeed anything else are 'perpetually troubled', and in this broad characterisation he is borne out by the sociology of religion. Note that, for our purposes, it is irrelevant whether strong opinions cause the troubled feeling (as Sextus believed), or vice versa; all that matters is that they correlate. Theology is often a driver for selecting a religious congregation, but friendship and social networks are the reasons for remaining there. Any religious leader must 'provide resonant teachings and worship to bring people in the door, but once in the door those people must find ways to connect with one another if they are to keep coming back'.[67] This is much more difficult for extremists than for moderates, because 'most of the issues that mobilize activists, who almost by definition have opinions and interests outside the mainstream, do not matter much to "regular" people, the vast majority of whom do not make politics [or theology] a priority'.[68]

The pull of the centre-ground is therefore even stronger than in Hotelling's example of the two shops on the high street. If a group's beliefs and practices are in harmony with the surrounding social environment, then there is little or no cost involved in participation for individuals. The adherent does not have to change his or her beliefs, morals, diet, daily rituals, dress code, language or the like. The benefits of religious participation—levels of spiritual and physical well-being, social recognition, solidarity, collaborative goods and so on—accrue with little to pay on the part of the individual.

It is all a matter of degree, of course. The Mormons place a number of duties upon their members. Children usually work in the church. When men are nineteen and women twenty-one, they do missionary work overseas for two years (eighteen months for women). They are not given a choice of destination, are allowed only two phone calls home per year and work at converting their hosts for sixty hours a week. Once that ordeal is over, they should provide 10 per cent of their pre-tax income to the church. These are tough requirements of the kind that used to be called 'character-building', when compared to those of more mainstream churches, but they will not necessarily put the believer in conflict with his or her host society. The growth of the Church of Jesus Christ of Latter-Day Saints is perhaps unsurprising given the bonds that such initiation helps forge. Yet they pale into insignificance in comparison to the demands and expectations of the more extreme offshoots.

Anything but the quiet life

Radical sects are likely to be characterised by a highly committed, voluntary and converted membership, a separatist orientation, an exclusive structure and an ethos of ethical austerity.[69] By contrast, a moderate church will most likely display such features as birth- or familial-based membership, inclusiveness and universalism, and an adaptive and compromising stance toward the larger society.[70] This distinction was even used as the basis for an influential distinction between churches and sects. 'A church is a religious group that accepts the social environment in which it exists. A sect is a religious group that rejects the social environment in which it exists.'[71] In particular, those who insist on persisting with the founding principles of a group are likely to find themselves marginalised within their groups, and to feel increasing pressure over time to splinter away.

This is inevitable in any kind of large-scale collaboration. In his review of collaborative strategies in the online environment, which were discussed in Chapter Two, Charles Leadbeater sets out the importance of the relation between a core unit which defines the group's mission and a larger periphery of less-committed collaborators.[72] Each is essential to a large-scale successful non-hierarchical collaboration. Yet we can see the roots of the CSC in Leadbeater's analysis; if the less-committed periphery is sufficiently large and diverse, then it may end up diverting the group from the mission determined by the core—this often happens in industry, where a product developed for one purpose ends up being used for another. And if the core is sufficiently devoted to the mission it has defined, it may have little choice but to give up on the large-scale collaboration and try to start another.

The proximate cause of this pressure to splinter is often doctrine and practice. To take one example, the Branch Davidians catapulted to infamy in 1993 when, under the leadership of David Koresh—born

Vernon Wayne Howell[73]—they burned down their compound in Waco, Texas, after a protracted siege by US security forces. The Branch Davidians were an archetypal millennial fundamentalist cult, and its history neatly illustrates the CSC. It did not appear miraculously out of thin air, despite much being made at the time about Koresh's magnetic personality and brainwashing abilities. Rather, it arose as a reaction to moderating trends in the parent group.

The Branch Davidians were a splinter group of the Shepherd's Rod sect. They split from the latter group in the 1950s after a schism over doctrinal interpretation and the requirements of belief. The Shepherd's Rod group was an excommunicated splinter from the Seventh-Day Adventist Church. That split was caused by the teachings of émigré Victor Houteff who, in 1929, criticised the Church for departing from its own teachings and attempted to inspire a revival of its original messages and practices. The Seventh-Day Adventists were themselves formed from a backlash against the mainstream Protestant denominations in the United States during the middle part of the nineteenth century, advocating a return to more austere religious observations and values, both in terms of doctrine and lifestyle. The Seventh-Day Adventists were considered at the time to be a radical new sect, but their stance gradually moderated as they sought acceptance from the mainstream and an increase in membership. Each resulting splinter (summarised in Figure 2) occurred in an effort to re-establish the initial austere position. It is telling that both the Shepherd's Rod group and the Branch Davidians sought to recruit most of their new members from within the Seventh-Day Adventist mainstream.[74] The doctrinal heritage was very important; continuity with the founding beliefs was the most important thing for the splitters. However, this continuity is often in the eye of the beholder— splitters often also produce dramatic novelties as well (Koresh allowed himself alcohol, formally banned by earlier groups in the tradition).

Although we have taken examples so far from Christianity, the CSC can be observed in all major religious groups. In August 2005 the British government announced its intention to ban the radical Islamic sect al-Muhajiroun. In an act of accommodation to the mainstream the group quickly wound itself up shortly before its leader Omar Bakri Muhammad was banned from the UK. Bakri had originally established al-Muhajiroun in 1983 in Saudi Arabia and brought it to the UK in 1986 because of doctrinal and political disagreements with the leadership of Hizb

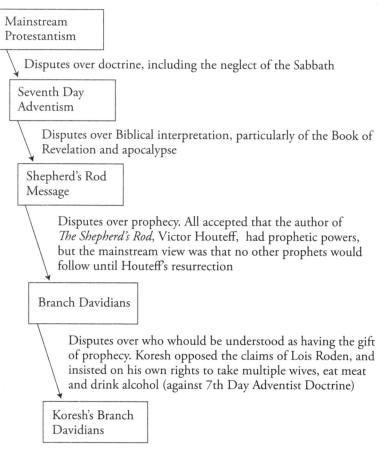

Figure 2: The Church–Sect Cycle in action

ut-Tahrir, of which he was an active member. Hizb ut-Tahrir, though itself a radical group—founded by Taqiuddin al-Nabhani in Jerusalem in 1953 after a period with the Muslim Brotherhood organisation—had demonstrated a moderating tendency, attempting to stay within the bounds of legality, especially within the UK, via such means as the denouncement of terrorism as a means to create an Islamic caliphate. When al-Muhajiroun disbanded in 2005, it gave rise to two subsequent sects, the Saviour Sect and Al-Gurabaa—both of which were subsequently banned.[75]

In Algeria, the Armed Islamic Group (GIA) was a ferocious and coercive Islamist terror group in the mid-1990s, but in an interesting departure, it moved away from conventional notions of jihad by being too extreme; its conflict with other rebel groups against the government led it to denounce all civilians as apostates and legitimate targets of violence. It disintegrated under this absolutist notion and was displaced by other groups, including the Salafi Group for Preaching and Combat (GSPC), which by 2001 was seeking a negotiated end to its struggle. This led to a power struggle within the group, and its eventual rebranding as al-Qaeda in the Islamic Maghreb (AQIM).[76] In the Philippines, the compromise between the Islamic rebels in the region of Mindanao and the central government (of a largely Catholic nation) has led to several splits with increasingly, no doubt unintentionally, comic acronyms. The Moro National Liberation Front signed a peace agreement in 1996, prompting the creation of the rejectionist Moro Islamic Liberation Front, whose participation in peace talks in 2013–14 produced another belligerent outfit, the Bangasamoro Islamic Freedom Fighters.[77]

The costs of rejecting rapprochement with a wider social consensus include sacrifices in such aspects as diet, dress, rituals, voluntary work, proselytising missions, time commitments and so forth, as well as an enclave mentality and being on the receiving end of group persecution. For example, in his study of al-Muhajiroun, Quintan Wiktorowicz lists the contribution of resources required by each and every member: one-third of all salaries; one two-hour study session per week; several hours per week of individual theological, ideological and political study; the hosting of at least one public study circle per week; the manning of a propagation stall in their local community every Saturday (12–5 p.m.); participation in public demonstrations every Friday afternoon; other 'outreach' initiatives appropriate to the community; and restrictions on diet, clothing and the performance of religious observations. In addition, members suffer the costs of potential arrest and detainment on a regular basis; higher instances of marital breakdown; the risk of breaking family and friendship ties through being ostracised. Specific social activities discouraged include listening to music and radio, smoking, sleeping too much, chatting on the phone for hours, playing games, aimlessly browsing the Internet and window shopping.[78] Yet the benefits are perceived by members of radical sects to be much higher. High costs deter free-riding; those who continue as members are playing their part through costly participation.[79]

Culture and the CSC

When combined with the understanding of recruitment incentives in a free religious market, the appeal of strictness as a means for creating group solidarity and overcoming free-riding helps explain the continual emergence, fracture and re-emergence of religious groups and the persistence of small radical sects. However, it is worth noting that not all radicalisation and fundamentalism is necessarily attributable to the CSC, although the mechanisms are related. The fulcrum of the CSC is the mores of the embedding society, yet any religion with global pretensions will be embedded in a number of societies, whose cultural norms will pull in various directions. What is radical in one place might be reactionary elsewhere.

To take one current example, Anglicanism is experiencing a crisis at the time of writing because of a more tolerant attitude in Europe and the United States to gay people, clergy and marriage, and because of the increasing likelihood that, following women clergy, women bishops will be ordained. Clergy from elsewhere, particularly in Africa, are resisting these innovations which are intended to keep the Anglican Church congruent with movements towards greater social equality.

At first glance this looks like another instance of the CSC splitting a church, with the Africans as the fundamentalists and the Europeans and Americans as the growth-pursuing moderates. But this interpretation would be mistaken. In this case there is a split between the rich world and the developing world, and it is merely cultural imperialism to assume that the cultural norms of the rich world should determine the shape of a church which may be larger in the richer countries but is growing more quickly elsewhere. In fact, the anti-gay, anti-women-bishops position adopted by conservative clerics in Africa and elsewhere is driven not by a desire to live in tension with their embedding societies, but rather by the desire to maximise congruence. It is because such clergy live in societies where women's rights mean little and gay rights less, that they oppose liberalising moves in the UK and the United States. If these churches were subsidised they could probably go along with the liberal tide, but in the hard-fought free market of religious ideas in most such nations the clergy receive stiff competition from illiberal Muslim clerics.

In the case of this dispute, the liberalisation of Anglican belief has been rationalised by a device similar to that used by the Church of Jesus

Christ of Latter-Day Saints to justify its own moves away from polygamy and racial discrimination. Whereas the Mormons cited continuous revelation, the Anglicans of the rich world choose to understand the Bible not as a text to be understood literally, but rather as a source of allegorical wisdom to be interpreted in the light of the spiritual needs of Christians in their environment. Yet—again for cultural reasons—such a move is not congenial to Anglicans in the developing world, where the Bible's tales of war, exile, forced migration and natural disaster ring horribly true.[80] In such societies, the Bible speaks loudest when it is interpreted most literally.

Hence the need for global religions to grow can also lead to tensions not only within a particular community, but also when it exists within two or more contrasting cultures. Islam as a growing religion can be found across the world from West Africa to the Pacific Islands—but also, as Olivier Roy points out, a remarkably large number of Muslims live as minority communities in non-Muslim societies, and reactions to and against these societies, as well as to and against globalised and decontextualised influences (such as satellite TV news, as well as radical sermons to be found online) will of necessity be complex. Disentangling the causes of fundamentalism, radicalism and extremism will not always be simple.[81]

The CSC and implications for policy

This account of the CSC raises the question of whether government regulation or intervention to this end is an effective method for attaining the ends of the policies described in Part I. Once the state begins to sponsor religious groups or to regulate the religious sphere, it introduces a negative incentive with regard to the recruitment of believers that produces unintended consequences. We have seen how religious groups compete for members from among the pool of potential adherents in much the same way as businesses compete for customers and political parties compete for voters. When income is generated purely by reliance on the contributions of members, this provides a heavy incentive to recruit vigorously because survival depends upon gaining and maintaining a sufficiently sized flock. This mechanism does not remove religious radicalism entirely—indeed, some radical views are a necessary part of any healthy religious environment—but it exercises a moderating influence.

However, when the state offers financial support, the clergy tend not to turn to their flock, but to their new paymasters for the source of their security (in the same way that nationalised industries tend not to produce efficiently, because it is easier to lobby politicians to make up financial shortfalls than to make money in a competitive market). 'In simplest terms, the providers of public religion are insulated from competitive pressures and the preferences of those they ostensibly serve. To the extent that their remuneration is fixed, they will tend to provide suboptimal effort and, hence, suboptimal quality of services.'[82] If the providers of religion can increase their financial benefits or reduce their responsibilities by lobbying their government sponsors, this is what they will do. State funding encourages socially wasteful rent-seeking behaviour (the investment of resources in an effort to secure the benefits of a monopoly) on the part of religious groups. Because this rent is valuable, firms can be expected to invest resources to secure a monopoly position from the government.[83] They will be able to reduce output and increase price. But rent-seeking benefits the rentier, not the wider society.

If rent-seeking is characterised by increased costs and lower productivity, there should be a tendency for state-sponsored churches or religious groups to follow suit in comparison with non-state-funded groups, and a growing and significant body of empirical evidence in religious sociology bears this prediction out. Indeed, exactly this tendency was in evidence during the early years of the United States. Levels of theological training during this period were much higher—and hence much more costly—for established churches than for new sects.[84] Overall, they were more costly to run and produced lower levels of participation, allowing the new sects with their poorly trained, less costly, but zealous preachers to sweep the board and to shape the religious environment in their favour. Rent-seeking is currently evident among Christian churches in an array of European countries with established churches (the Scandinavian countries being an obvious example). The knock-on consequences of rent-seeking include low levels of religious participation and activity, and a shift of membership from moderate established churches to more radical or austere sects, such as the Evangelists.

Taking the lower levels of participation first, it is clear from work in this area that the higher the degree to which a religious economy is monopolised, overall levels of participation—counted by various measures including church attendance—within that faith will tend to be low. As Stark and Iannaccone show in their comparison of European and US activity in the mid-1990s, a notable drop in activity is visible where state sponsorship exists.[85] Until 2000, for instance, Sweden funded the Lutheran Church of Sweden from taxes. The integration of church and state was close. Taxes paid the wages of the clergy and covered church infrastructure costs. Direct contributions from the congregation amounted to almost zero. Wages were high, and the clergy were employed as civil servants; productivity was low. Church attendance in Sweden ran at approximately 6 per cent. Similar stories hold in Denmark, Norway, Finland, Iceland and Britain.

With regard to the location of membership, the vast majority of the 6 per cent of Swedes that did attend church during this period did not attend the Church of Sweden, but preferred the free churches (predominantly the evangelical denominations). Of their membership, these free churches regularly turned out well over 70 per cent of their membership for Sunday services. This is evidence that religious monopolies push expansion at the fringes, not the moderate centre. Again, this pattern is repeated in other European countries where established churches exist or existed. Moreover, it is not a phenomenon limited to Protestant churches, as the pattern is also observable where the Catholic Church is established.

Nor is it a phenomenon limited to Christianity. In Muslim-majority nations, religious demand looks very similar.[86] Even in Saudi Arabia— an Islamic country that, on the face of it, appears to be an example of religious monopoly where Wahhabism occupies a position of state establishment and control—a plethora of competing forms of Islamic teachings exist, indicating a thriving religious market. State-sponsored clerics compete with an unregulated private sector, 'offering all shades of Islam from ultrafundamentalist to moderately liberal, different interpretations of Wahhabism, and even frank opposition to it, not to mention the presence of both non-Wahhabi Sunni minorities and Shi'ite minorities'.[87] Consequently, Saudi Arabia has recently undergone something of a religious re-awakening ('the Revival').

The practice of the Islamic faith within Europe similarly varies with the level of state regulation or establishment of religion. This is not only true of societies where the dominant religion is non-Islamic, but is also likely to create a double bind when the state—as in the case of Britain— has an established Christian church and sponsors other Islamic groups.

As Chaves et al. observe, 'more regulation of the religious market is associated with lower levels of religious participation *even among minority segments of the market*.'[88] Chaves takes participation in the *hajj*—the required pilgrimage to Mecca—as one indicator of religious participation, and the evidence shows that this is affected (once social class is controlled for) in the same way as religious participation among Christians. 'In societies with "freer" religious markets, Muslim participation rates are higher. The effect of a free religious market apparently is not limited to the numerically dominant, Christian segments of the religious markets.'[89]

Where state-sponsored churches or groups exist, this creates incentives for rent-seeking. In terms of the intended effects of reducing the pull of religious radicalism by offering a viable alternative moderate religious message, rent-seeking is pernicious in that it pushes potential adherents to lose faith and radicalises those who remain. It is possible to predict that under government sponsorship of moderate Islamic groups we would see higher costs, lower attendance rates and the production of members with lower levels of religious knowledge. Increased costs will result as the consequence of higher wages for officials, and increased training costs because of the perceived need to counter radical Islamic doctrine at the theological level. Some evidence of the latter is already present in proposals to sponsor university degrees in Islamic studies and Islamic theology, and to train Muslim clerics. Moreover, increased participation would be seen in the more radical groups or sects, rather than in these moderate groups. Evidence of this is already apparent from the limited studies of radical Islamic sects, such as al-Muhajiroun in the UK where membership flourished and activities multiplied.[90] This is directly contrary to the intentions of most policy proposals, and provides considerable reason to reject them.

If state regulation or involvement reduces religious participation and pushes adherents to the more radical fringes, then the reverse side of the coin is that less state intervention—a freer religious market—leads to more participation and an increase in more moderate views (in terms of adherents). Regulated markets are inefficient and hinder production, engendering fewer and inferior services. They also remove consumer control over the product, thus decreasing the value of participation. Furthermore, sponsored or subsidised groups or sects are likely to arouse suspicion regarding their motives among potential adherents. Taken together, these mechanisms create an environment where those who do bother to participate are drawn to groups that are more radical in their orientation rather than less.

If this is correct, then we should expect conditions of religious monopoly to produce situations where strict and ultra-strict sects flourish at the expense of the more moderate or centrist groups. Even in countries where drastic action has been taken against non-established theological variants, radicalism and extremism have flourished. This is largely because they are willing to make sacrifices (for all the reasons of group benefits that we have already discussed), and so can operate underground, whereas much of their competition is less willing to risk exposure and persecution. Consequently, those moderate groups in the opposition fade away and their membership becomes available for recruitment. Under Saddam Hussein, for example, the Iraqi state attempted to eliminate all independent religious organisations during the 1980s. Those groups that did survive were the ultra-radical and semi-terrorist ones, including some branches of the Muslim Brotherhood, just as the model predicts. 'Extremist ultrafundamentalists are thus able to meet a large segment of religious demand, with virtually no competition, and are paradoxically reinforced by the same legal measures that are aimed at eliminating them.'[91]

Taking the market model further

This chapter has described the market model of the religious environment, and argued that the myriad different groups, sects and doctrinal positions—including very radical ones—that we see within all religious traditions are fruitfully conceived as competing in a kind of market in religious ideas where the providers and consumers of religion act in ways reminiscent of suppliers and consumers in economic markets. The model has provided us with an explanation of the seemingly eternal moderation–fracture–schism process that is observable among the major religions. The debate which began between Adam Smith and David Hume about how to moderate religious communities has been won by Smith. When left to run without interference a free market in religious ideas tends to bring people to 'centrist' positions that minimise tension between the religious group and the host community. However, as the history of many churches testifies, the free market cannot eliminate extremism because the Church–Sect Cycle will always continue, resulting in the constant turnover and formation of new sects.

This model will be used in Part III to explore the characteristics of religion online. However, and again there is an analogy with economics, this bald statement of the market philosophy gives the misleading impression that religions move about in order to capture adherents with fixed preferences. This is not so—naturally, the preferences of potential adherents will change. A younger person may be more inclined to rebel against his or her surroundings than in later years. Having children or amassing property may increase the incentives of living in harmony with neighbours. Solidarity with co-religionists who are perceived to be under attack, or perceptions of unjustified economic inequalities or other types of discrimination may decrease such incentives. In the middle of these changing relations between the person and their environment, religions themselves will naturally attempt to change the preferences of those they feel may become adherents. The next two chapters will accordingly look at the issue of dynamic religious preferences, beginning with the ways in which religious groups work to set the terms of debate.

5

THE SUPPLY SIDE

FRAMING AND THE CONSTRUCTION
OF THE CENTRE GROUND

Are religious ideas really irrelevant to the problem of extremism? The picture we have drawn so far has minimised the role of ideology both in motivating individuals to join radical and extreme religious groups (even to sacrifice themselves to a cause), and in the decisions that groups make with regard to their methods of operating (whether to be peaceable or violent). Although the ideals themselves have little direct input in this sense, they do enter the picture indirectly. In this chapter we discuss the role of ideas in one particular dimension, namely their contribution to 'framing' a particular issue. The way an issue is framed—the language and concepts used to represent what is going on, and the images popularly used to illustrate it—can have a direct impact on how it is perceived, and where it is placed in the spectrum of debate. Part of the competition between groups is to secure their preferred conceptualisation as dominant.

What constitutes the moderate centre-ground is not somehow fixed or frozen, or set externally to the religious discourse of a given society. It is actually constructed by that discourse. A given group could either move toward the centre-ground to accumulate adherents, or it could move the centre-ground to its position. The strongest examples of framing come from politics. In his consideration of framing strategies in party politics, Andrew Hindmoor argues that 'by priming the use of particular frames, parties can change their position without changing their policy. A party whose policies are viewed as extreme when one frame is used may appear moderate when another is put in its place.'[1] Pioneering theorists Nelson and Oxley concur: 'Part of a successful communicator's job is to frame issues so that certain beliefs, concerns, values, and goals take precedence over others.'[2]

This is of obvious relevance to the view of religious groups we have put forward; groups can reframe issues by employing various tools in order to moderate their position. This is not just sleight of hand. Rather, no actual centre exists in an objective sense. The centre is constituted by perceptions of issues or policies. The Internet and associated technologies provide a plethora of communication tools that allow religious users to reframe issues in ever-sophisticated ways. Religious groups are in the business of communicating, and as we have seen, the Web is their new terrain.[3]

How does framing work? Language conveys much more than the literal meaning. Does a terrorist organisation 'admit' or 'claim' responsibility for an attack? The latter word implies a positive attitude without shame, while the former has connotations of shamefulness. The UK government and the IRA spent many years not only fighting each other, but also trying to frame the narrative of the troubles in Northern Ireland (criminal actions or an anti-colonial struggle?). This was not just a war of words; as part of the government's aim to establish the IRA as violent criminals, IRA prisoners were denied Special Category Status (analogous to prisoners of war) and treated as criminals. They in turn reacted by refusing to use prison facilities, such as uniforms and the showers, and ultimately began a campaign of smearing excrement on the walls, undermining the British narrative of normality.

In another well-known example, in the immediate aftermath of the 11 September 2001 attacks on the World Trade Center, the Bush administration began to plan its response not as a 'war on terror' but as the investigation and punishment of a crime. The notion of a war on terror came later, as a better way of framing the objectives of the administration in responding to events. 'War' conjures images of enemies, attacks, challenges to territory and sovereignty, and suggests armed, military response with strategic objectives of control and conquest.

'Crime', by contrast, suggests investigation, policing, trial, conviction and punishment.

The Web is well suited to framing and reframing issues, particularly political and religious ones, and not always with positive results. For example, in 2009, after the disputed re-election of President Ahmadinejad of Iran, protestors took to the streets, reporting and coordinating their activities via social media and microblogs, notably Twitter. Of course, for the young, educated and generally urban protestors, the use of smartphones to record the events was completely normal behaviour, in the same way as earlier generations of anti-authoritarians worked with faxes and *samizdat* publications. However, the story of what was happening in Tehran was interpreted in the Western world, particularly the United States, entirely through the lens of Twitter. Blogger Andrew Sullivan quickly argued that 'the revolution will be Twittered'.

That a new information technology could be improvised for this purpose so swiftly is a sign of the times. It reveals in Iran what the Obama campaign revealed in the United States. You cannot stop people any longer. You cannot control them any longer. They can bypass your established media; they can broadcast to one another; they can organize as never before.[4]

As a wave of tweets, YouTube videos and blogs supporting what became known as the Green Revolution washed over the world's smartphones and computers it appeared that authoritarianism was doomed. One member of the Bush administration began a campaign to give Twitter the Nobel Peace Prize.[5] Yet all was not what it seemed.

Twitter's penetration into Iran was not actually that large—only a few thousand accounts, largely in Tehran—and many of the Iran-related tweets and retweets were from outside the country. One highly prominent Iranian journalist, oxfordgirl, was actually based, as her online name suggests, in Oxford in the United Kingdom. A large proportion of tweets came from the United States, from anti-Islamist sympathisers and members of the diaspora. The 'story' emanating from Iran was actually false—the Green Revolution was not overwhelming the authorities, and as we now know, President Ahmadinejad was able to ride the storm, albeit not without difficulty.[6]

The narrative of the revolution was framed in a particular way, just as that of the war on terror. Positioning technology centre stage—although it is usually referred to as the Green Revolution alongside the other 'colour' revolutions that had swept the world in the years preceding it, it is also often known as the Twitter Revolution—implies a series of contrasts between modernity and conservatism, young and old, the free flow of information and censorship, and non-violence (tweeting and posting video) and violence (the oppression that was videoed and posted), with the revolutionaries on the 'right' side each time.

That frame succeeded simply by weight of numbers—the authorities were not prepared to erect a counter-frame, and the tweets apparently coming from Iran were taken to be the whole picture.[7] Yet it is only a frame, not an accurate depiction. The Iranian government is not anti-technological, and the Iranian blogosphere—a largely independent commentariat—contains many supporters of the original Islamic Revolution and many nationalists who fully support their government's stance toward the United States, Israel and the Iranian nuclear programme. Most obviously, the frame assumes a causal role for the tweeting that is not justified; protests did occur, tweets were sent and the regime did wobble for a few days, but it does not follow that the tweets played a causal role in either the protests or the weakness of Ahmadinejad. The frame encouraged overstatement of the case, as ultimately the Twitter Revolution did not succeed.

Framing in action

On one level there is something obvious, almost commonsensical, about the idea of framing—that an individual's judgement about a given issue depends upon how the information is presented. We might be dismayed by the thought that, far from our views being arrived at impartially based upon objective information, we are incapable of cutting through the rhetoric, and are led in what to think by politicians, marketing gurus, clerics or whoever. Yet social scientists have been showing the effects of framing for over sixty years:

Many examples of issue framing are familiar to even casual followers of contemporary politics. Affirmative action has been framed variously as 'remedial action' for the continuing effects of discrimination, 'reverse discrimination' against whites and/or males, and as an 'undeserved advantage' for women and minorities. Welfare has been framed as a 'helping hand' for those in poverty, and as a 'government handout' that encourages dependency. Foreign engagements may be framed as tools for promoting American values and interests abroad, foolish wastes of taxpayer dollars, or humanitarian gestures to the needy of the world.[8]

120

The 'frame' is not neutral; it smuggles in a narrative of what an issue is about and what is irrelevant in order for individuals to understand it, 'weaving a connection' between the various events.[9] When framing is used by recognised authorities, the results could also be described using sociologist Pierre Bourdieu's concept of 'officialising strategies': attempts by authorities 'to manipulate the collective definition of the situation in such a way as to bring it closer to the official definition ... and thereby to win the means of mobilizing the largest possible group'.[10] However, when thinking about this definition it is clear that there is nothing about the situation that means only the authorities could use such strategies, and that minority or extremist groups could not do the same (except then the target would not be congruent with the official definition).

In his insightful work about how New Labour was able to stage a remarkable turnaround of political fortune in the 1990s under Tony Blair in overturning a decades-long perception of political incompetence and untrustworthiness, Hindmoor identifies how framing effects allowed New Labour to reframe various issues on which it had historically been seen as overly radical. New Labour moved to the perceived centre of politics, and simultaneously moved the centre ground to its policy position:

Frames influence what it is that people notice about an issue, how they interpret it, the significance they attach to it, and their subsequent memory and recall of it. Because different individuals have and use different frames they construct the political world in different ways and, crucially, develop different policy preferences over it.[11]

The importance is the effect that framing has on the observer: 'a framing effect is said to occur when, in the course of describing an issue or event, a speaker's emphasis on a subset of potentially relevant considerations causes individuals to focus on these considerations when constructing their opinions'.[12] For example, test groups shown footage of Ku Klux Klan marches tended to be more tolerant if the issue was framed as relating to freedom of speech rather than as a potential public order problem.[13]

In this sense frames are like maps in that they help an individual to understand the terrain by representing the contours and major points of significance, a short-hand method of orientation, but they are not the terrain itself. And, just like maps, it is possible to draw them in different ways. Think of those strange-looking maps drawn upside down to overcome north–south or west–east bias, or where area is proportional to ownership of wealth rather than geographical space. Individuals see an issue or a problem in different ways, pick out different salient features and give more weight or importance to some over others. Although frames and policies are not necessarily tied together, often the representative bias of a particular frame privileges a single policy preference.

How do frames work? What leads one person to frame a particular issue one way, and another person to frame the same issue a different way? Although this is still something of a black art, various possible explanations are emerging that shed some light on the issue. One possibility is that framing primes a particular vantage point within the mind of the observer or subject.[14] This could come about via a link between a particular frame and a recent or easily accessed memory; something that is at the 'front of one's mind'. An effective frame resonates with something already in mind—or easily recalled—and is more likely to influence opinion than frames that do not connect.

Here research ventures into the realms of cognitive psychology, where this is well-trodden ground. So-called affective priming, which affects the speed of classification of particular words or events via preceding words or events (so that it takes longer to classify the word 'happiness' as positive if it is preceded by the word 'cockroach' than if preceded by the word 'flower') can be done with social groups. Negative stereotyping of, say, black people, obese people, immigrants and the elderly (all of which do prompt negative associations for surprisingly many people), and positive stereotyping of other groups can have worryingly powerful effects on the judgements of experimental subjects. The Implicit Association Test is a widely used measure of implicit attitudes,[15] and many people find it disturbing when they discover how often these attitudes contradict their publicly stated values. Other research has shown that juries are less likely to convict attractive people, and when they are convicted, judges are more likely to give them lighter sentences.[16]

The introduction of words or phrases into the subject's mind can prime them to interpret separate issues in a manner that reflects those words, what Nelson and Oxley call 'the temporary activation and enhanced accessibility of concepts and considerations in memory'.[17] Faced with bounded rationality, finite attention and limited information-processing abilities, humans select from a constrained set of possibilities within their memory, and are therefore more likely to select ones that are more recently accessed for this interpretive role.

So far, so good. As we said at the outset, there is something commonsensical about the idea that how we 'see' an issue or problem can be changed by the 'filter' through which the information comes to us. Yet there is an interesting complication to this story, which recent social science has pointed out. When tested under laboratory conditions, there is no significant link between recently accessed concepts and the interpretation of issues measured in terms of reaction time.[18] If frames are linked to recently accessed concepts in the way suggested, then the expectation is that these concepts would be accessed faster in cognitive terms than under different frames. But this is apparently not the case. What this points to is a more complicated explanation that may allow for some element of priming in the sense adumbrated above, but where the function of framing is to select from the options at the front of our minds. Thus Nelson and Oxley argue that the 'real contribution [of framing] to opinion is in establishing which of the many possibly competing considerations at the top of the head should assume priority in one's opinion'[19] and that 'frames affect opinion by selectively enhancing the *psychological importance, relevance,* or *weight* accorded to specific beliefs with respect to the issue at hand'.[20] On the limited experimental evidence available, framing effects seem to select or positively weight certain ideas or concepts already in existence. Frames may even help to change the beliefs individuals hold. To see how this operates we will explore a few examples. But first we will set framing more fully into the context of the religious economy.

A house built on shifting sand

Framing has obvious importance for our topic of religious groups. The development and use of particular frames by religious leaders, ministers, publicists, theologians and proselytisers in their speeches, writings, interviews, sermons, websites, person-to-person communication and broadcasts can prime individuals to employ or adopt particular concepts and images. If individuals are exposed to frames recently or frequently, then they are more likely to adopt them as a means for understanding a particular phenomenon.

Framing complicates the spatial model of the religious economy and its centre-ground we have been working with so far, and it is worth spelling out its explanatory realism in greater detail. Hindmoor has researched framing relative to another spatial model, the so-called Downsian model of democratic party politics where parties compete for votes and gravitate towards the moderate centre-ground where the median voter resides.[21] His insights are illuminating.

On the Downsian model, political preferences, like religious preferences in the religious economy model presented in the last chapter, can be arranged on a one-dimensional continuum from left to right.[22] When faced with a particular policy issue we can make the simplifying assumption that voters are rational actors with fixed preferences. But is this realistic? Hindmoor's application of framing to the Downsian model is instructive:

> There is no possibility here of parties reframing the issue. What the issue is about is fixed and is fixed by Downs. ... The assumption of a simple, predictable, and shared rationality jars with the idea that different people with different frames will notice, interpret, recall, and weigh information in different ways. The assumption that preferences are fixed allows Downs to make predictions about how parties and voters will behave but it is obviously inconsistent with the idea that different frames generate different preferences.[23]

Yet the spatial model does not preclude the incorporation of framing effects. It is quite possible to conceive of different frames leading to different policy outcomes without abandoning the model. The proliferation of different frames simply shifts the distribution of preferences along the continuum, so that the median voter may not be in the centre. As we saw with Hotelling's model of business competition on the high street, the distribution of shoppers is assumed to be equal along the road, hence both shops should locate as close to the centre point as possible. However, the use of one frame rather than another over a particular issue can cause the distribution of preferences to shift along the continuum. Thus, for example, if the dominant frame in an abortion debate is that of the 'right to life' of a foetus that is understood to be alive, then preference distribution will be weighted more heavily towards a policy that bans or severely restricts abortion. Similarly, if the dominant frame is one of the 'right to choose' whether a non-alive foetus is brought to term, then the preference distribution will be oriented toward a policy that is more permissive of abortions.

Hence parties will compete to establish a framework that favours their preferred policies:

One way in which parties can present their policies as centrist is by framing the issue that a policy relates to in a particular way. Because frames affect the way issues are interpreted and so understood, frames affect the way policies are seen. They affect whether a policy will be seen as politically moderate. Whether a policy will be seen as a reasonable one will depend upon the frame being used to view the underlying issue. Whether a policy will be seen as a part of the political mainstream will depend upon the frame being used to view the underlying issue. … By successfully reframing an issue, parties can change beliefs about the location of the political centre.[24]

Thus parties compete to prime the electorate with frames conducive to their own policy positions, and to link them to the moderate political centre. Parties can consequently lead voters to use one frame rather than another. William Riker's seminal *The Art of Political Manipulation* tracks these framing efforts through twelve historical stories, from Pliny the Younger's political efforts in the investigation of Afranius Dexter in ancient Rome, to Abraham Lincoln's successful attempt to divide the opponents of the anti-slavery bill by reframing the issue (and others) to divide the Democratic Party.[25]

This does not mean, however, that any party can be constructed in such a fashion as to occupy the political centre. There are limits to the extent to which voters can be led by framing. A party that is trying to reframe a debate that has long been viewed in particular terms will find this task more difficult than if the issue is a new one where no previous frame of meaning is established. Similarly, a party that tries to reframe a debate in competition with a large number of alternative parties and other groups, each of which is also attempting to establish an alternate frame, will find it much more difficult than if no, or few, other competitors are so engaged.

What does this tell us about the types of religious groups we have been discussing? It clearly does not mean that groups looking for support are going to throw themselves up and down the spectrum of possible positions in order to try to secure the moderate adherent. Groups are, to a certain extent at least, tied to particular positions and often change those positions only very slowly. Nevertheless, religious groups compete in another way, by seeking to control the agenda of religious issues and debate. This is especially true where religion and politics butt up against each other. For example, the abortion debate in the United States provides fertile public ground for religious groups to attempt to wrest control of an agenda in order to gain public support. Moreover, there is a certain amount of spillover in play here. Groups can prime a particular frame by utilising it—by using the words and concepts associated with it. But a less direct method is to use a frame for analogous or related issues. So, for example, sanctity of life frames might be primed for the abortion debate by using those frames in terms of healthcare or family rearing issues.

Three examples

How have these insights been used in religious discourse? In particular, how has extremism been rendered acceptable to communities in religious contexts? In this section, we will consider three areas where parties supporting violent action have arguably achieved a level of public acceptance for their position.

Palestine

One significant example of successful framing is provided by the Palestinian case. Many groups eschew terrorist tactics in general, and suicide missions in particular, because of the costs of alienating the support of the wider community. However, this has not been the case in Palestine, where suicide missions and terrorist tactics seem to have drawn considerable support from at least parts of Palestinian society over a not inconsiderable period.[26]

In general, those groups which require and enjoy a certain degree of support from within their socio-cultural milieu are unlikely to employ suicide tactics, while those who do not rely upon such support are correspondingly less constrained by public condemnation of their actions. This assumes a reasonably contented embedding society. But sometimes attitudes within the wider community are so embittered that it reaches a consensus where the only workable solutions to the situation it faces are likely to include violence. When this happens there is likely to be a wave of enthusiasm for any tactic that strikes back against the enemy. This is arguably the case with regard to Palestine.

Whereas most political and religious activists hold stronger views than their supporters, the views held by the supporters of Hamas and other groups do not appear to be any more moderate than those of the group and its operatives themselves.[27] There are a number of reasons for this at the broader social level, including: the rules of engagement followed by the enemy, such as very harsh reprisals for attacks and the indiscriminate use of violence; high levels of social, economic and political repression; a perceived lack of viable intermediate options; and a growing number of individual grievances based in revenge for prior wrongs.

These features are in evidence to a greater level in both Palestine and Lebanon under Israeli occupation than they were, for example, in Northern Ireland or in the Basque region. Israeli reprisals have often been harsh and random, and therefore unpredictable. In the face of such an enemy, drastic measures can seem the only possible method of reliable counterattack.[28] Indeed, along with professed religious calling, Ricolfi lists feelings of humiliation at the hands of Israelis, and a deep involvement with the Palestinian cause and frustration at the moderate position of the PLO, as motivating reasons for would-be suicide bombers.[29] The Kurds, Chechens and Tamils have also been subjected to extensive repression and suicide missions have been employed in their respective causes. But the Palestinian case is more extreme:

Military occupation town by town and neighbourhood by neighbourhood, uninterrupted growth of settlers, networks of checkpoints, curfews, travelling restrictions, control of water and energy sources, and confiscations of property and bank accounts have not just humiliated the Palestinians but produced a drastic, extreme, and tragic contraction of an individual's set of options.[30]

Combined with the heavy economic reliance on Israel, this leads to a lack of remedies and low life chances. It is an obvious hypothesis that 'the worse the level of political repression and economic misery, the more likely it is that an organization will find volunteers' for a suicide mission.[31]

The level of economic and political repression in Palestine, with widespread restrictions on association or movement and systematic economic deprivation as a group, is likely to warp the preferences of the group considerably, and drive support for more extreme methods of resistance.[32] Similarly, the aims of Israel and Palestine seem to admit of few intermediate goals or possibilities for compromise, so at times widespread violence must appear the only viable tactic. With target hardening, suicide missions become more widely accepted as an efficient means of perpetrating attacks. Furthermore, despite flouting most interpretations of international law (for example, by building settlements in occupied territory), Israel is rarely put under serious pressure by its chief backer the United States, and so there is only a small possibility that the Palestinians would view any externally applied arbitration as fair. Finally, the motive of revenge for specific losses and grievances should not be underestimated in the Palestinian case. A large number of atrocities can build widespread support for retaliations in kind. The murder of twenty-nine Palestinians by Baruch Goldstein in 1994 sparked the first Hamas suicide mission. Fathali Moghaddam has formulated a general five-stage psychological theory of how an individual might come to accept and even undertake violent extremist political actions. According to this theory, an individual first becomes conscious of injustice ('how do we fight this unfair system?') before rationalising violence as the only viable option ('the ends justify the means') and ultimately valorising and legitimising the individual's contribution ('this heroic act will improve the world').[33] What is extreme for almost all societies becomes the norm, and individuals re-orientate themselves to the new social conditions.[34]

This suggests that suicide missions are likely to dwindle when these conditions are reduced or removed, albeit slowly as the frames are reset gradually. As social, economic and political conditions change, and other options become available, then the trade-off between support from and alienation within their communities must be re-thought. There is some evidence of this in the case of Palestine, where support for suicide missions is on the wane. The lack of success of suicide missions in achieving the end of driving Israel back into the sea has led to a wider questioning of whether the benefits really outweigh the costs, and whether more feasible options exist.

Violent tactics suggest themselves either when support from the embedding community is not a necessary condition for the extremist group to flourish, or when support from the community for violence is unusually high due to the presence of factors that push the mainstream to extremism. When these conditions do not obtain, as for example with the IRA during the Troubles in Northern Ireland, extreme groups need to maintain a delicate balance between maintaining support and violent tactics.

Al-Qaeda and framing jihad

Another example of framing in religious terms is offered by the issue of violent jihad and the justification of terrorism using Islamic theology.[35] Wiktorowicz argues that al-Qaeda has undertaken a concerted and specific reframing process of jihad in order to furnish support for its attacks on the countries of the West, especially in the form of theological backing to legitimise its actions. This framing contest takes place primarily around the issue of the theological expertise of Islamic scholars. Unlike Christianity with its denominational structures, religious authority in the Muslim world is decentralised. Religious scholars provide authority by offering scriptural interpretations to the faithful over the activities or commitments required to fulfil their duties to God. As public intellectuals without the equivalent backing of, say, the Catholic Church with its formal, hierarchical structure, their authority depends directly on their own credibility or reputation. Wiktorowicz identifies a fourfold set of framing strategies: (1) vilification—undermining competing scholars; (2) exaltation—praising in-group scholars; (3) credentialing—emphasising the expertise of the in-group scholars; (4) de-credentialing—casting doubt on the expertise of rivals.[36]

Al-Qaeda has undertaken a prolific campaign to discredit its peaceable reformist competitors and to call into question their expertise, while simultaneously seeking to boost the credentials of its own scholars to pronounce correctly on the scriptural directives for jihad. Everyone debating when and where violence is justified (if ever) agrees the need for scholarly support for their legitimacy. In al-Qaeda's public pronouncements, many Islamic scholars, particularly in Saudi Arabia, are accused of having been deceived by the political authorities around the time of the First Gulf War, and the organisation consequently argues that their fatwas are mistaken because they are based on false information. The knowledge of competing scholars is thus called into question. Interestingly, al-Qaeda itself has suffered something of a credibility problem with its jihadi scholars because many of those who support the position through scriptural interpretation are Western-born, self-educated scholars who returned to serious worship and study after an early life at some distance from religious teachings. Consequently, they do not have a formal education from an established Islamic university, and cannot boast the many years of experience of their more successful reformist competitors.

In the absence of expertise comparable with the reformists, al-Qaeda often attempts to discredit the characters of competing scholars as 'unworthy of the sacred trust of religious interpretation'.[37] It implies that they have selfish interests, or links to political regimes or authority structures (in particular to the Saudi authorities) that undermine claims to neutrality of scriptural interpretation. Scriptural condemnation of those who would conspire with Jews or Christians, even for peace, is often used to make the link to the interests of the enemy. By contrast, al-Qaeda scholars are esteemed publicly as bastions of moral and religious fortitude in a corrupt world. Their courage, dignity, truthfulness and sacrifice are frequently mentioned in speeches, statements and other media. That its supporters are willing to die for the cause—for God—demonstrates their ultimate credibility. Thus they are the only ones capable of interpreting Islam in a truthful way, free from corruption, self-interest or deceit. When these scholars call for violent resistance against the crusading aggressor, they are to be believed.

The Web is important for al-Qaeda because it serves as a vital means of communication for an organisation denied access to most mass media. The lack of hierarchy in Islam which aids al-Qaeda in general is useful online because it means that websites receive less benefit from the strength of offline brands. In Web-based communication in, say, the United States or the UK, news is generally if not always taken from sources which are branded by existing mass media outlets—*The Guardian, Daily Mail,* the BBC, *Wall Street Journal, New York Times*—and religious communication can also benefit from branded 'official' religious sites such as those of the major religions. This infrastructure is a serious barrier to entry for new entrants to the marketplace of ideas,[38] but is less of an obstacle in the Middle East.[39]

El-Nawawy and Khamis report at least some instances where heated discussion over theological intricacies (for instance about the Sunni–Shia relationship) were carried on in the absence of 'traditional Muslim scholars', which they argue 'can increase lay people's confusion and disagreement around such a controversial issue, and can undermine their understanding of it'.[40] Hafez, writing of suicide missions in Iraq, argues that the main weapon in the fight to recruit would-be martyrs and gain support within the Islamic world is the emotional appeals that tell a 'grand narrative of humiliation' suffered by Muslims at the hands of foreign powers and of government betrayal. 'Such masterful framing of the conflict in Iraq is intended to shame the passive bystander and call into question his masculinity and honor. The only way to erase the shame is by redeeming himself and the nation through sacrifice on the battlefield.'[41]

It is also worth noting that the al-Qaeda framing strategy is echoed by a set of voices in the West which couch the conflict in terms of a 'clash of civilisations', a concept developed by political scientist Samuel Huntington:

the post-Cold War world is a world of seven or eight major civilizations. Cultural commonalities and differences shape the interests, antagonisms, and associations of states. The most important countries in the world come overwhelmingly from different civilizations. The local conflicts most likely to escalate into broader wars are those between groups and states from different civilizations. ... The key issues on the international agenda involve differences among civilizations.[42]

This directly supports al-Qaeda's strategy of marginalising less reductive voices which see cultural difference as one of a number of competing political factors. The fact that a remarkably large number of Muslims live in non-Muslim societies, for instance, has been held by some to render the notion of a clash between Islam and the West implausible 'because of the dissolution of prior notions of distance and frontier'.[43] We can see the potential of political violence in this context to trigger a series of tit-for-tat retaliations, which would render nuanced accounts of conflicts redundant as populations from differing ethnic backgrounds crystallised around these perceived political poles to create new 'virtual' frontiers based on sympathy and opinion. It is no surprise that Huntington's thesis was welcomed as prescient in the aftermath of the September 11 attacks in New York and elsewhere.

Equally, we must consider the converse relationship between rhetoric and violence. Would al-Qaeda's violent tactics have any serious effect, beyond the appalling destruction, if there was not already an extremist trope attempting to frame the debate and marginalise moderates? If groups are to polarise in the aftermath of political violence, then there must presumably be available a basic, broad, reductive politics to act as a focus for coalition-formation in the face of the violence. As has long been known, creation of a common enemy is an extremely effective tactic for uniting diverse and conflicted people into a collective group with a common goal.[44]

Even non-violent thinking sometimes plays into the hands of extremists when it legitimises Huntingtonian reductionism. Since 2001 there has been an assumption that we need 'dialogue' between the Islamic world and the Western world. Yet framing the requirement in this way 'retains a strategic orientation, for all its communicative overlay'.[45] The rhetoric is about dialogue, but the real aim of the discussion is persuasion. It envisages not a liberal exchange of ideas with respect for divergent ideas, but rather an attempt to persuade the 'other'. Marc Lynch cites Habermas's distinction between strategic communication, manipulating others to promote one's own interests, and communicative action, taking part in a genuine dialogue. 'All too often, U.S. public-diplomacy efforts have fallen crudely into the strategic category and missed their mark for that very reason. Information has gone in one direction; the target's views and thoughts have been of interest only insofar as they could be molded.'[46] While Western politicians often appear on television in order to promote their views, such appearances can be counterproductive if they are simply perceived as lecturing on a specific issue:

especially because all too often such appearances only confirm the viewers' worst stereotypes. On one recent al Jazeera program, for example, a running survey tallied votes on the question, 'Is the United States acting as an imperialist power in Iraq?' The longer a prominent former U.S. official talked, the more voters said yes, with 96 percent voting yes by the end of the show.[47]

The post-2001 dialogue is certainly not Habermasian in spirit; the strategic aim underlines the idea that two civilisations are clashing. As Olivier Roy puts it: 'at a time when the territorial borders between the great civilizations are fading away, mental borders are being reinvented to give a second life to the ghosts of lost civilizations'.[48]

Apostasy

A third example of religious framing on the Web is provided by Douglas Swanson in his analysis of apostate sites.[49] Apostasy is the rejection of a part, or the whole, of an individual's former faith. It is more than simply a question of church membership or attendance: it is, rather, the rejection of one or more of its central values. Disengagement from a religious group is the ultimate stage of questioning and rejecting belief. One would expect to see websites for apostates, justifying their actions and providing support, information or options, providing content that 'would strongly frame a condemnation of particular religious groups, urge followers to leave specific churches, and offer alternative opportunities for worship'.[50]

However, in Swanson's study of ten apostate websites, these expectations failed to be met. Only two framed their message in terms of apostasy, religious dissent and rejection, or disengagement from the particular group or church in question. By contrast, the others framed their messages very much as an intellectual exercise in theological uncertainty, without promoting disassociation from the parent church, and did not overtly seek to encourage apostasy. In terms of framing this is highly interesting because it appears as though there is a common strategy of replacing the frame of apostasy and disassociation, recasting it as a more moderate, less threatening, questioning. Typically, the sites do not refer to apostasy directly, and concentrate on providing information, creating dialogue between believers, scripture study and so forth. Where apostasy is touched upon, justification is often phrased in terms of rightness, spiritual reward, acceptance, human rights and lifestyle improvement.

This indicates an attempt to change the terms of debate by placing the actions of disengagement in a less confrontational light, perhaps with the intention of attracting those still within the group who seek a version of their religion that is less in tension with the social surrounding. Or alternatively, rather than enticing people to disengage, the aim may be to cause incremental change within the original group to help it moderate and make it more attractive. All the apostate groups in the survey were related to relatively strict sects or churches such as the Southern Baptists, Christian Science and Jehovah's Witnesses. Thus these framing contests play an important role in the moderating phase of the church–sect cycle.

Online cognitive restructuring

At the psychological level of explanation, the theory of selective moral disengagement is a valuable tool for understanding framing.[51] Moral disengagement is the process by which an individual disengages his filter against immoral action, and as a consequence is able to carry out inhumane acts without suffering cognitively dissonant emotions such as guilt or compassion. The inhumane action is valorised or reconceptualised as a good or worthy act. It is seen not in isolation (as an act of murder, say), but rather in a context in which it is the lesser of several evils, a means to an end, or a way of saving lives (killing twenty now to save 2,000 in the future).

Extremist websites can support this process by framing their analyses of political and religious realities to suggest the appropriate cognitive restructuring required. Gabriel Weimann summarises the tactics that allow this as follows (documented with examples from al-Qaeda, Chechen rebels and Aum Shinrikyo).[52]

- *Displacement of responsibility.* The need for violent action is blamed on someone else (the authorities, the victims, social forces), not the violent actor.
- *Diffusion of responsibility.* The responsibility is shared between a network of extremists, so that no single person is responsible for the outcome of the operation.
- *Dehumanisation of targets.* The attack is made impersonal, the victims are treated as symbolic representatives of an unfair system or an aggressive state.
- *Use of euphemisms.* The attack is described not as mass slaughter, but rather in terms such as 'engagement' with a 'target'. The campaign is an 'armed struggle' or 'resistance', whereas the enemy is described as carrying out 'mass murder', 'genocide' or 'massacres'.
- *Comparisons.* The attack is compared with far greater iniquities carried out by the enemy, for example comparing the relatively small scale of a typical terrorist encounter with the more efficient and bloody results of a military encounter. The resources of the extremist group are shown as being smaller than those of the enemy.
- *Interpreting the sequence of events.* The attack is described as an act of retaliation in response to an action of the enemy.

Each of these tactics underlines the extremist organisation's view of itself as a small, weak, persecuted minority group which is the underdog in a struggle for justice and freedom against an overwhelming evil force.

There are three ways in which the Internet plays an important role in the implementation of almost all of these tactics. The first is in the dissemination of these messages and the way they are framed, which is of course made easier by digital communication tools, by-passing the heavily edited and centralised mass media and facilitating anonymity into the bargain.

Secondly, the spread of the frame involves a large and open media environment where several sources independently adopt the euphemisms or dehumanisation trope. One website, newsletter, video, T-shirt or poster will make little difference, but if the extremists' terms for discussing an attack are adopted and spread by several outlets (for example, quoting from a spokesman), then the frame becomes available to more people. The mainstream mass media used to prevent this from happening by taking more care as to what they quoted. In today's vibrant online media world, such control of the terms of discourse is next to impossible.

Finally, the Web provides instant feedback and can establish an immediate narrative through the use of automatic tools, which becomes privileged because (a) it appears first before any other attempt to spin the events, and (b) its use of technology can give it an objective air. The instant reaction, collated over the Web, provides a debate with a named winner which is then reported alongside the event itself. The drama of the instantaneous reaction statistics of Twitter trumps even blogging (which itself was thought dangerously unconsidered when it began to upstage newspaper commentary). The 2012 US presidential election night was the most tweeted event in US political history and also produced what was at the time the most retweeted tweet ever (Obama's victory tweet).[53] The Web has brought us to a position where someone making a stump speech might find himself dealing with the fallout from the first part of the speech before he has concluded. Romney's 'binders full of women' comment became an Internet meme illustrated with animated gifs before the debate in which he made the remark had come to an end. Obama's poor performance in the first debate was nailed within minutes of its beginning by comedian Bill Maher's tweets.[54] Thus the framing war can be decided at the outset, if one side is a little less Web-savvy than the other.

6

THE DEMAND SIDE

THE CLUB MODEL

If there is something eerie about standing in an empty football stadium, and something electric about being there on match-day, then there is something slightly unnerving about seeing 60,000 people married in a Moonie wedding ceremony in one.[1] Stories of cults and their magnetic, megalomaniac or messianic leaders—think not only of the Moonies, but also the Hare Krishnas, Heaven's Gate, Scientologists—conjure images of psychological manipulation, preying on the weak and vulnerable, and 'brainwashing'. What could lead any reasonable, rational individual to join such a group? What could lead them to make the most dramatic sacrifices—often giving away all their worldly goods and turning their backs on their most-loved family and friends—in order to follow or join a group that seems at such odds with all socially accepted norms? Who in their right mind would join the Branch Davidians, Hizb ut-Tahrir or Joseph Smith's Mormons, let alone al-Qaeda or Hezbollah? What hold must the Reverend Moon have had over people to be able to persuade them to participate in mass weddings in football stadiums with the world watching on and, on the whole, sneering in disbelief? What psychological conditions must someone be labouring under in order to be persuaded to blow themselves up on a suicide mission?

So far we have looked at how groups operate in the religious environ-ment, moderating over time to gain more adherents (converging on, or perhaps redefining, the centre-ground), before a schism erupts and some members reassert a more radical version of their faith. This picture of the CSC and other aspects of the religious 'economy' has focused on the supply side of the story. We turn now to address the demand side—the view of the individual in the picture. We have alluded to the fact that radical groups will always be present within a flourishing and free religious economy. They will continue to persist because some people prefer a version of their faith that is in greater tension with the surrounding social environment. This begs two questions: first, why do some people prefer a radical version of their faith? And second, what is a preference in this context anyway?

Pascalian wagers for high stakes

In the 1960s to the 1980s, much media capital was made out of the claims of abduction, deception and brainwashing tactics attributed to groups such as the Moonies, as well as the irrationality and mental fragility of converts. No reasonable, rational person could ever join such a group with their odd New Age ideas; they must therefore have been irrational or deceived. The underlying picture that drives popular perceptions of radical cults and sects is one of cognitive inadequacies or failures, beliefs held on an irrational basis or by primitive minds—we earlier termed this the Dumb-and-Malleable (DAM) thesis.

DAM was a precursor to the dominant belief among psychologists and sociologists that religious belief is correlated with a lack of education and intelligence. Douglas and Brunner, for instance, described the 'emotional sects'—the evangelical congregations of the United States—as a 'backwash of sectarianism' that are to be found only in certain quarters, particularly 'the more backward sections of the nation'.[2] Then as now, it was thought that as the population became more educated and information more widespread, religious belief would decrease until the point of extinction.

The rise of novel religious or New Age cults in the '60s and '70s also fuelled the popular imagination in terms of solutions to what was seen as the threat of impressionable teenagers being carried off into the back woods of America by madmen who would work their particularly powerful magic on them. Professional 'rescuers' emerged who would kidnap the loved ones from a cult's clutches and then 'deprogramme' them via

CIA-style interrogation or 'therapy'. After all, if such DAM kids were dumb-and-malleable, then they could be manipulated away from the cult using similar techniques to those which caused them to join in the first place. This type of remedy will re-emerge later when we examine government responses to religious radicalism.

It should come as no surprise that we reject the DAM thesis. Religion has not faded away as those early commentators hoped and predicted. Indeed, religious belief has increased in the last few decades. Religiosity—an individualised, personalised devotion—has displaced mainstream religious signifiers and practices to an extent. Despite its massive advances in the same period, science has not proved to be the vanquisher of religion that it was expected to be. Indeed, a significant proportion of science faculty members at US universities express a belief in God.[3] The fact that many US citizens believe in Intelligent Design in preference to Darwinian evolutionary theory is a case in point.[4] Religion is evidently holding its own.

This is not a surprise for many thinkers. Some, such as Roger Scruton, have long argued that as the Enlightenment deist view of God as an abstract, rational being ('a creature of the head rather than the heart') has grown in influence, the sacrifices associated with mainstream religious practice have dwindled, resulting in the failure of the mainstream religions to satisfy the need for belonging and membership, a need which has inevitably been pursued elsewhere.[5]

The DAM thesis ignores the weight of empirical evidence from over four decades of research into radical groups and cults. The initial assessments of New Age cults rapidly gave way under that weight to a more plausible explanation of why individuals chose to join such groups, and in the vast majority of cases it was a conscious and reasoned choice. Eileen Barker's monumental study of the Moonies and their recruitment practices, based on nearly seven years of field research, found no evidence of abduction, coercion, imprisonment or deception.[6] Despite their best efforts, and much media sensationalism, the cults of the '70s were actually quite bad at recruitment. At the height of their prominence, the Moonies never numbered more than a few thousand members. Of the individuals who undertook the two-day 'retreat' less than 25 per cent joined the group for more than a week, and a mere 5 per cent remained members for more than a year. Of those who simply visited a Moonie centre, less than 0.5 per cent were still members two years later. With a retention failure of over 95 per cent, the most successful cult of its age experienced massive defection.[7] This is less than impressive.[8]

According to more recent studies, those who contemplated membership of radical sects and cults came to their decision after a careful consideration of the significant costs involved, including giving up all of their private possessions, and the benefits they would gain. As a mass of research has shown, lack of education, ignorance or poor reasoning skills were not common factors; indeed, a notable feature of converts was their relatively affluent, educated background. Potential recruits made the same kinds of judgements as anyone else. One of the most significant studies in this area reports one young man from the Moonies as saying in interview:

You know, sometimes at night I wonder what if none of this is true. What if Rev. Moon is not inspired by God? Maybe all of this is for nothing. But then I say to myself, if it's true then I'm in on the ground floor of the greatest event in history. And if it isn't, so what? I was probably going to spend the rest of my life working in that plywood plant anyway.[9]

These remarks are extraordinarily revealing. There is clearly a straightforward cost–benefit analysis being performed here. Membership of the Moonies required the complete dedication of an individual's time and property to the cause. The interviewee did not underestimate the costs involved in his decision, but bore them as the price of a high-stakes wager. He simply sought to maximise his outcomes—a Moonie form of Pascal's wager.

Reflections such as these are apparently commonplace among members of religious groups where participation is costly. Friendship, social interaction, a sense of belonging or solidarity, self-worth and being valued by others are often cited as tangible benefits from membership and reasons for joining.[10] Many of us receive these benefits of belonging from family, friends, work, social activities and sports. A large number find an important source of belonging in religious groups. Indeed, studies of radical religious groups indicate that those who do join are often those with few or relatively weak social ties, but who have pre-existing contact with other group members, and no strong attachment to any other movement.[11] New, all-encompassing religious groups provide an overwhelming sense of belonging.

Research over the past two or more decades shows that the actual religious message only plays a minor role in an individual's decision to join a radical religious group. The primary motivation for joining is often the personal benefits associated with group membership. Members depend on collective inputs in order for these to be satisfied. The closeness of the social interaction and the feelings of solidarity, common purpose, mutual commitment and so on are significant benefits from participating in close-knit groups. The higher the level of commitment required, the more intense the experience because each individual must sacrifice a great deal to be part of the group. When the benefits are outweighed by the costs, however, members drift away. Many Moonies did in fact leave the group—contrary to popular legends of brainwashed captives of faith—particularly when they began the process of raising a family.

This fact is often lost amid the hype about recruitment and retention practices, and the dangers of 'evil' ideologies, as well as the retrospective accounts of individuals of their own conversions and decisions to leave. Iannaccone argues that 'As long as the group views belief as central to its mission, converts will face strong pressure to make doctrine the centre of their subsequent testimonies ... [but] [s]ocial attachments are the horse that pulls the cart of ideological change.'[12] The same applies when individuals decide to leave radical or deviant groups, a decision which they often describe as some kind of 're-awakening' after a period of delusion. As Stephen Holmes observes, 'Sometimes people do what they do for the reasons they profess. But private motivations cannot always be inferred from public justifications.'[13] This does not mean that individuals necessarily misrepresent their intentions (though some undoubtedly do)—either deliberately or not—but that many choices admit of both religious and secular explanations, and it can be difficult to ascribe dominance to any single type.

Ed Husain, who left Hizb ut-Tahrir after many years of commitment and activism, and whose Quilliam Foundation now campaigns for governments to tackle Islamic radicalism and extremism at the ideological or theological level, is an excellent example of such mixed motives. In his book Husain often describes his farewell to fanaticism as being driven by a deeper learning and capacity for critical thinking about religion and politics.[14] Yet in other places in the book he describes his decision to leave the group in question as coming not from ideological challenge during the time and location of his membership and activism, but upon his removal from that environment. Relocation to university, new friends, different social networks and a romantic relationship seem to have been some of the drivers of change in this case.[15] With many devotees, the sources of provision of social goods can diversify, at which point the opportunity costs of continued participation may outweigh the benefits. We do not discount Husain's considerable introspection and reasoning about this process; these are very personal matters. But nor should we discount other explanatory features as part of the slow and painful experience of change in the general case. As with decisions on other features of our lives, people continually weigh their options in the balance. Consequently, they sometimes change their mind.

The club model

This model of religious belief and membership, termed the club model by its leading academic exponents,[16] provides a better explanation than the DAM thesis for the persistence of religious belief. Unlike the DAM thesis, the club model renders belief and religious participation consistent with autonomous, rational agency. Religious groups offer products for potential customers to select from based on their individual needs or preferences, like clubs providing benefits to members for their participation. As a result, small, radical groups will continue to survive because they meet niche interests down the long tail, and they offer particular individuals benefits which they perceive as outweighing the costs of participation. Different groups cater for different preferences, and no one religion can meet all the diverse preferences of each potential believer.

If religious doctrine is conceived as a range of products that cater for different sets of preferences, then radical groups can be characterised by the degree of tension which their offering produces relative to their surrounding community; in other words, how far their products differ from the societal norm. The greater the tension, the more radical the group. In extreme cases, such as the early Mormons, the tension generated may bring outsiders to hunt down members of the group.[17] We noted in Chapter Four that the costs of rejecting rapprochement with a wider social consensus can be significant.[18] Yet the benefits are perceived by members of radical sects as also being much higher; those who continue as members show commitment to their fellows through costly participation. As a consequence, the goods of belonging, and higher spiritual worth gained through sacrifice, are hardly earned.

THE DEMAND SIDE: THE CLUB MODEL

Religion is a collectively produced commodity. However, in order to receive its benefits an individual is not required to participate in its production. An individual can benefit in proportion to the collective effort, rather than their individual efforts. Those who do so are free-riding on the efforts of others. The strictness that causes tensions between radical groups and the embedding society raises the overall levels of commitment, increasing average levels of participation, and enhancing the net benefits of membership.[19] The more committed the membership of a group is, the more value each member receives from participation. Members who do not contribute to the same level of intensity as the most committed detract from the overall level of the group's resources. Everyone suffers a reduced level of value.

However, in strict sects the level of commitment required tends to deter free-riders. Because the criteria of strictness are visible to others, there are no hiding places for those who would prefer to contribute less but take the same reward. As Iannaccone points out, potential members are forced to choose whether to participate fully or not because the middle-ground is removed.[20] Evidence of this has been found in game-theoretic studies comparing levels of effort in religious and non-religious *kibbutzim*,[21] as well as within ultra-orthodox Jewish communities in Israel.[22] As Stark and Finke observe, 'high costs make membership sufficiently unattractive to chase away the apathetic, and in doing so make the rewards for belonging far more intense'.[23] Radical groups can penalise alternative activities that compete for members' time and resources. Particular behaviours can be stigmatised, or other practices enforced—dress codes, socialisation taboos, dietary requirements—that make participation in other activities socially difficult.[24] Such costly strictures mitigate the externality problems that most religious groups face. This pattern can be seen repeated across many unconventional groups, such as the Jehovah's Witnesses, the Mormons, the Moonies and the Shakers, and is one of the most crucial breakthroughs of the club model—cost–benefit calculations over membership apply to all religions regardless of denomination, theology or history.[25]

What does the club model explain?

The explanation the club model provides has huge significance for understanding the religious side of human existence. It puts another piece of the jigsaw in place because it explains why individuals choose to join radical religious sects and cults. This is one of the most persistent questions about religious behaviour, one which has vexed governments and policy-makers in their search to understand the appeal of radicalism, extremism or fundamentalism. The reasons are not primarily spiritual or theological, but rather the comparatively mundane ones of social goods and belonging. For those who desire such goods, radical groups provide them in spades; the experience is just so much more intense. The level of commitment demanded excludes free-riders, so members of such groups receive an exponential return on their investment. Strictness is a belonging multiplier. When understood in these terms it is easy to see why some people choose high-tension versions of their preferred faiths.

Some will no doubt find this view disappointing. Many look for explanation rooted in the pernicious influence of religious beliefs or ideas, or maybe even the truth of certain religious beliefs. Religion is often viewed as a special sphere of human existence that cannot be reduced to such mundane motivations. Yet this would be a mistake. We need not deny that religion is special or important in accepting a simple explanation of human motivation. Simplicity is, in this sense, a virtue. We should, all else being roughly equal, prefer an uncomplicated explanation to a complex one, and remember that people do not cease to be people when they enter their places of worship.

A note on trust, coercion and the plausibility of the DAM thesis

In Chapter Four we discussed the importance of trust and costly signals of trustworthiness within radical groups in supporting such groups and helping them prosper even in the face of pressure from the wider embedding society. If we look at such groups through the lens of our model of trust, this can also help explain why the club model is so often ranged against the DAM thesis, according to which people are coerced into joining. The reason is broadly that the distinction between trust and coercion can be extraordinarily fine.

To illustrate this, let us begin with a definition of rationally based trust by a political scientist, the rational choice theorist Russell Hardin. He talks of trust being a result of the trustor believing that the trustee's interests coincide with her own:[26]

I trust someone if I have reason to believe it will be in that person's interest to be trustworthy in the relevant way at the relevant time. My trust turns, however, not directly on the Trusted's interests per se, but on whether my own interests are *encapsulated in the interests of the Trusted*, that is, on whether the Trusted counts my interests as partly his or her own interests *just because they are my interests* (in philosophers' jargon, the Trusted counts my interests as his or her own qua my interests).[27]

This definition expresses a notion of rational trust that obtains on some occasions (however, not all trust is rationally placed or properly warranted), and is indicative of a kind of trust relationship between people. It is certainly more plausible as a description of how trust works within a small group of radicals or extremists who define themselves in opposition to the embedding society. To them, from the inside, this concept of trust looks like a paradigm of selfless devotion.

However, consider the following definition of coercion from another political thinker, F.A. Hayek:

Coercion occurs when one man's actions are made to serve another man's will, not for his own but for the other's purpose. It is not that the coerced does not choose at all; if that were the case, we should not speak of his 'acting.' … Coercion implies, however, that I still choose but that my mind is made someone else's tool, because the alternatives before me have been so manipulated that the conduct that the coercer wants me to choose becomes for me the least painful one.[28]

What is striking when we look at Hardin's definition of trust and Hayek's definition of coercion is that they seem identical. In each case there are two agents—X and Y—and Y serves X's interests not because they are Y's interests, but because they are X's interests. From outside the group, Hardinesque trust may appear like Hayekian coercion. The same set of relationships can easily be conceptualised as either trust or coercion, depending on one's sympathies and point of view. To some extent this helps to explain why brainwashing and other coercive mechanisms are often postulated by outsiders distressed by the unwillingness of a group member to 'escape' or 'come to his senses'.

The development of preferences

Individuals choose a view that best suits their preferences from a range of religious options. Religious groups manoeuvre to cater for those preferences, while individuals follow the logic of finding the best means to achieve their fulfilment. As we noted at the end of Chapter Four, this assumes that people's preferences with regard to religious beliefs are in some sense fixed and stable.[29] Is such an assumption realistic, however?

It is in fact highly unlikely that people seeking religious support will enter religious environments with fixed sets of preferences that are not up for negotiation with religious authorities or communities. Their preferences are likely to be shaped by the environments in which they grow up, and in which they live as adults. This is evidenced by the phenomenon of 'switching'—the process by which people change their religious affiliation. This phenomenon indicates that preferences do change over time, and are no doubt influenced by events around them. Hence the framing strategies we discussed in Chapter Five.

An individual's religious preferences are inferred largely by observation. The fact that individual A chooses good x while both x and y are available to them reveals that they have a preference for x over y. This inference from choice to preference is the 'revealed preference' approach, which can seem counterintuitive from the point of view of an agent, as Amartya Sen points out:

From the point of view of introspection of the person in question, the process runs from his preference to his choice, but from the point of view of the scientific observer the arrow runs in the opposite direction: choices are observed first and preferences are then presumed from these observations.[30]

Preferences tend to be adaptive; we come to desire that with which we are familiar, or is within easy reach.[31] We tend, by contrast, to develop an aversion for things that are alien to us, or are difficult to obtain. Crucial to this notion of familiarity is proximity to others who also share particular preferences, and from the occupation of social roles with which particular preferences are commonly associated. In terms of religious preferences, this indicates that early influences, such as parental beliefs and denominational commitments, as well as the closeness of the relationship between parents and children, will reinforce the tendency of children to accept their parents' beliefs. As several pieces of research show, religious choices across generations are more stable if they exist against a background of childhood familial belief and commitment.[32]

Thus people often adopt the religious affiliations of their parents, but when switching does occur, it tends not to be to a competing group too far from that of their parents' affiliations (though see Chapter Four, and Putnam and Campbell's remarks on 'churn').[33] This also helps explain the choices individuals make when the religious landscape does change, as it has in recent years. In the United States, for example, many conservative denominations have become more liberal as they have moved to occupy a position closer to the centre-ground. These changes are made in response to many stimuli, such as the changing social mores of the surrounding society and the need to keep pace with the social profile of their members and potential members. Some members of these groups feel left behind by such cultural and social changes, as the CSC shows. Many members no doubt find the more conservative alternatives attractive and opt to join splinter groups, or to switch to other conservative groups. Those with lower levels of previous involvement or weaker religious beliefs will tend to favour the liberalising movement as it provides a better fit with their social networks.

If preferences are adaptive rather than fixed, can they also be revealed by choices? The position is complicated by the uncertainty and bounded rationality with which we make our decisions. Choices are made by individuals not only on the basis of their desires, but also on what alternatives exist and what they know about them. People often change their preferences because of new information; once they try a new practice, they come to prefer it. Conversely, without knowledge of alternatives, they are likely to retain their original preferences. Recommendations from trusted others are important catalysts for change.[34]

Thus not only is information about alternatives important, but the medium of communication through which it is transmitted also plays a crucial role. As we have seen in many cases, from the Mormons to the Moonies, ties of friendship and family are crucial to conversion. Outreach programmes, such as the Moonie weekend retreat, attempt to convey information in the hope of reorienting the available options to individuals, and thus affecting their preferences. Religious preferences are consequently governed, at least in part, by the richness of information available, as well as the trust in the sources of that information.

The key issue is how we interact with the information about the options available to us. The notion of fixed, revealed preferences assumes that choices are rational and involve voluntary considerations of costs and benefits, reflecting a clear schematic ordering. This is a simplifying assumption which ignores the fact that our choices are structured in a significant way by our social surroundings.[35] Individual welfare is just one consideration among many when choosing. Our choices can be influenced by how our decisions will impact on the consumption of others—we choose, that is, in part on the basis of what good or ill it will do for others; and this, in turn, might have some secondary indirect reward for us. Hence children may adopt or reject the religion of their parents to please or spite them. Or we might go to church to set an example to our children. Alternatively, our choices might be socially shaped by the norms surrounding groups and affiliations that either supply incentives or hold open the threat of sanctions, as argued by the club model.

Five types of religious commitment

Preferences for the social goods provided by religion are complex and are hard to determine from the evidence. However, analysis by Massimo Introvigne has shown that we can cluster religions in terms of the type of benefits they provide, and the attitude towards free-riding that they show. The result is a framework of niche positions that partitions the marketplace.[36]

- *The ultra-liberal niche* in which individuals prefer a religion that does not require large sacrifices, and are tolerant of different perceptions of God and ways of worshipping. They do not require their religion to impose a moral framework that is much more restrictive than that of the surrounding society. Financial contributions outweigh time commitments. In Christianity this niche includes the Episcopalians, the United Church of Christ, and the Methodists, and in Islam, the liberal wing of Sufism. All of these are largely in decline, despite once being vigorous sects.
- *The liberal niche*, characterised by a more demanding version of the faith, occupied by people who tend to limit their participation to specific times and places (attendance, prayer, etc.) and reject strict requirements of faith that place significant burdens upon them. Christian examples here include most Lutheran groups, Baptists, some Methodists and the more liberal wings of the Southern Baptists. Conservative Jews and Sufis also fit here.
- *The moderate-conservative niche*, where people take upon themselves significant burdens in pursuit of their faith, enduring certain forms of stigma, sacrifice and ridicule. Diet, clothing and social restrictions are common (e.g. over drinking, Sabbatical observation, entertainment, consumables and dietary restrictions). Contributions of time

resources are considerably increased in comparison with the other, more liberal, versions of faith. Their religious views tend to pervade all aspects of their life, providing a moral compass to daily living, rather than compartmentalising religious belief and daily existence. This is where we can locate many mainstream versions of Islamism, or conservative political Islam.

- *The strict niche*, where most splinter groups formed during the CSC tend to congregate. Wesley and Calvin were positioned here. Adherents of strict faiths usually see religion as shaping and guiding every aspect of their lives and interactions with others. Substantial sacrifices of time and financial resources are incurred. Stigma for believers is significant, and they clearly signal adherence by mode of dress, speech and habits. Much of their life is given over to church business or proselytising. Christian examples in this niche include the Jehovah's Witnesses, the Mormons and Pentecostal groups such as the Assemblies of God and the Nazarenes. Orthodox Judaism is located here, as is Wahhabi Islam. Starke and Finke argue that 'This niche tends to be overproductive of religious organizations, and competitive forces are thus severe, but this ensures the vigor and market appeal of those bodies that emerge from the pack.'[37]
- *The ultra-strict niche*, in which the other-worldly who reject the trappings of society find as many ways as possible to demonstrate their devotion to the divine via extreme sacrifice and incurring the strongest stigma. Physical separation is often part of this (rural communes, compounds, cloisters, etc.), as is extremely different attire (as adopted by the Amish, Hare Krishnas and Hasidic Jews). The niche is characterised by very small, obscure and very unsuccessful groups.

By and large, those who resort to violent extremism in the modern world tend to be those in the strict and ultra-strict niches. It does not follow from this that there is a necessary or essential connection between religious radicalism and religious extremism. In the first place, only a tiny number of religious and non-religious radicals are violent. More to the point, the spread of political tolerance has removed much of the pressure from religious moderates, who are generally able to continue their practices (which by hypothesis do not place them in a great deal of conflict with the embedding society) without hindrance. Less tolerant societies, such as those of medieval Europe, generate greater conflict, which forces even relatively moderate religious groups into opposition, and perhaps more readily into violence.

This chapter has explored the notion of religious preferences in order to understand why some individuals choose versions of their faiths that exist at very high levels of tension with their surrounding social environment. The reason seems to be the earthly benefits of belonging that membership in such groups brings. If correct, then this minimises the role that the religious ideas or doctrines themselves play in influencing choice, and it also implies that controlling the supply and medium of information about choices can play an important role in policy. It therefore follows that when concerned policy-makers address the issue of violent extremism, they should be concerned less with matters of theology and more with issues surrounding the framing of choices for the religiously inclined, and alternative modes of supply for the goods postulated by the club model, especially for groups in the strict and ultra-strict niches. Such a conclusion is of course inconsistent with the DAM thesis.

However, this point indicates one final lacuna in our discussion of the mechanics and dynamics of religious adherence. We have discussed radicalism, but it might be claimed that violent extremism is a different matter. It is certainly the case that violence is the main driver for governmental action in the regulation of religion and of the Internet (the UK government was relatively insouciant about radical Islamists before 2001, which led to criticism, particularly from the French, that its multicultural policies were bringing about a radical enclave that became known as 'Londonistan').[38] It is quite plausible that ultra-strict groups' relations with the embedding society are so stretched as to demand qualitatively different responses from those directed towards the non-violent majority of radicals. The next chapter will therefore consider violent extremism as a special case of the religious mind.

7

THE DEMAND SIDE

THE MOTIVATIONS OF SUICIDE BOMBERS

So far we have focused on radical religious groups, which occupy the strict and ultra-strict market niches in supplying a particular type of religious good. However, it is important that we also consider violent extremists, who are more likely to belong to radical groups, because violence is the key driver of government involvement in the marketplace for religious ideas and the regulation of the Internet. We have defended the marketplace model of religious discussion, and the club model of demand for religious goods, which imply that there will always be a supply of radicals. The question we need to address is why some individuals or groups turn to violence or terrorism in pursuit of their ends.

As these individuals are vanishingly small in number it is hard to generalise. However, it is important to consider this question because overreliance on the DAM thesis, combined with the trope that the Internet creates echo chambers which amplify the attraction of antisocial ideas, seems to imply that there is a slippery slope from radicalism to extremism and that government action can be effective in preventing radicals from becoming extremists.

Violence in pursuit of a cause takes many forms and is not the preserve of the religious. In this chapter, we will focus on one particular type of violent intervention—those that involve the sacrifice of the extremist's life. Although suicide bombing is the most common such phenomenon, extremists have also sacrificed their lives in other ways in the pursuit of a particular cause, as was the case with the September 11 attacks in the United States. We concentrate on suicide for three reasons.

The first of these is that suicide is a game-changer, as Joseph Conrad wrote in his great novel on terrorism, *The Secret Agent*. Those who wish to live will always be restricted as to the violence they are able to perform—whatever they plan would need to include an escape plan. The suicide bomber, on the other hand, is all-powerful.

'I have always dreamed,' [Yundt] mouthed fiercely, 'of a band of men absolute in their resolve to discard all scruples in the choice of means, strong enough to give themselves frankly the name of destroyers, and free from the taint of that resigned pessimism which rots the world. No pity for anything on earth, including themselves—and death—enlisted for good and all in the service of humanity—that's what I would have liked to see. … And I could never get as many as three such men together.'[1]

The lack of pity completely transforms trust and the understanding of risk in the host population. Aeroplane travel, for instance, has been made almost intolerable since 2001 because of the threat of the suicide bomber. A crowded public place is crowded because it has utility for the crowd; any attempt to screen it off to ensure safety will reduce the utility.[2] The suicide bomber threatens either the utility of the space, or the safety of the people in it. As Ulrich Beck points out, there is literally no protection against a person with explosives concealed about their person:

From the perspective of the victim, [suicide bombing] amounts to a strategy of threat maximization because the space of possibility of the deeds becomes boundless and the institutions of prevention, calculability and control are circumvented. With still relatively 'low' numbers of victims and deeds, the *felt violence* and *felt war* are maximized and explode in the centres of the felt peace, both literally and in the mass media.[3]

Secondly, there is something of an explanatory gap with respect to suicidal terror. Bryan Caplan has argued that terrorist sympathisers hardly deviate from typical models of rationality—if they are non-violent but supportive of terrorists and their aims, then they are in effect free-riding on the violence of their colleagues to achieve their long-term aims. Violent extremists are also rational, at least to an extent. They adopt violent tactics because they conclude that non-violent ones are unlikely to achieve their goals. Their violence has unpleasant consequences for the politics of a region, but the costs of their actions are external to them (they would happen anyway, assuming there is a sufficient supply of extremists who think in a similar way). They can be judged more or less rational in so far as the cost to them of their irrational beliefs is not high, following Caplan's model of 'rational irrationality' in which 'people consume less irrationality when the price rises'.[4]

However, even on that model, which concedes that people can be irrational while still making rational choices, Caplan concludes that 'suicidal terrorists probably are simply irrational. ... They do not buy less irrationality when the price skyrockets, suggesting that they believe their doctrines all the way down.'[5] On a rational expectations model, which assumes unbiased beliefs, they fail the rationality test by systematically overestimating the probability that they are right. 'Bin Laden is not certain about conclusions that turn out to be right 95% of the time. He is certain about many conclusions that are probably false.'[6] Suicidal terrorists stick to their beliefs in the face of very high costs.

Hence although there is little to add to the marketplace model and club model, which assume at least some rational economic thinking on the part of religious adherents, to explain violence, there is perhaps a little more to do on suicidal terrorists whose rationality is in question.

Third, the purpose of this book is to explore the contribution of the Internet to violent terror, and its potential regulation by governments. Suicide bombing is arguably the driver for regulation, because if the aim of governments was simply to prevent terrorism, and if violent extremists were rational, then deterring them or 'buying them off' would be a possibility. It is the apparent irrationality of suicide bombers which leads to government efforts to prevent them from being infected by the 'bug' of radicalism in the first place, because once they are infected there is no possible way of deterring them from self-destructive and violent actions (because they are irrational) and no possible way of ensuring security (because they have no interest in escape). The push to regulate the Internet would be much less powerful if there were other means to deter or prevent violence, but the imperative, on standard models, is to prevent radicalisation in the first place.

Hence it is important to understand why a small minority of groups turn to violence or terrorism in the pursuit of their ends. A plausible set of explanations in this area will provide us with the foundations for measuring the input of the new technologies into these processes. In particular, we will continue our analysis of social goods as the foundation of the preferences that inform religious choices, including the choice of violent confrontation.

For the reasons given, we will concentrate on the use of suicide terrorism by some violent groups. Suicide missions have received a large degree of attention in recent years, and we will attempt to summarise the burgeoning literature. Once more, we will focus on the question of what evidence has been unearthed to suggest that ideas are the main causal agents.

Taking it to the extreme

We introduced Nozick's analysis of extremism in Chapter Two;[7] he focuses on the willingness of a person to live in extreme tension with the embedding society in such a way as to become a perceived threat. This leads to the policy conundrum that the perception of threat from the extremist group will affect the politics of the society, even if the group is small or insignificant. In particular, the society may move in the direction of greater confrontation in order to protect itself.

Nozick lists eight characteristics of extremism. These characteristics depict an extremist as someone who strongly rejects conventional wisdom and whose reaction to events is disproportionate. Two characteristics should give pause to the authorities—extremists, he argues, persist in occupying the far ends of the political spectrum, however the spectrum changes (thereby limiting the potency of a reframing initiative), and they are less interested in any particular position or issue than in being extreme. These go some distance in denying the DAM thesis, and predicting that apparently primitive and irrational thoughts will survive despite enlightened hopes that they would wither with time and 'progress'.

Other important characteristics include the fact that the extremist will use extreme means to override the rights of others, and will believe both that there is a literal force of implacable evil (and whoever does not work against this force implicitly works with it) and that there is no worthwhile trade-off of positive goals to achieve partial success. In the religious sphere, this combination of characteristics is likely to drive someone into an ultra-strict group, as set out in Introvigne's theory, as we argued in Chapter Six.

In terms of the public policy issues in the context of digital technologies, if the Internet contributes to the likelihood that a religious group will adopt more rather than fewer of Nozick's characteristics, then it will legitimately be a matter for public policy to consider. Extremists would be legitimate targets because, as Brasher puts it, 'they happily employ the futuristic technological products of contemporary rationalism to champion ideas that—in rationalists' eyes—erode the underpinnings of rationalist thought'.[8] We will consider the online world in Part III; our task now is to examine the level and type of threat from violent extremism. A society's response to vipers in its bosom needs to be proportionate to the threat; hence this chapter will consider the extent of the threat itself. This will lead us to the additional question of whether a response that does tend to contain or eliminate the extremist threat will also be damaging (a) to the embedding society itself (perhaps by unduly restricting freedom or privacy), or (b) to the infrastructure of the Internet, if it is perceived to facilitate the spread of extremist ideas.

The main reason that extremists contemplate violent methods is because they think they are the most effective way to achieve their goals.[9] Terrorist methods are often contemplated and adopted when the ultimate political goal seems so distant that normal social and political mechanisms appear impotent for achieving them (and as noted, compromise is ruled out). The existence of a short-cut route to the destination can prove very alluring, even if it will be costly. The larger the distance to be travelled and the fewer the number of acceptable intermediate steps en route to the final destination 'the more the group leaders will tend to be indifferent to the sacrifices of human life by both victims and members, because the potential gains to the group from reaching its goals will be large compared with any conceivable losses'.[10]

Hence the complete exclusion of a group from the regular political process, with no possibility of bargaining, often explains the resort to violence. When the ANC took up arms in its early years to resist the Apartheid regime in South Africa, it cited its complete inability to make any political inroads through the normal political channels of discussion and compromise for its aim of political equality for all. It started to abandon violence when dialogue began to take place and intermediate goals seemed possible.

This raises the tricky question of whether, and to what extent, governments should speak to terrorists. Governments will clearly want to avoid being seen as rewarding violence, but the value of maintaining this principle needs to be assessed accurately and, as Caplan argues, the costs of making such concessions are often much smaller than imagined.[11] In policy terms, this indicates that creating situations where large-scale disenfranchisement is likely should be avoided. Similarly, providing intermediate goals or compromises may take the wind of frustration out of extremist sails.

Suicide Bombing

Extremists' adoption of violence seems to have rational roots, and analysis seems to suggest that there are ways in which tension can be defused, thereby reducing the risk to the embedding society even if there is no effective way of removing the threat altogether. Yet as we argued above, suicidal terrorism still remains a conundrum. If groups adopt violence to further their political objectives because of a lack of other means to achieve indivisible goals, then why do some of them adopt the particular tactic of suicide bombing?

On any definition of rationality based on narrow self-interest, suicide missions seem utterly inexplicable; what definition of rationality could apply to a person who is willing to die for the cause? There is nothing, it is safe to assert, less conducive to one's well-being than blowing oneself up. Yet when looked at through the same lens as other terrorist acts, they offer a direct route to the final destination. The return on the sacrifice of a life, in terms of immediate slaughter, media coverage and the fracture of trust in the embedding society, is exponential. However we define rationality, it cannot be in terms of narrow self-interest. Equally, suicidal terrorism cannot seem rational to too many people, because if it did then we would have to explain why there is so little of it.

It is thus important to begin by asking why some violent groups, and not others, use the tactic. Why does a group like al-Qaeda adopt suicide missions, when a group like the IRA did not?[12] This is not a straightforward question. The IRA (Irish Republican Army) employed a broad range of terror tactics in its attempts to achieve a united Ireland, as did ETA in Spain. But neither organisation employed suicide missions.[13] In fact, when the IRA began to target civilians, it started to lose popular support. When it toyed with the use of human bombs—such as the use of kidnapped individuals to deliver and detonate explosives while their families were held hostage—the tactic did not last long.[14] This is to be contrasted with the vast majority of contemporary suicide missions that claim backing by Islamic doctrine. Such missions often receive explicit support from the communities in whose name they are perpetrated.[15]

If the explanation resides in religious conviction after all, then this would fit with the DAM thesis and popular conceptions of suicide bombings as perpetrated by brainwashed jihadis or individuals so attracted by the promise of heavenly rewards that they are willing to meet their maker, and sooner rather than later. By contrast, political groups such as the IRA do not have such arcane and costly metaphysics at their core.

But this explanation is unlikely to be accurate. It ignores all the considerations we have gathered from an extensive discussion about the demand for religious goods in Chapter Six. More importantly, the suggested cleavage between religious groups with peculiar supernatural elements willing to utilise suicide missions and secular groups which are reluctant does not stand up to scrutiny. Some religious groups that are prepared to use violence do not resort to suicide missions, and some non-religious groups have utilised them. Indeed, religious extremists were not the primary users of suicide tactics until fairly recently. Writing before the ultimate defeat of the Tamil Tigers, Robert Pape noted that 'Islamic groups receive the most attention in Western media, but the world's leader in suicide terrorism is actually the Liberation Tigers of Tamil Eelam (LTTE), a group who recruits from the predominantly Hindu Tamil population in northern and eastern Sri Lanka and whose ideology has Marxist/Leninist elements.'[16]

Specific to Islam?

Yet there is still a suspicion that doctrine plays a role in the use of suicide by Islamic terrorists. Certain populist thinkers, for instance, have suggested that Islam differs from Christianity in being amenable to suicide bombers. The manner in which many contemporary American politicians and commentators received news of the apparent religious claims of bin Laden in the post-September 11 statements was telling in virtue of their astonishment that 'Muslim extremists seem actually to believe in God, pray to Him, and even invoke His assistance.'[17] The idea that Islam provides justification for suicide bombings is not necessarily an absurd claim. Christianity and Islam are just two different religions with two different contents. Their internal value systems vary, so perhaps they permit different actions. The Christian injunction to forgive, while permitting defensive warfare, would seem to rule out terrorism of any kind.[18] Yet, on the other hand, the vast majority of Muslims interpret their religion as peaceful, and as opposed to violence, just as Christians do, and abhor the violence that is often committed in the name of their religion by those who seek to do harm.

In fact, neither religion has been immune to doctrinal innovations that allow religion to be employed as ideological backing for violence. The Crusades are the most obvious example of violence being committed in the name of Christianity. In recent times radical Christian groups and individuals have not been averse to blowing things up to create terror effects. Eric Rudolph killed two people by bombing the Olympic Games of 1996, two abortion clinics and a homosexual nightclub, as part of his pro-life (*sic*) campaign. In his various statements he linked his actions to his religious beliefs, often quoting scripture, and received wider support from the Army of God and its spokesperson Reverend Donald Spitz.

So not all Christians abhor violence and turn the other cheek. Perhaps, however, things are different with suicide missions. Christianity might impose an absolute prohibition on such actions, thus giving reasons that constrain action, while Islam might ultimately be consistent with such actions. Is this a plausible reading of the two sets of doctrine? A quick sketch should cast sufficient doubt on this explanation to open up space for a more plausible explanation.

Thou shalt not kill thyself

On one level the Christian tradition appears steadfast in its prohibition of suicide. Both Roman Catholicism and Protestantism condemn the willing of one's own death. Augustine understood the sixth commandment, 'Thou shalt not kill', as referring to everyone, including oneself. Aquinas read Deuteronomy xxxii. 39, 'I will kill and I will make to live' to mean that God had the exclusive right of determining which lives were to end. Suicide, he noted, was the worst sin because it could not be repented. Is this prohibition on suicide within the Christian tradition an effective constraint on individual motivations with regard to carrying out suicide attacks?

It seems unlikely—after all, the sixth commandment has not enjoyed total success in Christendom over the years. Indeed, the Thomasian position is subtly crafted and admits of different forms of action. Suicide is but one member of a set of actions which share the property of certain death, and Aquinas and Augustine sought to tease out such distinctions in order to allow certain actions in some cases but not in others. Consequently, suicide missions could not necessarily be ruled impermissible on the basis of the biblical texts.

The Bible itself tells of six self-killings, and the writers neither condemn nor commend these actions. Saul impaled himself in preference to being captured by the victorious Philistine army, and Samson pleaded with the Lord to take revenge on his Philistine captors with his one final act, pulling down the pillars of the temple of Dagon on himself and his captors.[19] Furthermore, a particular conception of martyrdom was a crucial part of early Christianity, helping reinforce the faith via demonstration.[20] Ignatius, the second-century bishop of Antioch, travelled at a leisurely pace to Rome after being condemned to death, writing letters along the way imploring fellow Christians not to intercede on his behalf in case he lost this opportunity for martyrdom. 'What a thrill I shall have from the wild beasts that are ready for me!' he proclaimed.

I shall coax them on to eat me up at once and not to hold off, as sometimes happens, through fear. And if they are reluctant, I shall force them to it. Forgive me—I know what is good for me. Now is the moment I am beginning to be a disciple.[21]

The Augustinian position sought to differentiate these types of action, condemning those who chose suicide in preference to defilement or suffering as mistaken, but affirming actions that retained the integrity of the individual. Samson was adjudged special because he was directly commanded by God. Otherwise he would have erred in seeking revenge.

Islam also implicitly forbids suicide,[22] but like Christianity it includes a historical tradition that keeps open the distinction between suicide and martyrdom. The attempts to frame suicide bombings as martyrdom operations are indicative of this. The intention of the actor once more comes to the fore in narratives. As influential Sunni theologian Sheikh Yusuf al-Qaradawi claimed in an interview: 'They are not suicide operations. These are heroic martyrdom operations, and the heroes who carry them out don't embark on this action out of hopelessness and despair but are driven by an overwhelming desire to cast terror and fear into the hearts of the oppressors.' The conceptualisation of such events as martyrdom rather than suicide is vitally important.[23]

The notion of jihad was apparently an innovation of Muhammad's prior to the Battle of Badr, where defeat would have meant the extinction of Islam.[24] The Prophet Muhammad told his followers that a death in a battle for their faith would be a very special kind of death: 'No man will be slain this day fighting against them with steadfast courage, advancing not retreating, but God will cause him to enter Paradise.'[25] Within Christianity, the decision of the Church of Rome to attempt to wrest the Holy City from the Saracens was underpinned by a wholesale shift in the notion of martyrdom in justification of holy war.[26] Pope Urban II urged the Franks to unite in 1095 and recapture Jerusalem from Islamic control. In words reminiscent of Muhammad, Archbishop Turpin is accredited in *The Song of Roland* as saying prior to battle that 'if you die, you will be blessed martyrs/And take your place in paradise on high'.[27] Drawing on the examples of the early Christian bishops singled out for persecution and martyrdom, such motivations provided the theological backing for all the Crusades.[28]

It has been argued that a similar process in modern Islam is key to understanding the recent apparent discrepancy between the two religions. Scruton's analysis of the Islamic revival in terms both of doctrine and political events laid the blame squarely on Ayatollah Khomeini and argued that the doctrine of martyrdom together with the powerful symbolism of the Iranian Revolution created a perfect political storm which spread far beyond Shi'ism. 'Sunni Muslims, who believe on the authority of the Koran that suicide is categorically forbidden, have nevertheless been sucked into the Shi'ite maelstrom to become martyrs in the war against Satan.' According to Scruton, the result was actually beneficial to the spread of Islam:

It is not too great an exaggeration to say that this new confluence of Sunni orthodoxy and Shi'ite extremism has laid the foundations for a worldwide Islamic revival. For the first time in centuries Islam appears, both in the eyes of its followers and in the eyes of the infidel, to be a single religious movement united around a single goal.

The importance of Khomeini was that 'he endowed the Islamic revival with a Shi'ite physiognomy, so making martyrdom a central part of its strategy'.[29] Scruton was writing in 2002; since then any apparent Islamic unity has fallen apart, with conflict between Sunni and Shi'a being far bloodier than the so-called 'clash of civilisations'. Nevertheless, this is not to say that his analysis did not ring true at a particular historical moment.

Through a glass, darkly

Having surveyed the evidence of doctrinal interpretations of Islam and Christianity that remove possible barriers to self-sacrifice, the strategy explaining the use of suicide tactics via doctrine looks less than robust. Perhaps, however, the doctrinal explanation should be in terms of incentives rather than barriers, as it may be possible that there is something unique to certain religions that motivates individuals to undertake such actions in pursuit of their cause. Much is made in the popular literature, for example, of the Islamic martyr, having secured his place in paradise, securing at the same time access to the seventy-two virgins that await him there. The hypothesis is that Islam incentivises suicide bombers in ways that other religions do not. Can this explain the difference?

This is a more difficult claim to assess, largely because we are, once again, in the murky waters of judging preferences and motivations rather than behaviour and outcomes. What someone says motivates them may be very different to what does, in fact, motivate them; the preferences that someone reveals by their actions or choices often differ markedly from their stated preferences. But let's look through a glass, darkly, into the mind of the suicide bomber and see what we can see.

Jon Elster, who has addressed this issue directly, views such spiritual rewards as consolatory rather than motivational—as having a disinhibitory effect on usual normative constraints. Three such considerations lend weight to this idea. First, if entering heaven did bear the motivating status often attributed to it, then surely we would see more instances of selfless suicide:

If those who claim to be religious believers were as sure of the afterlife as they are that the sun will rise tomorrow, *and* if they thought they could get there by performing good actions, we would observe a vastly greater number of martyrs than we actually do. Before the fall of Communism, Christians from the West would have overrun the borders of the Soviet Union to spread the gospel, knowing that the worst that could happen was that eternal bliss would begin sooner rather than later.[30]

Religious belief may have certain positive effects such as preventing back-sliding among would-be martyrs or of relaxing the normal moral constraints on killing. Even there, however, the strength of those effects should not be exaggerated. Many would-be suicide bombers do not go through with the act, despite being bolstered by religious belief (this has led to the use of remote detonation), and in any case there are not massive numbers of suicides despite the extravagant promises of future goods in heaven for those who die for their faith (which, *ex hypothesi* would-be bombers must believe). History simply does not bear out the idea that the promises of Islamic metaphysics are irresistible.

Mohammad ... promises paradise to all who fall in a holy war. Now if every believer were to guide his conduct by that assurance in the Koran, every time a Mohammedan army found itself faced by unbelievers it ought either to conquer or to fall to the last man. It cannot be denied that a certain number of individuals do live up to the letter of the Prophet's word, but as between defeat and death followed by eternal bliss, the majority of Mohammedans normally elect defeat.[31]

It could be that each believer pursues his own individual rational self-interest in defecting, which collectively produces the worst group outcome, in a prisoner's dilemma-type situation. But, as Caplan suggests, it is not that such believers do not actually believe the truth of their doctrine, it is rather that the psychological costs of holding the belief that the fallen are in paradise in peacetime is negligible and no doubt comforting, but during war and in the face of death it has significant costs: 'He is literally *better off dead*. As danger approaches, then, the Muslim warrior does not act *more* selfishly; he revises his beliefs about *how* to pursue his self-interest.'[32]

Disbelief is rare among supposed believers. The idea that such people do not believe in what they say is implausible simply because their public professions of belief are so frequent, powerful and uncompromising. Caplan asks, rhetorically, 'is the typical fundamentalist of any religion merely *pretending* to embrace its doctrines? Try arguing with one.'[33] The point is rather that radical religious ideas are easy to hold when little in the way of real-world costs turn on them, but not so easy to pursue when there are considerable costs. 'A few Muslims sacrifice their lives for their faith, but a billion do not',[34] as Caplan's theory of rational irrationality predicts.[35]

Second, the reward of seventy-two eternal virgins will only be attractive to a very limited set of would-be martyrs. It is unlikely that the four Palestinian women who perpetrated suicide bombings in 2002 or the female suicide bombers utilised by the Tamils, or the Turkish Workers Party (PPK), or in Chechnya, were overly interested in the prospect of being received into paradise by the *houris*. The biographies of each of these women, including their personal jihad messages, are replete with references to social and political oppression, the murder of Palestinians by Israeli forces, and a sense of hopelessness, but mention virtually nothing of spiritual incentives such as entering paradise.[36] Although extremist organisations such as al-Qaeda and Hezbollah make much of Islamic doctrine and the various spiritual incentives and rewards allegedly contained within it—a feature that has been picked up by Western observers when attempting to understand the phenomenon—the notions of martyrdom it peddles are in large degree alien to the Islamic canon. Similarly, those groups such as the LTTE that lack a significant religious element would on this account lack any such incentive, despite being a leading proponent of suicide missions as a tactic.[37] The fact that incentivising religious beliefs are neither necessary nor sufficient for the use of suicide tactics is evident from these cases.[38]

Olivier Roy's suggestion that extremist notions of martyrdom have less to do with the Koranic tradition, and more with the Western tradition of individual and pessimistic revolt for an elusive ideal world, has the ring of truth.[39] Martyrdom can be given a wholly secular foundation, and provide an overwhelming sense of obligation to the cause, if we need to furnish a motivation at the level of individuals' ideas.[40] For example, pessimism and individual revolt together explain the curious combination of views often on display in such groups as al-Qaeda, Hezbollah, Hamas and so on, which see Israel and Zionism as an overwhelmingly powerful force in history, but which still could be driven from the land and into the sea by the people of Palestinian territory. From this perspective, al-Qaeda looks more akin to the anarchist revolutionaries of nineteenth-century Europe than an Islamic group.[41]

Taken together, these points suggest that spiritual rewards do not play an actual and effective incentivising role in the ready supply of Islamic suicide bombers; nor does there appear to be anything inherent in Islam which explains the use of that tactic by Islamic extremists.

Opportunity knocks

If this casts doubt on the theological explanation of why extreme tactics such as suicide missions are employed, is there a more plausible explanation of the decision violent extremists make to employ suicide tactics? We believe that there is indeed such an explanation, backed up by considerable social scientific research, which fits with the model of religious belief we have adopted throughout. In simple terms, the social, political and economic repercussions of violence in general, and suicide missions in particular, are so high that for most groups such a course of action is prohibitively expensive. Only in cases where social context renders the repercussions minimal are such tactics viable.

To see this we need only consider the fact that far fewer Christians live as a minority group in their country of residence than Muslims. This is not to say that Christian groups and sects do not live in tension with their surrounding society, but this tension is often less high, and the sects are rarely completely alien or unfamiliar. Certain practices, beliefs, observances or dress codes may appear extreme or outlandish to the mainstream, but they are usually instances of radical interpretation of familiar ideas clearly rooted in the social, cultural and religious tradition of the wider society. For example, despite being one of the most radical recent Christian sects in the United States, the Branch Davidians saw themselves, and more importantly were seen by the wider community, as an extension of the more mainstream and familiar Seventh-Day Adventists. Many observers of the protracted siege came to identify with the Branch Davidians because they were attempting to live according to the principles of Christian doctrine. This shared heritage made the group understandable to that wider community, at least in principle. Koresh often appealed to this wider community for support.

Christianity did not always enjoy this relative level of social embeddedness. In the years immediately following Jesus' death, his followers were a tiny minority movement starkly at odds with the pagan, Jewish and other religions of the time. The notable features of this early existence were the large sacrifices required of followers, and the stigma attached, as well as the degree of persecution. No doubt inspired by the example of Christ's Passion, many of the early Christians followed suit in terms of preferring death to the renunciation of their faith.[42]

The modern Muslim experience is very often that of an outsider, with which Scruton illustrates a conservative critique of modernity:

In short, Islam offers an unparalleled form of membership, and one whose appeal is all the greater in that it transcends time and space, joining the believer to a universal *umma* whose only sovereign is God. Even if it may appear, to the skeptical modernist, as a medieval fossil, Islam has an unrivalled ability to compensate for what is lacking in modern experience. It rationalizes and validates the condition of exile: the condition in which we all find ourselves, severed by the hectic motion of mechanized life from the age-old experience of membership. Nothing evokes this more clearly than the collective rite in which the faithful turn to Mecca with their prayers—projecting their submission and their longing away from the place where they are to that other and holy place where they are not, and whose contours are defined not by geography but by religious need.[43]

Constituency costs of violence

An important variable is consequently the level of integration that exists between a given group and its surrounding society. From the point of view of the suicide mission, integration is a point of weakness, as the nihilistic Professor points out in *The Secret Agent*:

Their character is built upon conventional morality. It leans on the social order. Mine stands free from everything artificial. They are bound in all sorts of conventions. They depend on life, which, in this connection, is a historical fact surrounded by all sorts of restraints and considerations, a complex organised fact open to attack at every point; whereas I depend on death, which knows no restraint and cannot be attacked. My superiority is evident.[44]

The majority of terrorist groups depend upon the support of a substantial section of their host societies, sometimes within a particular ethnic or religious group, in order to function, maintain legitimacy and receive the economic and political means to accomplish their ends. This imposes restrictions on possible actions. Group leaders may be willing to undertake or sanction actions that the supporters from the wider social context would reject, for example because of the differences in moral norms between group and social background or in the intensity with which preferences are held.[45] A group's leadership, for instance, might prefer rapid political gains via the indiscriminate use of violence and a disregard for civilian casualties, whereas its supporters might share the same goals but refuse to countenance certain measures because they are ethically unacceptable, or because they would make their politically reasonable aims less achievable. There is a trade-off between levels of support and the intensity of violence or types of tactics employed.

The challenge for groups that operate with a given level of integration is to achieve a balance that gives them sufficient financial, political and social support and legitimacy while reserving the right to employ sufficient political and violent means to achieve their ends. This is a *modus vivendi*—a strategic compromise liable to be revised if circumstances change—rather than consensus between supporters and leaders. Stepping beyond the *modus vivendi* jeopardises legitimacy, and risks haemorrhaging necessary resources. When gains can be made in other ways, adopting suicide missions will likely cost more than it can benefit. Kalyvas and Sánchez-Cuenca term these constituency costs.[46]

For instance, Chechen forces adopted suicide missions in 2000, leading to claims of al-Qaeda alignment or support. Despite the presence of some Saudi radicals in Chechnya which no doubt helped to radicalise the tactics of certain groups, these missions were ultimately halted when the leadership of the Chechen resistance recognised that other more profitable tactics existed.[47] Local conditions played more of a determining role in this case than the presence of external fighters in the area.

The IRA is another example. While it employed a number of tactics, it achieved its highest level of support when it targeted the British military or state apparatus. The struggle was framed as a conventional war fought between two opposed armies. The nationalist population that supported the cause had preferences about acceptable means. This is the 'normative' form of constituency cost, where 'supporters could reject [suicide missions] simply because they object to suicide or do not see themselves, and thus do not want to be seen, as fanatics or extremists'.[48] At times these preferences conflicted with those of the leadership. When other tactics such as the targeting of civilians or the use of kidnapped individuals to plant bombs were adopted, support quickly ebbed away. Such tactics failed to fit the narrative of a symmetric struggle. The IRA leadership, though often more radical than its grass-roots support, consistently recognised and observed the constraints placed upon its actions in pursuit of its goal.[49]

There is a sense in which the rise of the popularity of suicide bombing in other arenas hastened the peace process in Ireland. As other groups came to the fore that were prepared to use such tactics against the British, the IRA could no longer compete. Fear of alienating those who supported it both at home and abroad prevented the IRA from adopting more extremist methods and made peace discussions look more profitable. As the *Economist* argued shortly before the attack on the London Underground in 2005, this is a much more delicate and complex situation to negotiate for both terrorist and government:

In Britain, the threat posed by Islamist terrorism is both simpler and graver than the familiar menace of the IRA. Simpler, because there is no argument about whether the terrorists can be reasoned with. A group that tries to bomb its way to the negotiating table presents politicians with a dilemma, as John Major's government discovered in the early 1990s; a group that wants only to blow up the table does not. Graver, because of the power of the suicide bomber and the disorganised nature of Islamist terrorism. IRA bombings can be blamed on the IRA. Islamist bombings are more likely to be blamed on the security services and the government.[50]

As a third example, consider the so-called pro-life lobby in the United States. No Christian anti-abortion group has ever come out in unequivocal support of violent means, let alone planned them. The closest such groups have come is the offering of occasional and qualified support for violent actions by individual preachers, despite well-developed theological underpinnings for the anti-abortion position and the fact that millions of Americans, who are willing to spend substantial amounts of money in support of the cause, are told from the pulpit each Sunday that abortion is murder. Again, the reason is the wider social context upon which such groups depend for their support. Even the radical Army of God went to extraordinary lengths to deny that its so-called 'Nuremberg Files' website—which listed the contact details of abortionists and crossed them out when they had been killed—was in operation prior to the deaths of those listed. In such cases the opportunity costs of any violence, let alone suicide missions, are too high to be adopted.

Such groups recognise that association with violent means would cause them to suffer huge losses in terms of public support, reputation, influence, membership and financial support. The social, economic, political and legal realities of the United States make concerted efforts in this direction counterproductive; the opportunity costs would simply be too high to countenance such tactics, even if the more fervent among the leadership wished to hasten matters. Crucial to this is the existence of other worthwhile mechanisms for achieving those ends. If alternative mechanisms exist for change, and the final goal admits of decomposition into intermediate reforms, then support will ebb from the potentially violent.

The lure of violence

We have argued that suicide missions are driven neither by doctrine nor spiritual incentives, and that opportunity costs are likely to play a prominent role in constraining would-be violent extremists. The final question to address is why violence occurs when it does.

The lure for organisations

An explanation from the social science literature with a strong fit with the empirical data is that suicide missions overcome certain barriers to the advancement of the terrorists' cause. In a recent study of an array of cases Berman and Laitin argue that terrorist groups tend to employ suicide missions when the chosen target is virtually incapable of being attacked in any other way.[51] In the face of terrorist threats, governments take steps to make potential targets harder to attack (target hardening) by increasing the level of defence employed, and preventing undetected escape. The greater the probability of attackers being killed before achieving their goal or of being apprehended either before or after the fact, the higher the tendency for a given group to adopt suicide missions. Although suicide missions bear a cost to the group because of the sacrifice of a committed member, not to mention the cost to the individual themselves, the success of an attack on an otherwise impenetrable target is a considerable gain.

Furthermore, the use of suicide missions is an obvious extension to the often elaborate organisational structures that terrorist groups employ to maintain secrecy and anonymity. This is lent further plausibility by Berman and Laitin's observation of a decline in standard insurgency tactics following target hardening. The expected utility of individual operatives declines through an increased probability of apprehension.[52] Similarly, suicide missions are rejected even by organisations with no distaste for violence when they can achieve their ends without them.[53]

As we would expect, far from having a doctrinal base, it follows from this analysis that:

suicide terrorism is strategic. The vast majority of suicide terrorist attacks are not isolated or random acts by individual fanatics but, rather, occur in clusters as part of a larger campaign by an organized group to achieve a specific political goal. Groups using suicide terrorism consistently announce specific political goals and stop suicide attacks when those goals have been fully or partially achieved.[54]

The lure for individuals

It is all very well making a strategic organisational decision to turn to violence and suicide; but that does not explain why an organisation is able to gain recruits who are willing to undertake violence, let alone blow themselves up.

Why do individuals undertake such missions? If religious rewards contribute only partial motivation at best, what is the key factor? Once again, the explanation is rather mundane: it appears to be largely for the benefits of belonging. The club model still applies to this even more radical sacrifice. A great deal of research has indicated that participation in such a group brings benefits that are perceived to outweigh the costs.[55]

Whatever spiritual benefits membership in extreme religious sects may bring, they also bring tangible social benefits to individual members. Recent work on the internal structure and workings of radical groups has identified two overriding features. First, unsurprisingly, the members of the group share a set of extreme beliefs. There is homogeneity, with little or no dissent. Second, they are characterised by high levels of belonging, solidarity and social cohesion.[56] Belonging in this sense is a 'unity' or 'oneness of purpose' among group members.[57] This might be motivated by empathy, or by self-interest. In general, whatever the underlying cause, the greater degree of belonging that exists, the more able the group is to work coherently as a social machine toward a particular end state or common goal.

Many are attracted to the intensity of belonging that such strict groups supply. It is possible to see the willingness on the part of the individual to engage in suicide missions as the ultimate extension of the desire for belonging. To gain the collective benefits of participation in a strict group requires self-sacrifice, often to extreme levels, but getting people to die for a cause has never been overly problematic (otherwise military recruitment would be much harder than it is), while conversely there is little evidence that capital punishment has ever acted as much of a deterrent in preventing even relatively minor crimes. Hence the expected benefits of a suicide mission can exceed expected costs. Belonging confers benefits such as honour, praise and moral status (all as judged by fellow group members),[58] plus the harm and suffering caused to one's enemies, and the benefits to close acquaintances (welfare assistance, compensation, fame).[59] The experience in some parts of the world of being able to observe the posthumous paeans to bombers doled out not only by fellow members of the group but also by spontaneous public demonstrations is no doubt invaluable in stiffening spines and increasing confidence that these benefits will continue to accrue. As Hugh Barlow observes, 'All forms of martyrdom are potentially both selfish and altruistic.'[60]

In short, attaching a psychological profile to a suicide attacker is not difficult: He lacks empathy for his victims, is altruistic toward his own cause or side, and is a little deluded about his importance in the grand scheme of things. Unfortunately that profile is not at all helpful in screening for possible suicide attackers—those three characteristics are simply too common in conflict-ridden areas of the world.[61]

While suicide bombers in the UK do not receive much support from their surrounding community—far from it in fact, as their actions are widely and vociferously condemned by the Islamic community—such individuals have often turned their backs on traditional support networks. Instead, new friends, drawn from different backgrounds, with an intense devotion for their often newly found or reawakened religion, provide the lion's share of the tangible benefits of praise, honour, status and assurances of posthumous earthly rewards. Moreover, as Cole and Cole argue, support from the wider, global community can be important:

The so-called 'martyrs' are not celebrated within the Muslim population of the UK as they are in the Palestinian territories, Sri Lanka and Lebanon. Indeed, there is widespread renunciation from the majority of the Muslim population for acts of terrorism in the UK. Instead, the memory of those who die is kept alive within the collective memory of the radicalised networks of which they were part and the *ummah*.[62]

Websites such as Caravan of Martyrs and Islamic Awakening list the names of Islamic 'martyrs', including some from the UK.[63]

Perhaps there is something in George Bernard Shaw's quip that martyrdom is the only way for those without ability to be famous.[64] As Ricolfi points out (citing Gambetta), in the Palestinian case the volunteers often seem to be civilians rather than militants.[65] Part of the 'symbolic' process associated with suicide missions—a final, often video-taped statement, posters, photographs and other public displays of heroism—lends itself to creating fame for martyrs as they leave their signature on events:

This type of motivation reveals an individualistic aspect of martyr operations, and helps us understand why [suicide missions, or SMs] manage to attract individuals lacking religious motivations … Furthermore, if it is true that, among the motivations of suicide operations, revenge occupies an important place, it might be reasonable to believe that SMs are preferred [to other more traditional militant forms of resistance] indeed because a signed operation is more effective in satisfying the thirst for revenge than an anonymous one.[66]

The individual's rational decision to take part in such a mission depends not just on a simple calculation of costs and benefits, but also on the system of behaviour and symbolism that surrounds the act. Once again, there is a similarity with the explanation of why individuals chose to become and remain members of early Christian groups, despite significant stigma and widespread persecution, with many of their number facing death for their beliefs:

[T]he fruits of the faith were not limited to the realm of the spirit. Christianity offered much to the flesh, as well. It was not simply the promise of salvation that motivated Christians, but the fact that they were greatly rewarded here and now for belonging. Thus while membership was expensive, it was, in fact, a bargain. That is, because the church asked much of its members, it was thereby possessed of the resources to *give* much. For example, Christians were expected to aid the less fortunate, many of them received such aid, and all could feel greater security against bad times. Because they were asked to nurse the sick and dying, many of them received such nursing. Because they were asked to love others, they in turn were loved. And if Christians were required to observe a far more restrictive moral code than that observed by pagans, Christians—especially women—enjoyed a far more secure family life.[67]

Conclusion to Part II

In this part of the book we have discussed some of the prominent explanations for religious behaviour, narrowing our focus through the four chapters from explanations of general religious commitment, to religious radicalism, and finally to violent extremism. Along the way we have narrowed the type of explanations that seem best to fit the facts. The benefits of belonging seem to drive types of violent religious behaviour that a liberal society must legitimately wish to prevent, which in turn has policy implications. If this analysis is correct, then there is *prima facie* little mileage in attempting to boost certain types of religious ideology, theology or doctrine, and to suppress other types, as doctrine is not a key variable. Moreover, looking to spot which religious groups might have violent tendencies seems a largely fruitless task for government—

the equivalent of looking for the needle in the haystack, but with the additional complication that the needle might not even be in the haystack. If the DAM thesis is false, then government efforts to forestall or detect violence need to be aimed elsewhere than religious motivations.

However, the argument does not end here. The work on echo chambers reported in Chapter Two argued that the Internet is a game-changer in that it not only allows the spread of ideas, including bad ideas, but also changes the nature of debate and political interaction, because personalisation and group polarisation make it more likely that individuals will adopt extreme positions. This is the ground for the development of the Prevent policies discussed in Chapter Three.

The task of Part III, then, is to examine the nature of religious belief on the Internet, and to consider whether the technological context should cause us to rethink the conclusions of Part II, or the theories and policies discussed in Part I.

PART III

8

THE LONG TAIL

In this part of the book we examine the specific effects of the Internet on the religious environment. If, as we have suggested, it is useful to conceive of the religious environment as a market in ideas, in which believers can be characterised as displaying market-type behaviours, then the Internet could have a massive impact in the field of religion. It has dramatically influenced economic markets in recent years, as we argued in Chapter One; in this chapter we examine these effects in more detail. If debates over religious ideas function like a marketplace, then the long-tail thesis will be relevant to the argument from Cass Sunstein's work on echo chambers and polarisation. We shall see that, in the context of religious ideas, Anderson's and Sunstein's work is mutually supportive.

We begin by expounding the long-tail thesis in detail, and applying it to predict what shape the religious marketplace might take. This has crucial implications for the Church–Sect Cycle (CSC) as a feature of the unrestricted religious marketplace of ideas. In this chapter, our aim is solely to set out the thesis, while in the next we will subject it to critical analysis.

The long-tail thesis

E-commerce has snowballed in recent years. The world's first online shopper, the aptly named Mrs Jane Snowball from Gateshead in the

UK, bought groceries from Tesco online in 1984; three decades later e-commerce is worth hundreds of billions of dollars.[1] Although retailers have been keen to break into the area, and those without an online presence are often dismissed as too old-fashioned to flourish in today's business world, there has been remarkably little analysis about the wider effects of bringing commerce online. One important recent contribution is by the then editor-in-chief of the IT magazine *Wired*, Chris Anderson, in his book *The Long Tail*.[2]

Anderson's argument is simple and compelling. Compare an offline retailer of a good, such as books, with an online competitor. The offline retailer has a store or a chain of stores with a certain amount of shelf space. Its aim is to maximise book sales. Some sell more heavily than others—all things being equal, *Harry Potter* will outsell an esoteric thesis about modal logics weaker than S3. Furthermore, for each bestselling title there are many works whose sales are minute. The retailer may wish to preserve variety on its shelves—variety is attractive to the book-buying public—but however big its stores, the limitations on shelf space mean that it will prefer to stock bestsellers rather than the esoteric. Customers browse, and the chances of a modal logician interested in weak logics actually entering the right shop and seeing the perfect book on the shelf and buying it are much smaller than a *Harry Potter* or Dan Brown fan coming in. The modal logician is very likely, if she does wander into a shop, to be disappointed in her quest (or more accurately, for every esoteric type who finds what she is looking for, there will be thousands who do not). In a world of browsers it makes sense to cater for the numerous rather than the rare. Each copy of the modal logic book in the shop takes up precious space that could be occupied by *Harry Potter* or Dan Brown.

Now consider the online retailer. Online customers are able to search, rather than just browse, so the Dan Brown fan and the modal logician are on equal terms—they put their key terms in the search engine and see what comes up. The bestseller has no advantage over the niche product in terms of availability, because neither demands physical space: all they need is their own webpage, which is actually created automatically by the customer's browser, rendered from information from the retailer's database, thereby incurring minimal costs. The economics of retail are no longer driven by scarce shelf space in purpose-built shops; all the online retailer needs is a warehouse and a distribution system. The online presence of the modal logic book is not an opportunity cost, because it does not prevent a million *Harry Potters* being stored alongside it. Warehouse space is abundant, unlike shelf space in shops.

This analysis led Anderson to postulate that the structures of markets will change. In an offline market, the scarcity of shelf space means that the number of esoteric titles is artificially lowered—potential readers of books on modal logic, medieval icon painting, local history, avant-garde poetry or repair manuals for the 1949 Cadillac Coupe deVille find them particularly difficult to find. Instead they are stuck with their second-choice books. They are less happy, as are the esoteric authors. But when book retailing migrates online, the esoteric readers can find what they want, which increases the sales of their favourite books and slightly lowers the sales of the blockbusters (assuming they have a more or less constant book budget). The sales of the esoteric do not increase much as they still have very few readers, but that small number of readers has greater opportunity to buy the books that really excite them. The online market caters for the long tail of the demand curve which consists of all those thousands of books written every year for a tiny number of readers. Customers are more satisfied because they can find the niche products which interest them.

The end result is yet another instance of the democratisation of the Internet. People get what they want. The distribution of goods formerly rationed by price and space is now only limited by price. In Anderson's phrase, 'a long tail is just culture unfiltered by economic scarcity'.[3] Demand that was latent in the offline market because transaction costs were too high is now satisfied online.

In technical terms, minus transaction costs, one would expect the curve of a market to be in the form of a scale-invariant power law, with sales of goods declining rapidly as we move down their rankings. Any section of the graph will obey something like Pareto's 80–20 rule, which says that 20 per cent of the goods will make 80 per cent of the sales (it is called scale invariant because any fragment of the graph will look more or less like the graph as a whole). A corollary of this is that there is no meaningful average of sales of the goods; different samples will have wildly different mean sales. When goods are distributed as a power law, the way becomes open for the appearance of what Nassim Nicholas Taleb has called black swans,[4] outliers beyond the range of regular expectations which carry extreme impact (very large sales, in the case of a commercial

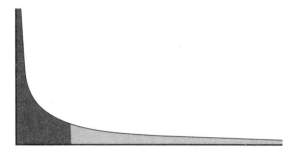

Figure 3: A scale-free power law graph. In the darker grey are the popular blockbusters and in lighter shading is the long tail

market). If we carry this logic through to the marketplace of religious ideas, this would mean that religious ideas which have very large and completely unpredictable effects only appear very rarely. Taleb himself has suggested that Christianity is a black swan under his definition.[5]

However that may be, the upshot is that the tail of the market lengthens. Given the view of the marketplace of religious ideas expounded in Chapter Four, this has major implications for the migration of religious views online. When the marketplace of religious ideas moves online, the hypothesis is that it will manifest properties of online markets; in particular, minority views will be better catered for. This is certainly not a vision to over-enthuse Cass Sunstein, who writes that it 'is best understood as a kind of nightmare'.[6]

Anderson is right to emphasize that the Internet can greatly increase niche marketing, in a way that offers extraordinary economic opportunities from the long tail. He is also right to suggest that communities can form around highly specialized tastes. What is remarkable is his near-complete lack of self-consciousness about what might be wrong with a world of niches. Anderson writes as if the power to choose the particular good that each particular person particularly wants is an unambiguous good—as if there is little to do but to notice and celebrate this process. Anderson's analysis appears implicitly premised on the idea that freedom and the good life are promoted by, and maybe even captured in, the opportunity to choose what is specifically sought on either the large head or the long tail. Of course he is right to celebrate the increase in available options, but from the standpoint of democracy, the assessment is not so simple.[7]

We consider this controversy in some detail in the next section, beginning with the mapping between the online long-tailed markets and the online marketplace of ideas, before looking at the mechanisms that might produce the relevant phenomena. In each case we use Anderson's analysis to try to understand how religion might adapt to the online world.

Fitting the model

Anderson sets out what he calls six themes of the 'Long Tail age'.[8] Taking these in turn it is possible to characterise long-tailed markets and to understand the marketplace of religious ideas in their terms.

Anderson's Theme 1: More niche goods

In virtually all markets, there are far more niche goods than hits. That ratio is growing exponentially larger as the tools of production become cheaper and more ubiquitous.

There is no clear-cut distinction between niche goods and hits of course, but the slope of the graph is such that it is still relatively easy to draw. In terms of the religious marketplace, 'hits' in the dark area of Figure 3 correspond to the major global religions, while the niche goods in the lighter area are the smaller sects. The religious marketplace certainly looks to have a power-law shape, as there are a very small number of religions with a very high number of adherents; there is no 'average' religion. Table 1 shows us the shape of religious adherence as estimated in 2008. What we see is a few mega-religions with billions or hundreds of millions of adherents, a small number with a few millions, and then many smaller ones. The largest of the 'niche' religions, Zoroastrianism, has a couple of hundred thousand adherents, mainly in Asia, while if we add up all the others, the total is under 1.4 million, half of whom live in North America with the rest scattered about the globe. Note also that some of the larger groups here, such as the ethno-religions, are actually aggregates of many smaller religions, as explained in the footnotes.

Furthermore, the subdivisions of Christianity and Islam show a similar pattern. When we aggregate Christians, they are the biggest of religious 'hits', but even when we disaggregate, some of their sects are important forces. Catholicism, the largest Christian denomination, is followed by about one in six of the world's population, a little smaller than the Muslim population.[9] There are many niches, however—nearly 122 million Christians are unaffiliated (1.8 per cent of the world's population), while there are 33.6 million marginal Christians (0.5 per cent, these include Unitarians, Mormons and Jehovah's Witnesses) and 411 million who consider their churches independent of historical or mainstream denominationalist Christianity. Meanwhile, the 1.4 billion Muslims can be subdivided into 84 per cent Sunnis, 14 per cent Shi'ites and 2 per cent from other schools.[10]

Table 1: Worldwide adherents of all religions, mid-2008[11]

Religion	Number of adherents worldwide	Percentage of world population
Christianity	2,254,535,000	33.4
Islam	1,434,081,100	21.2
Hinduism	913,671,000	13.5
Non-religious	769,614,000	11.4
Chinese universism[12]	387,294,500	5.7
Buddhism	384,318,000	5.7
Ethno-religions[13]	270,413,000	4.0
Atheism	148,322,000	2.2
Neo-religions[14]	107,269,100	1.6
Sikhism	23,835,300	0.4
Judaism	15,096,000	0.2
Spiritism[15]	13,669,900	0.2
Baha'ism	7,868,000	0.1
Confucianism	6,418,400	0.1
Jainism	5,579,100	0.1
Taoism	3,377,200	0.1
Shintoism	2,784,500	0.0
Zoroastrianism	180,900	0.0
Other	1,346,000	0.0

In short, there are some mega-religions and many minor ones with insignificant percentages of the world's population. The graph of religious adherence has a power-law structure with a long tail as in Figure 3. Anderson's first theme also includes a prediction that the ratio of niches to hits will increase. It is hard to measure these accurately, but the growth figures imply that is more or less true here. As one might expect, the mega-religions are growing most quickly, with Islam growing at an annual rate of 1.8 per cent, one of the fastest rates (only Baha'ism is growing more quickly).[16] The number of followers of the 'other' religions is growing faster than the average, and while the number of Christians is growing at about the average rate of population growth (so therefore stable as a percentage of the world's population), most of its growth is accounted for by the growth of the independents.

Hence in so far as these figures can reveal the movements, we can see that much of the growth in religious belief has come at the top and at the bottom—the mega-hits and the niches are growing, while those in the middle are stable (as are atheism and agnosticism), and therefore falling as a percentage of population.

Anderson's Theme 2: Falling costs of reaching niche positions

The costs of reaching those niches are now falling dramatically. Thanks to a combination of forces including digital distribution, powerful search technologies, and a critical mass of broadband penetration, online markets are resetting the economics of retail. Thus in many markets it is now possible to offer a massively expanded variety of products.

A religion as a set of doctrines and practices can be encapsulated by information. The distinctions between religions, whether doctrinal or based on practice, can usually be described, in which case they can be searched for. Religions, if not entirely informational goods, have strong informational components, and so a 'massively expanded variety' of faiths can flourish without too much cost.

There is a debate across many disciplines about whether organised religion is in decline. In general, it does not seem that religious belief itself is declining, despite the predictions of the DAM thesis. Religion does seem to be on the decline in Europe and parts of Asia, but in most areas of the world it is as powerful a force as ever. The debate has therefore focused on whether organised religion is being displaced by personal or customised sets of beliefs. Much of the drive toward fundamentalism stems from an urge for simplicity and a rejection of compromise, away from the nuanced and socially embedded doctrines of worldly priests and imams, and a return to the letter of early texts.[17] Alternatively, many people now simply adopt whichever beliefs they find most convincing. In sub-Saharan Africa, elements of Christianity or Islam are often grafted on to animistic beliefs. In North America, traditional modes of spirituality are conjoined with elements of popular science fiction, such as *Star Trek*. Scientology is a cult created almost entirely by science fiction writer L. Ron Hubbard. This increase in religiosity at the expense of organised religion is an expansion of choice for the religious consumer, and an increase in the numbers of 'products' in the market-place for religious ideas. The Internet cannot be cited as the cause for this increase, as the trend dates back to the period before its invention, but it may well have exacerbated the trend. One important aspect of the Web as a medium is that it is genuinely interactive (particularly since the development of Web 2.0 technology and culture), rather than relying on a broadcast model. The Web user need not only listen, like the user of radio, television or print, but can have their own say. This may of course render it a less attractive medium for religious traditionalists and/or authoritarians, but it is, as it were, a godsend for those with a desire to craft their belief system around their religious instincts or preferences.

The Internet facilitates the process of developing new religions, or new variants of old ones. Any type of religious pioneer will be aided by the technology. Dawson and Hennebry reported widespread surprise in the early days of the Web's popularity that 'cultists' (supposedly 'socially marginal' or even 'personally deficient' people) were able to use the sophisticated new technology.[18] We argued in Chapter Six that cultists are not brainwashed or deficient in some way, but even if they were it would be a mistake to assume that marginality or deficiency in one sphere of life is necessarily reflected in all others. It is not that the sophisticated websites of the cultists prove that they are all cutting-edge thinkers, but rather that they recognise a useful communicative tool when they see one.

We can see from Table 1 that many millions of people declare them-selves to be followers of non-mainstream religions. The point of Anderson's second theme is that someone who wishes to set up and populate a religion need only advertise it online. New religions turn up occasionally on Facebook and used to appear on its predecessors. For instance, in October 2009, someone known only as Sean set out the doctrines of Sexastrianism on MySpace, and predicted that within two or three decades it would be bigger than Buddhism and Hinduism (hence ~1 billion adherents by 2029). The fact that the new gospel was posted at 6.34 in the morning indicates a sleepless, and possibly inspired, night. The gospel, and associated metaphysics, ran as follows:

Chistianity and all the other religions out their are boring, false, dumb pieces of crap
join my new religion SEXASTRIANISM and become a proud SEXASTRIANIST
we will worship breasts and vaginas of every type
we will sacrifice nipple and pussy rings to the breast of flaknark
we pray and talk to our god through masturbation
and the vaginis of Gilgamesh
Our God King and Qeen is Lord Orgasamus and his bride Mrs. Fallopian Tubas
We do this so wen we die we may ascend to Nippleloppilos to serve princess Lilith and her Lesbian Incestual sisters Paola and Francesca
If you deny our religion your are doomed to Abstinentitus—ruled by the demon Chastity
u will forever be forced to watch porn naked but chained up and never allowed to attain orgasim, 4ever in horny torture
who wants to join me now and worship me as ur new Messiah[19]

Some may be tempted by a Pascalian wager on the Sexastrian creed, others less so. However that may be, as early as 2001 a Pew Internet Survey on Cyberfaith found that 28 million Americans had found information about religion online, and that more people had received religious or spiritual information than had gambled, used Web auction sites, traded stocks, placed phone calls, banked or used dating services online. Religious outsiders (those who see themselves as a minority, who say they have few people of the same religion in their local communities, or who say they have faced discrimination due to their beliefs) were particularly interested in using the Internet to meet others of their own faith and share items of religious interest.[20]

The Internet drastically reduces the costs of proselytising in five ways. First, search engines such as Google transform marketing from push to pull; the proselytiser does not need to spend money spreading the message to a wide variety of uninterested people in order to pick up the tiny number of interested ones. In the online world, the preacher need only post his or her message and those interested will pick it up via their searches for key words. The message is only seen by those searching for texts of a particular kind, as opposed to a roadside billboard, for example, which is seen and ignored by everyone who happens to be in that district. Furthermore, because search results appear immediately after a search is made, the message is discovered by the searcher at the exact point at which he or she is receptive to it (i.e. the point at which they felt inclined to do a search). A search engine is guaranteed to deliver results in a timely way.

Indeed, Google's model of advertising is also a cost-effective method of preaching online; adverts appear alongside particular searches, and so are targeted at those with adjacent interests (the advertiser's fee depends on the number of people who click through to the site). However, Google advertisements do not seem to be used by many small churches or sects (a search for 'Seventh-Day Adventists', for instance, brings up an advertisement for an Adventist dating agency, while a search for 'cult' brings up an advertisement for Cult Clothing). The way that search engines shift the focus from the preacher's perception of the interests of potential adherents, to the adherents' interests themselves via the search terms they have typed into the engine at the point at which they are receptive to information about the topic is probably the most important factor.

Second, the barriers to entry to the religious market fall drastically. A website certainly entails initial costs to create, and still more to maintain, but these costs are lower than those required to rent and maintain a physical building. More to the point, the ratio between the two sets of costs increases as quality rises—that is, websites not only cost less to build and maintain than buildings, but impressive websites cost massively less to build and maintain than impressive buildings. The Web's global reach also allows the proselytiser to address a worldwide audience, and not merely those with transport and access to particular buildings. A website has hundreds of millions of potential readers; no other medium gives the resource-poor access to such a potentially large audience.

Third, proselytising becomes more nearly a non-rival activity. Two activities are rival when only one can be done at a time (I either go to the pub or I tidy the garage—at any particular time I can only do one of the two); they are non-rival if that is not true (I can travel to work and do my emails at the same time, if I travel by train). In the religious world, much of the work of persuasion and conversion involves face-to-face discussions, a rival activity (i.e. face-to-face conversion of one prospect rules out face-to-face conversions of others—following up one opportunity has opportunity costs elsewhere). Online, even very deep discussions can take place in chatrooms and other environments where several people can be addressed simultaneously. The shift is only partial (face-to-face encounters remain extremely important, as we shall see), but there are fewer opportunity costs.

Fourth, a related point is that the Web facilitates personalised and individual presentation of information. It is, and was always conceived as, a multimedia space. Text, video, interactive forums, audio and synchronous and asynchronous discussion are all supported. Sometimes religion requires deep and intricate argument, sometimes the charismatic performance of a preacher in a pulpit, sometimes amassing evidence about a miracle, and sometimes training aids for particular types of action. The appropriate media for these different types of support are all available on the Web. Such materials do not need to be explicitly religious. For instance, the spread of radical Islam has been facilitated by online images of atrocities perpetrated against Muslim civilians.

The Web's effective linking mechanism allows documents generated by others to be incorporated into a canon. A religion that required, for instance, a particular interpretation of a passage from Isaiah could point without plagiarism or creativity to an already existing site with a different provenance. The Web is now accessed more frequently by smaller mobile devices, and the mobile Web is proving to be extremely important in the developing world. Imagine a location-sensitive app that texted the user whenever he was within 100 metres of a fellow-worshipper. Increasingly, many objects and buildings are annotated with photographs, comments and hyperlinks, allowing what is almost a running commentary on the environment. Imagine an app for Google Glass that gave such a commentary from the point of view of a particular religion as the user strolled through a city. Social networking means that many people routinely put data about themselves online; imagine an app that trawled through the Facebook pages of friends and friends of friends of fellow worshippers to predict which of them might be amenable to proselytisation.

Fifth, the costs of conflict with an embedding society, and of concealment from ill-wishers, are reduced. It is much easier and cheaper to conceal online activities than offline ones, when the proselytiser is based in a physical headquarters, or his activities require a physical presence (e.g. handing out leaflets). The al-Qaeda journal *Al-Jihad* could only be distributed at great cost in paper form in the late 1980s, whereas now there are many jihadist journals online with not only lower production costs but also a far less risky production and distribution system.[21]

Anderson's Theme 3: Filtering

*Simply offering more variety, however, does not shift demand by itself.
Consumers must be given ways to find niches that suit their particular needs
and interests. A range of tools and techniques—from recommendations to
rankings—are effective at doing this. These 'filters' can drive demand down
the Tail.*

The Web has a number of obvious filters, with search engines, message
boards and link directories prominent among them. Resource lists are
straightforward (such as the Internet Sacred Text Archive). Chatrooms
and other communication areas allow people to make personalised suggestions to others. As noted above, search engines also allow advertising,
although there is not a great deal of evidence that online religions use
them. Social bookmarking sites such as Digg and deli.cio.us are increasingly important crowdsourced resources. User tagging of resources is
decentralised and therefore perhaps of greater utility and sensitivity than
any centralised system.

Furthermore, the beauty of a website is that it is not only a statement
of a creed, but can also be an aggregator of key texts. A recent study of
hate groups (which is not to suggest any further parallel between religions and hate groups than their need to communicate) found that
around seven out of eight websites point the reader to a text library,
while three in four also link to like-minded sites.[22] Such sites act as filters
for searchers for information to hone their searches via links.

Security creates further problems for groups marked by particularly
high levels of conflict with the embedding society. For obvious reasons
it has proven extremely difficult to maintain militant jihadist groups'
websites at consistent Web addresses for any period of time, which
makes them harder to trace not only for the authorities but also for
like-minded followers. The key to function is flexibility of distribution.
The Ansar al Sunna Army, for instance, uses a mailing list which allows
its readers to access its site as soon as it appears, download all its content,
and upload it to other sites. Password-protected forums are another
useful filter for extremists.[23]

It should be noted that very extreme groups may actually prefer to
limit the number of adherents. Risk of infiltration is an important factor, and to mitigate this the extremist group may well feel it more
important to place major hurdles between it and its readers in order to

restrict its readership only to the most-trusted adherents.[24] Hence the readership of such sites might not grow as the long-tail theory predicts, but rather may be deliberately depressed by the group. The group works against, rather than with, the long-tail dynamic.

Cult recruitment is usually labour-intensive. Long periods of face-to-face contact with sect members play a large role in conversion; few click on a website and see the light there and then. Unlike information, faith cannot be downloaded.[25] The Web might alter the dynamics of conversion, but that has yet to be properly investigated. It is likely that the chief contribution of the Web is to put people in touch; this in itself is a useful function. Social networking and online chatting also afford surprising levels of persuasive power (consider the number of romances and crimes planned over the Internet between those who have never met), and so a long period of chatting and email contact may also be conducive to conversion. The would-be convert has probably already been searching for religious alternatives, and so may well be in a receptive frame of mind.

Note also that the dynamics of conversion are still favourable even if only a few connections take place outside of pre-existing acquaintance. Sectaries are particularly interested in people from elite social groups who are 'more likely to be involved in the kind of wide-ranging social networks essential for the dissemination of a new cultural phenomenon'.[26] Although recruitment 'happens primarily through pre-existing social networks and interpersonal bonds',[27] the Internet provides (a) an extremely useful method for bringing in new blood and new social networks, and (b) a useful medium for putting possibly socially marginalised sectaries in touch with social elites.

Indeed, it would be unrealistic to expect the Internet to put complete strangers in touch routinely, let alone open up vast new opportunities for conversions. Local networks of people in physical proximity are generally needed to support someone's use of a new medium or a new technology, and we interact online mainly with people we know, and who we are geographically close to.[28] It is a perhaps surprising property of online relationships that they tend to take place between people who live geographically close to each other, despite the 'World Wide' nature of the Web and its ability to 'disembed' phenomena from the constraints of location.[29]

Anderson's Theme 4: Flattening the curve

Once there's massively expanded variety and the filters to sort through it, the demand curve flattens. There are still hits and niches, but the hits are relatively less popular and the niches relatively more so.

Here we must be wary about what we attribute to the Internet in particular. There are many developments occurring across the globe to effect changes in religious composition. However, our long-tail hypothesis should be that the number and size of smaller sects (the niches) should increase while the size of the smaller major religions (the hits) decreases— in other words, the effects of the CSC will tend to increase, and the cycle will tend to speed up. Meanwhile, the size of the super-blockbusters should also increase, because of the ease of communication. The long tail and the blockbusters at the head should squeeze the middle.

Computational simulations of religious behaviour have also indicated that the powerful benefits of extreme religions are found to be worth the major costs of membership when the benefits are substitutable for public goods. In other words, when wider society does not provide the benefits that people actually want, extremist religions benefit because they can focus on providing such benefits without the problems that pervade the provision of public goods (e.g. small extremist groups can weed out free-riders).[30] Although an efficient and liberal marketplace of ideas, according to such simulations, tends to decrease membership of extreme groups (in accordance with Adam Smith's argument, the wider marketplace enables people to get the same goods from less extreme organisations at lower cost), clearly the more information available about the goods provided by groups whose membership is costly, the more substitutable its own benefits are for public goods.[31] Persuasion has free entry, so moderates have to expect to compete with extremists to attract their audience.

Anderson's Theme 5: The large market for small niches

All those niches add up. Although none sell in huge numbers, there are so many niche products that collectively they can comprise a market rivalling the hits.

The size of the niche market in religion is to some extent in the eye of the beholder. If we look at Table 1, it is striking how many non-standard religions appear in the table. Furthermore, it is clear that the growth of many of these is unlikely to be associated with the Internet in particular. For instance, traditional Chinese religions are characteristic of rural Chinese environments, and do not have a large online presence. However, there are clearly large numbers of people outside the standard religious space, including 122 million unaffiliated Christians, 34 million marginal Christians, 29 million Muslims outside the Sunni and Shia denominations, 107 million neo-religionists and 270 million ethno-religionists, so something in excess of half a billion people professing religious belief outside the bosom of the world's leading churches. Even if only 20 per cent of these have access to the Internet, that is still a nine-figure number, not a puny quantity, although the number of people per village, or per population unit, is small.

An individual group can be much more coherent online, especially as social networking technology is advancing all the time in its ability to foster communities (whether in persistent online environments such as Second Life, discussion spaces like Twitter or social networking sites such as Facebook). It also follows that as technology for community development improves, human beings are also adapting to the emotional costs and benefits of conducting relationships without actual social contact.[32] This 'death of distance' should not be overemphasised, but 'digital natives' find it increasingly natural to consort with, and to prefer to consort with, like-minded others via Web-based presentations rather than face-to-face.[33] As technologically mediated social connectivity becomes more prevalent, people will undoubtedly learn to read online signals in ways analogous to those offline signals which enable us to assess reputations and place trust relatively effectively.

In such a world, a small group is much more viable online. Imagine a type of thinking, call it type A, which is evenly spread throughout the world and which 0.00005 per cent of people are inclined to join. This means that in a relatively small place such as Funafuti, the capital of Tuvalu, the chances of there being any type A person is close to nil. In a medium-size place such as Luxembourg City, the chances are still less than one in twenty. In a small city, such as Nottingham in the United Kingdom, Fort Wayne, Indiana, Bordeaux in France or Firozabad in India, there would be a one in eight chance of there being a type A person. In New York or Moscow there would only be five of these people, while even a giant metropolis with 30 million people would yield only fifteen of them. In a world defined by buildings and face-to-face meetings, type As could never be any kind of force. Yet worldwide there would be over 3,000 people who could meet, interact and cooperate using the Internet.

Anderson's Theme 6: The liberation of demand

Once all of this is in place, the natural shape of demand is revealed, undistorted by distribution bottlenecks, scarcity of information, and limited choice of shelf space. What's more, that shape is far less hit-driven than we have been led to believe. Instead, it is as diverse as the population itself.

This last theme, that the natural shape of demand is revealed, is in effect to suggest that 'naturalness' of demand is what results when transactions costs are removed. This is as artificial a measure as any kind of demand—demand depends on all sorts of things, including other types of cost. But it is worth pointing out that if the benefits and costs of small religions are evident and transparent, it is likely to enable people to make more informed choices about the groups they join. The restriction of choice that inevitably results from high transaction costs, as people are driven to the narrow range of alternatives about which information can be gathered easily, has a much smaller effect online.

Exactly as with the world of long-tailed markets where people can find out about the niche goods, the unusual books, the indie pop songs, the exact piece of software or scientific gadgetry, the online religious marketplace levels the playing field a little. Catholicism can no longer play to its advantage that there is a church in virtually every town or province on the planet, while the extent to which proselytising Protestants are promoted by their visibility on the streets (e.g. Salvation Army bands, street-corner preachers) decreases. No doubt there are many Catholic websites, but the little type A church can also have its website, and search engines such as Google are quite effective at marrying up searchers and sites.

The preponderance of Catholic websites will help boost the presence of Catholicism on a Google search if they all link to each other because a site that is linked to by many others will tend to appear prominently in a Google search. But if the type A church site can be characterised by sufficiently differentiating keywords, the diligent searcher may reach the end of his spiritual quest online. In fact, the need to find differentiating keywords suggests that, all things being equal, the online marketplace for religious ideas will have a tendency to skew towards radically different religions, and away from moderate variations of the mega-religions (the 'hits'). A minor variation of Catholicism which continues to use Catholic vocabulary, yet which is not linked to prominently by Catholic sites, will tend to be swamped in searches by its orthodox brethren, whereas a more extreme religion which uses a less standard vocabulary could be found by searching for the new terms that it is using.

The democratisation of the forces of distribution

Anderson suggests three forces that produce the long tail.[34] The first is that the tools of production are democratised, which facilitates the production of niche goods. In our terms this of course means that heterodox thinkers with fewer resources than mainstream practitioners find the barriers to proselytisation lowered. We have explored the effects of the lowering of barriers to entry in the previous subsection. The second mechanism is that filters send the consumer down to the niches in the tail; again as we have noted, technology opens up the tail for scrutiny and search.

The third mechanism is the democratisation of the forces of distribution. The Web has always been decentralised and democratic in its linking structure in that a website's author can link to any other webpage directly. Hyperlinking has been augmented in the Web 2.0 environment by the growth of tagging and social bookmarking, which allow simple user markup of significant pages. Tags are also interesting in that they cluster into what have become known as 'folksonomies',[35] emergent taxonomies of tags which develop when naïve users categorise resources according to their own requirements and conceptual schemes. Folksonomies are by-products of individual tagging decisions, and correspond to the immediate and interested reactions of users—in other words, everything is categorised by everybody—and as such avoid the pitfalls of classification schemes developed by authoritative bodies and imposed on the domain from the top-down. Such categorisations of content may not respect the conceptual boundaries that make sense for small, heterodox communities, and may gloss over the distinctions that are important for them.

For the religious outsider, linking is still somewhat imperfect as a mechanism for navigating the Web. Google is a democratic tool in that prominence in its ranking is determined by the number of links from other sites, with a weighting that treats a link from a high-ranking site as more significant. Religiously marginalised communities may be unable to generate a sufficient number of links to deliver high rankings for their pages. Indeed, if we assume that the 'blockbuster' religions, and secular sites such as the BBC, will in general generate more traffic and be linked to more frequently, even searches for the names of marginalised communities are likely to have pages written by non-members of such communities at the top of the ranking. This is a techno version of history being written by the winners: for a small community, it is quite possible that hostile accounts will feature prominently in Google rankings.

This leads us to remember that though the tail is lengthened, it is still a tail. If we take the Web as a whole, although distribution has been democratised, the important commodity is now attention (or, in the jargon, 'eyeballs'). Everyone's opinion can now be put out there, and the key factor is who is being read. Discrimination against minority views still happens online; however, whereas in traditional media the discrimination happens at distribution points (i.e. minorities cannot get their opinions published), online discrimination happens at search and download time, so that only a small number of published writers, bloggers and so on find themselves read in any numbers. Popular writers are referred to more, appear more prominently in searches and are read more. This has been called the 'Matthew effect',[36] from Matthew 25:29, 'For unto every one that hath shall be given, and he shall have abundance: but from him that hath not shall be taken away even that which he hath.' It is certainly the case that the democratisation of distribution is offset by the Matthew effect.

The Devil's long tail?

There is therefore an interesting *prima facie* case to be made that the Internet has allowed the marketplace of religious ideas to cater more assiduously to the long tail of radical and extremist opinion. In that case, the echo chamber argument that it is a representative government's duty to combat such ideas online becomes more convincing.

However, although there is an important parallel between the economic and religious marketplaces, the case that the Internet is transformative has not quite been made in full. The next chapter looks at some of the issues standing in the way of the speedy endorsement of the echo chamber critique.

9

ECHO CHAMBERS AND LONG TAILS

A CRITICAL EXAMINATION

Given the general background to religion which we explored in Part II, Chapters Two and Eight developed a thesis about the Internet and its role in the spread of radicalism and extremism. It is now time to look with a more critical eye at these ideas, beginning with some thoughts about the long-tail thesis before moving on to the critique of the Internet as a technology which isolates. In each case the empirical evidence is somewhat more equivocal than Anderson, Turkle and Sunstein suggest, and in that light we must consider how the argument for government intervention against extremism is altered. Our conclusion takes into account the evidence that the Internet may well have altered some of the terms of trade, without producing a future which is fundamentally different from the past.

How long was that tail again?

Anderson's long-tail theory has not stood uncontested. Spurred by its striking and intuitive claims, a number of investigations have been launched to test its predictions, and in the commercial sphere at least these investigations have uncovered phenomena that it struggles to explain. A number of researchers seem to have discovered online markets in which the tail shortens.

Anita Elberse investigated sales patterns in two of the markets that Anderson discussed in most detail, music downloads and home video, reviewing sales data from a number of sources and countries.[1] She found that the tails of these markets had indeed lengthened in one respect—there were more niche products more easily available, thereby supporting Anderson's claim. However, she also discovered that the tail, though long, was very flat—very few people actually bought these items, again consistent with Anderson. But from a business point of view, her findings had significantly different implications. The extra sales from the niche products were relatively small, and the tail became flatter as the number of extra products increased. Both light users and heavy users of the services she studied preferred the blockbusters, the light users disproportionately so. For one music download firm, the top 10 per cent of titles produced 78 per cent of plays, and the top 1 per cent produced 32 per cent of plays. The firm had a million titles, so the top 1 per cent was still 10,000 titles—a high number. But Elberse concludes that return on investment will be greater for firms that focus on the blockbusters at the head of the curve, rather than the niche products down the tail. In other words, despite all the new properties of the market that Anderson described, traditional investment strategies would still make more money. Bentley et al. have also confirmed that when consumer preference is very changeable, the inventory size that maximises profit for a retailer is relatively small.[2]

Will Page and colleagues found similar phenomena in the downloads market. In particular, his argument concerned the distinction between two types of long-tailed curve. In a log-normal curve (a standard type of curve) most of the area below the curve is at the head, where the blockbusters are. As the curve of sales has the property that the area under the curve is proportional to revenues, a strategy to gain profit from a long tail would prefer the curve not to be log-normal, so the greater area is in the tail where the niche products are. Page discovered that the downloads curve was indeed log-normal, supporting Elberse's claim that even if more products appeared, the serious money was still to be made at the head. He phrased the dilemmas for the retailer very cogently.

For example, we found that only 20% of tracks in our sample were 'active', that is to say they sold at least one copy, *and hence, 80% of the tracks sold nothing at all.* Moreover, approximately 80% of sales revenue came from around 3% of the active tracks. Factor in the dormant tail and you're looking at a 80/0.38% rule for all the inventory on the digital shelf.

194

Finally, only 40 tracks sold more than 100,000 copies, accounting for 8% of the business. Think about that—back in the physical world, forty tracks could be just 4 albums, or the top slice of the best-selling 'Now That's What I Call Music, Volume 70' which bundles up 43 'hits' into one perennially popular customer offering! My argument, in summary, was that the future of business is definitely not selling 'less of more'. Scale matters.[3]

Page raises a number of interesting issues, not least the question of profit. But what is the analogue of this for the religious marketplace? As Adam Smith would remind us, there is a direct and crude connection between a parson and the size of his flock—'no plunder, no pay'—but these results have wider implications about what a small or growing sect wishes to do. They cut directly into the dilemma of whether the sect wants to grow, or would rather remain pure at the cost of growth and influence. Is availability the major question (i.e. putting a message out into the world, without compromise), or is the sect aiming to convince people of their message and entice them to join? The latter case is analogous to the business aim of profitability—the sect is trying to move away from the tail of the curve and get closer to the head. This is ever more imperative if the curve of popularity of religious ideas has the same property as log-normal curves, of having a greater area under the head than the tail—which it does, as Table 1 in Chapter Eight shows that 54.6 per cent of the world's population were adherents of either Christianity or Islam, the first two items in the list (even breaking down the figures into smaller groupings does not really disturb this conclusion, although the head will be wider). The longer and flatter the tail, the more competitive the sect will be to advance closer to the head. At any rate, the sect—assuming it lacks state support—will have to operate in a sufficiently business-like manner. It has to achieve and retain sufficient levels of membership to provide for its continuation over time.

This does not necessarily undermine the long-tail theory. An insight into what is going on is provided by Salganik et al., who looked at music downloads among a large sample of young people.[4] The volunteers were divided into groups, some of which received recommendation feedback based on the purchases of other members of the group, while others did not. The market shapes of the groups without recommendations had longer tails, so without guidance about the preferences of their peers, purchasers relied on their own guesswork and experimentation. The groups with recommendations had more traditionally shaped market curves with more hits and fewer niche products, but the hits in each group were different—the groups all showed a tendency to converge, but around different sets of songs.

This implies that intra-market communication is a key factor. Markets are short-tailed because of friction in the market; information does not flow easily. When this friction is removed by Web technology, information about products increases availability and, all things being equal, lengthens the tail and slims the head of the curve. However, recommender systems have the effect of restoring the friction by focusing preferences, especially in volatile markets such as music downloads, on items that have previously sold well. The collaborative filtering which underlies automatic recommendation uses historical sales data as input, so items that have not sold well are disadvantaged.

So the long-tail thesis remains unbowed. Information does alter markets. However, what seems to happen is that demand is conditioned by the type of information given. Information about the availability of products, such as might be found in a search, seems to lengthen the tail, but when the information is expanded to include information about others' choices, the tail shrinks once more. As Elberse has shown, people are generally more interested in products in which other people are interested; people's market-mediated behaviour is not completely individualistic, but, as Adam Smith argued, it contains a social element as well.

In light of this, Anderson's claim in theme 6, that the natural shape of demand is revealed by electronic commerce, looks like a naturalistic fallacy. What is 'natural' demand? Does it mean that it is uninfluenced by others? If so, why does that make it natural? Why should it be eroded by further information (information about others' purchases)? It makes sense to think that people investigate and experiment with products when they can find out about them easily (the lengthening of the tail)—after all, they are hardly likely to buy goods they do not know exist—but equally if there is a 'natural' type of demand which is independent of influence, why do people abandon it when they receive information about others' preferences? If everyone's demand is independent, then it seems silly for me to buy what I do not want just because everyone else has bought it.

Music downloads and films have the property that people are interested in what other people watch and listen to. They are sociable arts, and people like to discuss, share and proselytise their latest discoveries. Religion has at least some of these properties—it is a social practice, involving people congregating to take part in certain practices. This is even more true of the radical sects we have focused on, where the goods of belonging feature prominently in the explanation of why they persist. Hence the arguments of Elberse and others set out in this section would seem to apply to the long-tailed market of religious preferences. We cannot simply assume that bringing the market online will unleash the 'natural' preferences of consumers of religious ideas, thereby lengthening the tail. Many of these consumers will be interested in the choices of others, and will adjust their preferences accordingly, once more shortening the tail and fattening the head.

Echo chambers revisited

Long-tailed markets, then, might not quite be the 'kind of nightmare' that Cass Sunstein anticipated. Their properties in an online environment do not seem to be as prone to exaggerating the isolation and alienation of Sunstein's ideologically driven echo chambers. This section examines echo chambers in online settings in order to try to gauge how prevalent, how important and how deleterious their effects will be.

The 'Dean scream'

We should first note that echo chambers have a place; one can admit their existence without taking on the whole of Sunstein's pessimistic thesis. Echo chambers have a role to play. Technology commentator David Weinberger, who advised the presidential campaigns of Howard Dean in 2004 and John Edwards in 2008, directly addressed this issue after the collapse of Dean's campaign. Weinberger had been Dean's 'senior Internet advisor', and the campaign had gained a great deal of attention due to its then-revolutionary strategy of amassing grass-roots support using online communications. It was the first campaign to use the Internet effectively for both fundraising and motivating the troops; Dean raised more money than any other Democrat, even though the average donation was just $80. The momentum helped garner a number of high-profile endorsements, including that of former candidate Al Gore, despite a perception that Dean was towards the left of his party. However, his performance in the actual primaries was disappointing, being eclipsed by the more mainstream candidates, John Kerry and John Edwards.

The charge was made that the closed world of the Internet had magnified and exaggerated Dean's chances of winning. In fact, according to popular narrative, he was on the far left and too eccentric to be acceptable to the centrist swing voters who would decide the election, an impression famously confirmed by his overwrought scream during a speech following his disappointing third place in the Iowa caucuses.[5] Dean's brand of populist politics would supposedly appeal mainly to activists, who by definition are unrepresentative of the citizenry as a whole. The primary season does appeal to politics nerds, and Dean's tactic of using the Internet to communicate and organise meant that the nerds were feeding their enthusiasm back to each other in the absence of dissenting voices. The scream, on this account, was just feedback from the echo chamber. After the scream but before his withdrawal, *The Economist*'s American correspondent Lexington suggested that 'the Dean campaign looks ever less like a political revolution and ever more like an internet bubble'.[6]

Weinberger dissented from this narrative in a piece published two days after the end of the campaign:

The play of agreement and disagreement is far twistier than this rationalist picture assumes. Conversations iterate differences within agreement. On the lefty mailing list, for example, the participants agree that the Bush administration is apocalyptically bad, so we don't spend time arguing about that. We do robustly argue about what can be done to change the country's direction. We'll happily engage on whether the e-voting machine issue could mobilize the country, or how campaign technology can be integrated. But someone who wants to argue that Bush is a great president is going to be told to 'take it offline.' The fact that conversations start from a base agreement is not a weakness of conversations. In fact, it's a requirement.

That initial agreement isn't always implicit; it can become a rallying cry. On the lefty list, for example, we don't send a lot of messages that say Bush is a jerk, because we already agree on that and want to talk about what to do about it. On the Dean comment board, though, there were frequently comments that said, 'Go Dean!!!', plus or minus a few exclamation marks. Yet even there, most messages iterated differences: How well the governor did in a debate, what he ought to say to Sen. Kerry, why a particular news story was unfair. A message board that only had variants of 'Go Dean!!!' (or 'Hillary sucks!' on a right-wing board) would quickly lose participants—it would be too boring.

This explicit repetition of the founding agreement is the only salient characteristic I can find of what are called echo chambers. And from this I conclude: So what?[7]

Beliefs are not simply propositions to which we assent, or somehow store in our minds, like the contents of some filing cabinet. They underpin action, sometimes are crafted post hoc to rationalise action, sometimes postulated by observers to explain action. Sometimes they co-exist precariously with doubt. Sometimes they promote solidarity. They exist, in short, in a psychological and a social context, which therefore needs to be taken into account. An echo chamber can be important for allowing someone to develop a political or religious position that may be in tension with the embedding society. In that event, it may be liberating for them, and may allow the development of a more authentic, less socially determined, character.

Dean's outburst clearly fell short of the ideals of the Habermasian public sphere, with its emphasis on discourse, rationality and universality. But then he was speaking in a private setting, as it were, to his supporters both within and without the room. In that sense, the problem with the Dean scream was that it was a private act occurring in public, with the cognitive dissonance that can create. The scream was unlikely to be persuasive in the Habermasian sense, but then—Weinberger's point—it was not intended to be.

This relates directly to the issues of online political communication and cyberpolarisation that we discussed in Chapter Two. Recall that there was a serious worry about political blogs only linking to others of a similar stripe, but if we revisit the evidence with Weinberger's critique in mind, the picture is not as clear cut as it might be. In a study of patterns of linking, Hargittai and colleagues discovered the expected separation between liberal and conservative blogs, but further analysis undermined many of the worries. To begin with, a typical blog will contain within itself what is called a 'blogroll', a list of recommended blogs that appears in a sidebar to the main text on every page of the blog. Hargittai et al. discovered that the blogroll (a) takes up a large proportion of the total number of links, and (b) links overwhelmingly to sites of a similar political creed. Because it is a fixed item, it will have the artificial effect of lowering the proportion of ideological opponents the blog links to.[8]

Secondly, although most of the other links that appear in posts also connect with ideological friends, we should not discount the minority of in-post links that do connect to opponents (in their sample, 12 per cent of outbound links from conservative sites and 16 per cent of outbound links from liberal sites). Only a very small number of sites never linked to opponents. Contrary to the thrust of Sunstein's thesis, Hargittai et al. also found that there was no evidence that polarisation was still occurring—although the data were not very comparable with other datasets; as far as could be seen the number of cross-ideological links was not decreasing.[9] One could certainly imagine discussion becoming more polarised close to elections, where the establishment of a Habermasian truth or consensus is somewhat less pressing a task than winning (no one has at the time of writing, to our knowledge, compared behaviour near elections with mid-term behaviour in that respect, although unsurprisingly it has been found that voters in the United States are more politically interested and aware in presidential election years as opposed to during the mid-terms).[10]

It is also worth pointing out that US politics has become vastly more polarised in the early years of the twenty-first century, for many possible reasons (political redistricting processes, which in many states amount to gerrymandering, are likely to have a lot to do with it), and of course against that background one might also expect that political blogs will reflect the polarisation. However, correlation is not causation, and few people have attempted to make the claim that the polarising forces of the blogosphere are causally responsible for the polarisation of American politics (although that would be a possible bold prediction of the echo chamber thesis). In any case, it would beg the question as to why the politics of other countries, for example in the EU where the Internet is also widely used and there are lively blogospheres, have not produced comparable gridlock in their own seats of power.

When the functions of the in-post links are examined in more detail, there is somewhat more evidence of interaction and conversation. Hargittai et al. found five types of in-post cross-ideological link:[11]

1. Straw man links: the blogger links to someone who he believes has said something particularly idiotic. These links made up 43 per cent of links from conservative blogs and 54 per cent of links from liberal blogs.
2. Disagreements on substance: the blogger links to a version of an argument or claim which he specifically challenges. 12 per cent of conservative links, 16 per cent of liberal links.
3. Non-political links: the blogger simply references a blog which contains text to which he wishes to refer (for example, the first report of an event). 5 per cent of conservative links, 6 per cent of liberal links.

4. Redirect links: similar to the above, except the blogger does not reference the other blog, but sends his own readers there to read the story. 26 per cent of conservative links,[12] 19 per cent of liberal links.

5. Agreements on substance: the blogger links to a version of an argument or claim which he specifically endorses. 14 per cent of conservative links, 5 per cent of liberal links.

The blogosphere has unwritten rules that the source of a story or viewpoint should be acknowledged, and even an attack as in types 1 and 2 above (which make up more than half of the links) is an engagement. The ideologically committed blogger, by linking to another blog that he has identified as nonsense or garbage, still risks his reader following the link and engaging with the opponent's claim or argument. The blogger is prepared to take that risk, and by doing so introduces the reader to the opponent, widening the reader's experience.

There is nothing in the analysis of Hargittai et al. that specifically undermines Sunstein's thesis, but his empirical work is relatively abstract. Even in the discovery that most in-post links are to negatively presented opponents, the detail of the interactions across the American political ideological divide still connotes a measure of civility and dialogue that suggests group polarisation is not necessarily a disaster for political discourse. This is backed up by polling evidence too. For instance, a study on the 2010 US mid-term elections showed that 55 per cent of voters believed that the Internet increased the impact of extreme views (against 30 per cent who thought it reduced it), but actually only 34 per cent of voters who used the Internet as a source of news websites admitted to seeking out websites that shared their point of view.[13]

Crowdsourcing

A second point to make is that many commentators argue that expert networks have a much greater tendency to produce echo chambers. Nassim Nicholas Taleb has complained, particularly with respect to the world of finance, that expertise results in groupthink, the restriction of possible outcomes or solutions considered, unimaginative prognoses for the future, a focus on quantifiable risk at the expense of unknown risks, an unwillingness to think beyond accepted expert models of reality and a tendency to mistake the models for reality itself.[14] British Parliamentarian Douglas Carswell specifically turns the argument about echo chambers around by 180º and argues for the liberating powers of the Internet. To someone who asserts that the blogosphere is a self-referential echo chamber, he replies:

And what … are MPs and all the other elite experts if not self-referential? What are those who like to interpret the world for us, if not full of their own prejudices and presumption? [The] elite is able to make decisions regardless of what voters actually vote for. … [T]hey often make decisions on the basis of recycled dogma and ideas—and often carry on making wrong-headed decisions because they are driven by secondhand ideas. The digital revolution is a coup d'état against the tyranny of this elite. It overthrows these secondhand dealers in other people's ideas.[15]

On the other hand, where a group of sufficiently diverse people is convened and their views aggregated in innovative ways, problems such as groupthink and self-reference are dramatically reduced. The intuition here is that everyone has a point of view, and everyone knows his own circumstances and preferences well enough to be an expert—indeed, the expert—on them. I may know nothing about you, but I know an awful lot about me. Hence although no one knows everything, everyone knows something.

Aggregation mechanisms that enable decisions or opinions to be sourced from the crowd can be found in many areas, but two well-known examples are market pricing and the Google PageRank system. In a competitive bidding market, the price of a good is set by understanding the balance of demand and supply for a good. Suppose we have a type of object—say, a bucket—and I am prepared to pay £5 for one. I know that that is what a bucket is worth to me. If the price of a bucket is more than that, I will forego it; if it is less, then I will buy one. The price will converge to a range where demand and supply will be in rough balance, and can then determine how many buckets should be made, and whether there is a better use for the raw materials. This crowd-sourced mechanism outperforms planned economies. No one knows everything about demand and supply, but each individual knows exactly what he is and is not prepared to pay for a bucket. Google's search engine works in a similar way. It takes the links between webpages to determine their relative importance. If many pages link to a particular page, that is *prima facie* evidence of its importance. If many important pages link to a particular page, that is evidence it is even more important. No individual decrees what must link to what; if you are the author of a webpage, you decide what pages you link to. You make your small contribution to the Google algorithm that ranks the pages for which you search, in the same way that you make your small contribution to determining the price of a bucket when you decide whether or not to buy one.

The key is feedback. Each decision—buying or linking—feeds back into the wider system, and the result is that a parameter—the price, the ranking of a webpage—is determined which will in turn affect further decisions. Experts, however, can insulate themselves from criticism. The Soviet planners' efforts to decide how much of each good should be produced and where raw materials should be diverted eventually bankrupted and polluted the country. And online, when the French government decided to replace Google with a less democratic search engine whose output would be determined by a group of experts, the result was a predictable flop.[16] As a community of users increases, planning for that community gets harder, while a system aggregating feedback from individual micro-level decisions is more likely to scale.

So if we look at the wider community, the Internet aids the wider scrutiny of decisions or ideas developed by small, inward-facing groups of people. Recall the discussion of Todd Akin, Republican senatorial candidate for Missouri in 2012, from Chapter Two. His views on rape and abortion were exposed as idiotic and offensive when opened to discussion by a wider audience than he was used to. In fact, the ideas of a group can even be challenged by the group itself. David Piff and Margit Warburg give the example of the Talisman discussion group devoted to examining the Baha'i faith's theology. This could have produced an echo chamber effect, but as a matter of fact it ended up exposing ideological divisions in the Baha'i community and questioning mainstream Baha'i views.[17] Introvigne backs up this point, arguing that anti-cultists tend to be more active and more numerous than those already in cults; his evidence leads him to conclude that 'so far, this Internet arena has exhibited a better potential for destruction than for construction when it comes to marginal religious movements'.[18] Once more, we must conclude that even if the Internet does create some opportunities for the creation of online echo chambers, it also creates opportunities to evaluate their output, and it is at least arguable that the latter effect is somewhat more significant than the former.

The global umma

The Islamic world provides an interesting twist on this debate via the notion of the *umma*, or global Muslim community, which has become the focus of some Islamist political actions, including but hardly restricted to violent terrorism.[19] It has been suggested that the Internet is allowing the *umma* to be reimagined online, creating a sort of virtual *umma* or community[20] facilitated by the compression of space and time by information and communication technologies that has been described by Anthony Giddens among others.[21] The diverse local experience of Islam in particular locations and specific cultural milieux will surely undermine the sense of global Islamic community, even as many Islamic practices can be functionally explained (e.g. facing Mecca to pray, praying five times a day, the *hajj*) as separating Muslims from their embedding geographical communities and uniting them with their co-religioners.

The existence of international communication networks that not only connect Muslims from diverse communities but also allow virtually instantaneous communication should support the pan-national solidarity that Islamic practice fosters. However, that very plurality undermines the idea that everyone will speak with the same voice. El-Nawawy and Khamis argue that the anonymity of the Web can occasionally lead to confusion about where authority lies;[22] diversity in the *umma* is not a problem, and is to be expected, but the whole idea of an authoritative Islamic source, already a very nuanced notion, is under threat because in the absence of agreed authority over doctrine, plurality of opinion very easily transmutes into a meta-level argument about who is authoritative.

So there are three outcomes of Muslims' use of the Internet for communication about religious matters: it can unify and integrate, magnify the sense of internal difference and foster a hybrid political identity consisting of attributes from the religion and the homeland.[23] To be sure, this isn't to say very much. Following Weinberger's account of the Dean campaign, the creation of a space in which people can discuss or argue is extremely important to them, irrespective of the echo chamber problem (or, perhaps better, the purposes of the communicants are met very well by spaces with characteristics of echo chambers). For immigrant groups, for instance, religion plays an important role in helping people construct and understand a new life in unfamiliar and sometimes hostile surroundings.[24] Such a function is surely prior to *any* kind of fruitful interaction between the embedding community and the immigrants, even if it simultaneously creates the potential for conflict.

The networked individual

Echo chambers consequently have their uses, and their effects may sometimes be counterbalanced. Decision-making and ideological choices are of course affected by the social circumstances of those making the choices, and so it may be the case that the Internet makes choices worse in the sense of being more radical, and more threatening to the embedding society by increasing alienation and *anomie*, as was argued by Sherry Turkle. It is therefore time to examine this thesis a little more closely. There are three questions we need to ask. First, how dangerous is this situation? Secondly, how prevalent is it? And thirdly, even if it is prevalent, are there offsetting tendencies?

Turkle's qualitative data was gathered through engagement with a cohort of youth and some of it is consequently anecdotal (although this does not reduce the veracity of the data). However, the quantitative data tells a different story. Sociologist Barry Wellman has studied the network connections between individuals, mainly in North America, and argues that the evidence shows the constraining scenario to be a partial picture. He claims that the simple interactions between people and other people, machines and virtual entities that Turkle describes are too simplistic to do justice to the full picture of our complex engagements. We have more friends than ever, we are still anchored in our local environments and our online friends tend to be our offline friends as well, so that the attenuated transactions between online individuals via sculpted avatars that worry commentators play a relatively small role in our lives. Indeed, the division between our online and offline lives is not easy to draw.[25]

Wellman argues that the growth of the Internet, and online social networking in particular, has provided an opportunity for people to leave tight-knit groups and live in looser networks instead. People have generally moved from being group members to become individuals, albeit ones who gain much of the meaning and support in their lives from their networks. The result is a gain for most people in terms of flexibility, choice and exposure to heterogeneous points of view. Social ties and events are now more likely to be focused around an individual rather than a social unit, such as a family, a neighbourhood, an employer or an organisation. Communications are person-to-person rather than place-to-place, and people organise their own communications networks rather than expecting heads of households or work bosses to provide (and sometimes monitor) communication for them.

The Internet is not completely responsible for this shift, which was a feature of the twentieth century and associated technologies such as the telephone, radio, television and mobile telephony. It has, however, exacerbated and even accelerated it. We now connect with people routinely not only at home or at the office, but at stations and in airports; furthermore, we connect with people who are not co-located with us. In fact, the physical context of a communication matters less and less.

This is consistent with Turkle's critique, but if we continue to dig, we find that the picture is not as bleak as it might seem. People often have several networks, and the tight connections that we used to expect between individuals in a single network are replaced with looser and more opportunistic connections with many others in a diverse spread of networks. The idea of a single 'home' community or identity is far less applicable. This jumble of networks is harder for the individual to manage, but it pays off via the spread of services and experiences they are able to receive.

Wellman terms such people, who have partial membership of multiple networks rather than permanent membership of settled groups, 'networked individuals'.[26] Relationships are more transitory, but they are more often rekindled after a dormant period. The number of people reporting very close ties with family members has remained broadly stable since 1967, according to Wellman's figures, while those with close ties with friends have increased in number, and those with close ties to neighbours have decreased. People reported that they had more offline friends on average in 2007 than they did in 2002, especially those who were heavy users of the Internet. Indeed, the real-world friendship networks of those heavy users not only grew faster than any other group graded by level of Internet use, but by 2007 they were also on average larger in absolute terms than those of the other groups.[27]

Households are now less like castles which allow a family to withdraw and avoid the attention of others, including the government and figures of authority, and more like aircraft carriers, bases from which exploratory forays can be launched.[28] The house is a place where family members network with others, including work colleagues; people bring work home increasingly often. Families spend less time doing things together (including, infamously, eating dinner together at the dining table), and tend to have less 'family time' in common. Yet this does not mean diminishing contact; families are together less, and parents spend less time at home, but actual contact has increased over the last twenty years via the use of mobile phones. In Canada, 35 per cent of families feel technology has improved connections within their families, while only 5 per cent feel it has not.[29]

Ties between people seem to have become stronger at the cost of a decline in the perceived value of weak ties. We are less interested in strangers, and less likely to help them and care for them. Indeed, strangers are often viewed with suspicion. The idea, common in many cultures, that one is required by laws of hospitality to show concern for strangers and try to meet their immediate needs if they require help is increasingly alien to most Westerners.

Hence even if a particular network has the problematic properties of an echo chamber, the chances are that its members are also members of other networks which provide support in areas other than politics, ideology or religion. In fact, the crippled epistemology that concerned Russell Hardin is rather less threatening in a Webby world than it was in more fixed societies. Although a community based on proximity, family and sameness of purpose facilitates very deep communication with a small number of members, it is hard for new ideas and knowledge to penetrate the group. On the other hand, if someone is interacting with multiple networks and communities, they, and ultimately everyone else in their networks, are exposed to new ideas all the time. Each person who is a member of more than one network connects, or provides a bridge between, all his networks.

This may provide an explanation of the oft-noted point that traditional religions are in decline alongside the fixed-proximity networks upon which they thrived, and that those religions with a do-it-yourself aspect are flourishing in comparison. Such religions provide more useful benefits for networked individuals, as well as supporting more flexible communication.

Wellman identifies three important revolutions which have driven the development of the networked individual.[30] The first of these is the personal Internet revolution, which allows the individual to personalise communications, gather information and broadcast opinion (this, of course, is the putative cause of the echo chamber problem). The second is the social network revolution, as people attach to networks rather than fix themselves within groups. Third, there is the mobile revolution, so that communications hubs can be carried around with the individual who can therefore access, and be accessible to, others at all times. Even if the Internet did have a potential to seal people in echo chambers, the other two revolutions, far from promoting *anomie*, have a tendency to expose people to new ideas.

To Wellman's three revolutions, we might also add an important fourth—the speed of the infrastructure. Broadband, which dramatically speeds up the transmission of information, also enhances the online experience to the extent that it is feasible to perform more tasks using the Web, which drives the development of technical and informational skills.[31] It becomes easier to embed online interactions into an individual's offline life; broadband helps prevent the Internet becoming a virtual ghetto such that when an individual is online they are out of touch with everything else. Speed of information flow helps reduce isolation. In the context of Sunstein's argument, it is worth noting that a study of the 2004 US presidential election showed that broadband users were more likely to be exposed to diverse arguments and viewpoints, controlling for other factors.[32]

The result is that, although people have many more relationships with people whom they know offline only slightly or not at all, they retain their relationships with their local community too. Many emails, instant messages, mobile calls and texts are between locals, often supplementing face-to-face contacts.[33] Indeed, a surprising number of texts precede a face-to-face meeting by a small number of minutes, as one person texts another that 'parking car be wiv u soon'. Wellman's examination of the data shows, *contra* Turkle, that 'traditional' personal relationships seem to be supplemented, rather than displaced, by the technology.

For our purposes, this seems to imply that even if some networks have echo chamber properties, and even if some individuals thrive on or seek out such networks, no individual would be trapped in such chambers without hope of relief by the technology alone. This is not an all-or-nothing thing, of course; for example, Putnam and Campbell found that for many Americans a number of their social networks were centred on their church.[34] And although:

political messages can echo through any network of like-minded people, whether based on occupation, group membership, or some other characteristic, ... not all networks are equal. We suspect that when religion is the common thread that has woven a network together, the political information that circulates carries more moral weight—and is thus more persuasive.[35]

Nevertheless, it is perfectly consistent with the fact that the local environment, though proportionally less important as a part of a person's social context, remains significant, and indeed many relationships are enhanced as a result of technological mediation. People find it easier to join, re-join and move between networks. Even if one network has an unhealthy effect on someone—which Sunstein and Turkle have established as plausible in many instances—it does not follow that the network is the only influence on the people in it. People move across and through a network of networks, membership of only some of which is optional, and this widens the set of influences upon people. The Internet and the Web have not changed this—in fact they have accelerated the trend of exposure to new influence.

Changing minds

If people are primarily situated within a network of social networks, then to assess the echo chamber thesis we need to consider how ideas travel through such networks. Several theories have been developed within social science with regard to how communication networks work,[36] and the echo chamber thesis makes fairly concrete assumptions about which of these are in operation. A network for radicals must, on Sunstein's account, have relatively poor communications links outside a central clique or cluster, and reasonably good ones inside. The clique need not be particularly strongly interconnected, so the radicals could be quite isolated, but it should be able to suppress communications from heterodox sources and provide good connections to adherents from approved orthodox sources. Under such circumstances, it is hard to see pure theories of self-interested communication being germane; the radical hardly looks as if he is trying to build up his social capital, for instance, or to implement a strategy of cost minimisation. Rather, the theories that seem appropriate to this type of phenomenon are those that postulate 'homophily' (i.e. love of the similar) and 'identity' as reasons to develop links to a network, and those that explain the growth or otherwise of networks as a type of contagion.

Network science provides insights to help explain how an individual can leverage his or her network in order to achieve particular effects. For example, one interpretation of the world of the radical religious group sees it as a public good problem. The issue for those convinced by the reasoning of the group's religious texts is that certain aspects of their theology are a public good (as a heaven on earth, perhaps), but society is organised in such a way as to provide incentives for individuals to work against the provision of that good.[37] This is unsurprising, given that our definition of radicalism is precisely living in tension with the embedded society. Hence the failure of the radical view to achieve popularity or political influence, from the radical point of view, looks remarkably like a public good problem such as the provision of clean air or water, or the preservation of fish stocks. For the individual, it is rational to behave in such a way (burning wood, disposing of waste, fishing competitively) so as to increase his own good while undermining the public good. Similarly, from the radical's point of view, social structures provide incentives for individuals to work against the radical's goal.

The problem for the radical, then, is how to work effectively for his goal (which he interprets not as a personal preference but as a general good), and the problem for the radical group is how to organise to produce the goal, given that most people will work against it. The mass of people, from the radicals' point of view, will be free-riding on their efforts. They, in contrast, will place value directly on what they perceive as the collective benefit—and from this point of view, once a sufficiently large number of people value the collective benefits so highly that it becomes a social norm (what has been called a public-good transformation),[38] conflicts of interest will disappear.

Cliques

The radicals' networks will surely play an important role in providing mechanisms to realise their goal.[39] It is likely that the radical group will form a clique or a well-connected cluster[40] in the wider network of communications across society, and it is easier to reach people with similar interests within cliques than across society. Hence spreading a particular message or pushing a line in a debate is easier when one has modest resources, when the problem can be reduced to addressing a clique. Indeed, a clique will help to spread the word beyond itself. Because communication within a clique is relatively cheap, a radical can conserve his resources and use members' weak ties with other groups to communicate, via them, beyond his or her own group.

When resources are limited, a clique enables the communicator to be selective. Although the ideal communication strategy is high reach and high selectivity—that is, many people are contacted, especially those who are most likely to be receptive to the message—such a strategy is clearly expensive. Marwell and Oliver's simulations have shown that the two pragmatic strategies of high reach and low selectivity (many people contacted indiscriminately) and low reach and high selectivity (special efforts made to contact those people who are receptive to the message) are both effective in getting agreement and action about a public good. When the radicals' problem is viewed as a public good problem, it is clear that a tight network of adherents is valuable.

Homophily

If a clique is important, how do radicals get one to form? The attraction felt by people of similar backgrounds is an important binding mechanism for groups. However, most work on homophily has focused on demographic similarities such as age, gender and race, although some researchers have also found strengthened ties based on offline religious observance.[41] This sort of connection mechanism based on attractors of physical proximity and demographic similarity does not provide a great deal of support for the echo chamber thesis, which says that these attractors can be displaced by attractors based on shared ideology, religion or nihilistic disregard of their embedding societies.

In a sense, homophily based on proximity is a protection against ideologically driven extremism, on the assumption that extremists are rare within a particular community. In this connection, it is interesting to consider the case of Thomas U, a German neo-Nazi who converted to Islam, joined the Taliban and travelled to Waziristan.[42] He eventually quit and gave himself up due to his disgust with his erstwhile colleagues' drug use, tendency to spit and lack of respect for women. It is possible that Herr U might still be a Taliban member if he had restricted himself to online contact, although he would have been less useful to the group itself in its struggle with the Pakistani forces. As it was, the German's cultural preferences trumped his ideological ones.

When we look online, we see consensus driven by more than ideological agreement. One example was described by el-Nawawy and Khamis, who analysed a small number of Islamic discussion forums, some of which were characterised by diverse networks, others by homogeneous ones (language turned out to be a useful proxy for diversity, English correlating with heterogeneity and Arabic correlating with homogeneity). Although their sample size was small, they were able to make some generalisations:

[The Arabic-language forums under study] attracted mainly Arabic-speaking, Muslim participants who shared similar views on key issues ... In other words, it was the ethnic, cultural, and religious 'homogeneity' of those participants that produced highly consensual, shared attitudes of pan-Arabism and pan-Islamism around certain key issues, within the realm of collective identities.

To the contrary ... [participants in the English-language forums under study] exemplified diverse ethnic, cultural, and religious backgrounds, and some of them did not have any religious affiliation. This, in turn, did not allow for any pan-Arab or pan-Islamic perspectives or attitudes to emerge among the participants in this forum, which was characterized by highly polemic, rather than consensual, discourses and attitudes around key issues, within the realm of divergent identities ...[43]

Hence if the Internet tends to produce echo chambers, the effect is not constant across groups. The second group of forums brought together a diverse set of people, including Islamophobes as well as Christians, Jews and various different Muslim sects, resulting in ill-mannered debates—unpleasant and intolerant behaviour from all sides, but hardly an echo chamber. The first group of forums was more like an echo chamber, but they had already gathered an ethnic and culturally homogeneous group of participants. In such a case, although this was not a finding of el-Nawawy and Khamis, the Internet might facilitate the development of extreme positions, but only within groups which were already, independently of the Internet discussion, exhibiting demographic and cultural homophily. The development of a forum into an echo chamber depends not on the technology, but rather on the social context.

This is the sort of result we should expect. Research into social networks and their facilitation by technology has tended to throw up paradoxes and ambivalent conclusions rather than direct unequivocal effects. The introduction of email and other digital methods of communication into organisations, for example, has resulted in both centralisation and decentralisation being detectable,[44] and similar contradictory effects were found with respect to earlier communication technologies such as the telephone.[45] More generally, Majid Tehranian has argued that technologies are very likely to produce effects that are completely opposite to each other at the same time and in direct contradiction. One effect might be more prominent than the other, depending on the context, but this 'dual effects hypothesis' has not been falsified by more recent communications technologies.[46] It is especially convincing when we consider it in the context of Wellman's account of networked individuals; the large number of networks in which we take part will influence us in a number of possibly contradictory ways. This may help us to understand how echo chambers both support authenticity, as Weinberger claims, and diminish it, as argued by Sunstein and Turkle, at the same time: they can do both.

Contagion

If homophily is at best an implausible explanation of how echo chambers develop (and also not an explanation that implicates the Internet), then we must postulate another kind of mechanism to disseminate attitudes through a network. In a contagion model of influence, various network properties allow views to spread at greater or lesser speed and efficiency—properties such as the strength of the connection between two people, whether it is symmetric or asymmetric, whether it is multiplex (i.e. whether they are linked by more than one type of connection), and the frequency of communication.[47] An echo chamber must include some kind of contagion mechanism, which would seem to explain why people within the chamber are more at risk than those outside (in the same way as those trapped in a quarantine zone are more likely to be infected than those outside).

How might contagion work? The echo chamber hypothesis implies that the group gradually reaches a consensus that is more extreme than the starting positions of many of the participants. This suggests more interaction leads to similarities of attitudes. However, in most contagion theories this principle is counterbalanced by a principle of reflected exclusivity—'the degree of influence person j has on person i's evaluation … is inversely proportional to the amount of time j spends with all others'.[48] Reflected exclusivity will tend to offset the inevitable homogenisation of attitudes across a network—and so in an echo chamber one would conversely expect that reflected exclusivity plays a relatively small role precisely because an echo chamber does homogenise attitudes. It follows from this that the influence of people within the chamber on each other is high and therefore that their external networks are relatively insignificant. This would contradict Wellman's discoveries, and suggest that the denizens of echo chambers are more likely to suffer from the kind of alienation that Turkle describes.

However, it is unclear how the Internet could be the cause of that alienation. If it was, then the implication is that a networked individual, as described by Wellman, enters the echo chamber and somehow loses his or her diverse connections, which are then replaced with more and stronger connections within the echo chamber. Turkle and Sunstein do not suggest that this is what happens, nor do they suggest a mechanism to make it happen. Such an account is tantamount to the brainwashing idea behind the DAM thesis, which we comprehensively rejected in Chapter Six.

Individuals in the echo chamber must also be somewhat more open to influence than members of a more typical network. In early models of social networks, Mark Granovetter suggested that people would have some kind of threshold below which they would not be influenced by others; if, within some network, they were influenced by a sufficiently large number of others (in a sufficiently large number of sufficiently strong communications), then the threshold would be breached and they would become likely to adopt the views they had been introduced to.[49] For an echo chamber to form, we must assume that a sufficient number of network members had low enough thresholds to allow such views to gain traction and begin to spread more widely.

Is such a model realistic? On the one hand, studies have shown that the religious environment in a church can correlate more closely with someone's political views than their own religious opinions.[50] It has also been noted that those religious practitioners who say they draw upon religion in making their political judgements are more likely to agree that religion influences other decisions in their lives, in areas such as family and career.[51]

But on the other hand, Monge and Contractor argue that contagion models are somewhat less plausible than they might initially seem, discounting rare and exceptional circumstances. The studies discussed in the previous paragraph describe tendencies rather than hermetically sealed deterministic intellectual environments. They warn against reductionist theories about the spread of ideas.

Missing in the contagion model is the typical ebb and flow of messages through networks that typifies human communication. In human interaction messages containing different ideas, values, and attitudes flow back and forth among people as they negotiate resolutions. The most typical outcome is modifications to the different positions each person held at the outset of the contagion process, modifications that influence both contaminators and the contaminated.[52]

Conclusion

To summarise the results of this chapter, a critical examination of theory and empirical work does a lot of work to undermine the theory of the Devil's Long Tail. The long-tail arguments themselves are not very well supported by the empirical evidence. And without ruling out the possibility of online echo chambers, the strength of Sunstein's thesis can be undermined. Some commentators, such as Weinberger, defend the value of echo chambers (which is not to say that all echo chambers are good, only that they can have benefits as well as costs). Research by Wellman and others has suggested that people typically join a range of networks, and that new technology does not seem to be creating hordes of alienated people who would be useful fodder for extremist echo chambers. Most people have many connections which tend to reduce the influence of particular sets of ideas, and as a matter of fact, the Internet facilitates making those valuable connections.

When we look at the mechanisms for spreading ideas through a network, we see that echo chambers will perhaps be more likely to develop where there are coherent cliques, and when ideas spread through homophily and contagion. But homophily seems to be primarily an offline phenomenon, requiring demographic contingencies in addition to technological mediation, while contagion seems to require an unusual degree of homogeneity, alienation and openness to influence. It is possible of course that the Internet could exacerbate problems with communities of such people, but it can hardly be held responsible for their existence.

10

THE HARDEST THING

Suppose a government felt the need to intervene on the Web to damp down extremism. How might it proceed? The difficulty it will always face is structural—as Part II of this book has shown, the ideas of the extremists are not the key variables. It is central to extremists' identities that they define themselves in opposition to mainstream society. This is always going to be a problem for any approach that eschews totalitarianism (locking up potential extremists as a danger to society) or paternalism (locking them up for their own good).

Governments feel pressed to act in the face of an attack—and so they should. However, there is no point acting for the sake of it, and nothing is often the hardest thing to do, especially in the face of relentless media pressure and the need to provide new stories to fill the airwaves. It is striking how little is known about so-called de-radicalisation or disengagement—what brings an extremist into the mainstream political fold and keeps him there. We do not know, for instance, whether it is essential to purge an extremist's mind of radical ideas, or alternatively whether moderating behaviour is a more sensible focus—does it matter what an ex-terrorist believes, as long as he is an ex-terrorist?

On the other hand, what is an ex-terrorist? Does a terrorist 'career' have an identifiable beginning and end, as the prefix 'ex' seems to imply? And if the model of a slippery slope from radicalism to violent extremism is flawed, could it be that de-radicalisation will not even achieve the cessation of violence it is intended to? There is little or no consensus on these questions, and we will not attempt to answer them. Even more frustrating, despite a number of initiatives to de-radicalise terrorists, especially Islamists, few of these have been evaluated, so we still do not know what, if anything, works.[1] Indeed, studies of previous waves of terrorism have concluded that they all died out for reasons other than the counterterrorism measures employed against them.[2]

In this final chapter we will revisit the results of our enquiries from Part II in the context of the technologies underlying the Internet and the Web that some have argued have played a part in spreading extremism. After all, policy interventions that 'adjust' the Internet need to be feasible, and also need to preserve the qualities of the Internet that make it such a valuable tool.

What not to do

Public spaces revisited

The Internet and the Web are creations of Western liberal thinking, as is reflected in both their governing ideals and their engineering. Untangling these will be difficult and may risk damaging their function of facilitating the exchange of complex ideas. It seems hard to imagine how they could work as means for transferring information and money while being infested with various chokepoints, editors, censors, snoopers and other Buttinskis who would scrutinise the flow.

That is not to say that laws curbing free speech cannot be applied to the Internet. There are protections against slander and libel, and restrictions on hate speech or speech designed to incite violence. Societies define and isolate unacceptable forms of expression and outlaw them. Whatever is said online can also be outlawed by individual societies. As the Web is worldwide, there will be issues of jurisdiction to be negotiated, and it would be hard for a British court to press sanctions on a Ukrainian website, for instance. But in principle it is not impossible for the general law of the land to be applied to the Internet,[3] and it is hard to think of a reason why new offences or regulations need to be formulated to tackle the particular problem of inappropriate online discourse.

Sometimes an offence is not really enforceable, but it can serve its purpose. To take a relatively illiberal example, Singapore has strict media laws which it applies to websites. These laws were strengthened in 2013, and the largest news distribution sites must now register and post a bond with the Media Development Agency and agree to take down offensive content within twenty-four hours of notice. It also uses libel and defamation laws to suppress dissent. In principle it would be relatively straightforward to circumvent these laws if the supplier and consumer of news were prepared to take a small risk (for example, using the anonymity network Tor—https://www.torproject.org/), yet the laws have the required deterrent effect to preserve the calm and orderly characteristic of Singapore. We are not arguing that such suppression is a good thing—our point is only that the application of laws restricting free speech online is not impossible. It should not involve drafting new laws or require enormous levels of surveillance, and any democracy with a commitment to liberty should be able to manage its online conversation without special attention.

It would certainly be beneficial if there were spaces in which extremists entered into constructive dialogue with more moderate members of mainstream society. Yet saying this does not mean that Habermasian spaces can easily be created (perhaps they only emerge out of pre-existing practice), or that they will necessarily be filled with the desired kind of polite interlocution. It is unusual for communities online or offline to focus exclusively on a single topic, problem or goal. A 'brochure' website which provides content for its users can restrict interaction, and many do,[4] but whenever content provision is two-way, the community of users contributes to the content and the site inevitably becomes an extension of the community itself. Its members are likely to have more in common than the narrowly circumscribed goal which is the 'official' reason for the site, and could easily be tempted to stray off-topic. One study found that religious websites 'use the Internet not only to transmit information about religious and community life, but also to communicate subjective community experiences augmented by visual and auditory geographic sensibilities'.[5] The community has a life over and above the shared theology.

As a result, it should not come as a surprise that el-Nawawy and Khamis found that the Islamic online forums they studied failed to adhere to Habermasian principles. 'Most participants … did not utilize these forums to engage in truly democratic discourse and open deliberations. Rather, they used their participation to release emotions, express anger, propagate an already existing viewpoint, or preach to others to adopt their views.'[6] After all, why should people who hold undemocratic views, or who might be emotional or angry, or who simply want their point of view to prevail, not use the forums to express themselves? Who—particularly someone who feels injustice and is annoyed about it—would go online in order to be 'de-radicalised' for the greater good?

El-Nawawy and Khamis argue that 'the anonymity and easy accessibility that were made possible through these forums have contributed to creating a nondeliberatory environment, rather than improving the quality of a truly rational-critical Habermasian discourse'.[7] Although it is impossible to disagree with their judgement, this is like arguing that the existence of two separate football teams each determined to score more goals than the other contributes to creating an antagonistic environment, rather than mutual cooperation between the twenty-two players. This is undeniably true, but antagonism is the entire point of football. If there was no antagonism, what would the players cooperate in doing? And similarly in the online forum—the point of the forum is that it was set up to discuss things that people care deeply and passionately about, and if they were engaged in a rational-critical discourse, they would have to discuss something else, something they felt deliberative about.

Punitive sanctions can of course be used to police discussion pages.[8] However, sanctions only work if they are perceived as punitive. A restrictive religious website has the potential sanction to throw someone off the site, or even out of the group, and that is a serious threat: the people on the site (in the group) want to be on it (in it). A site for open constructive discussion can be policed just as harshly, but the reasons for an extremist's participation are far less strong, and therefore the sanctions are much less severe. Conversely, if anonymity were prevented by moderators, or if accessibility were limited to people willing to go through a few hoops in order to prove their rational-critical faculties, then the discussion would be likely to be more Habermasian (if anyone remained to discuss anything). It is not clear, however, what would have been gained other than driving those who feel strongly about these particular matters on to other forums, maybe offline ones.

El-Nawawy and Khamis's response is to reject the Habermasian account as exclusionary, restrictive and anti-diversity,[9] and therefore inapplicable to the portion of the Web they investigated. This seems an overreaction, but we should not expect civilised discussion to emerge organically in sites which appeal to the committed.

An alternative response to chaotic and often unreasonable online discussion is to define the desired sort of Habermasian space and create a site to implement it. As an example, consider the unimplemented proposal of Jay Blumler and Stephen Coleman for a civic commons to promote active democratic citizenship.[10] This would be an accessible common ground in which people could articulate their energies and aspirations, replacing what the authors consider a hollowed-out public sphere. In this, their idea is certainly congruent with Sunstein's emphasis on the importance of public spaces for democracies, as we described in Chapter Two.

Blumler and Coleman's aim, therefore, is to specify a Habermasian space disconnected from government and other vested interests such as big corporations. This space, in their vision, would become an important representation of public opinion, one which could be used by legislators and local government for the purposes of consultation, for instance. It could be used to scrutinise government policies, even legislation itself. It would be transparent and accountable to a range of stakeholders, an exercise in civic learning and consultation, and would explore, moderate and perhaps even regulate new methods for online deliberation and consultation. It would be run by an agency with a light-touch regulatory function, which would have to ensure inclusion, ensure that discourse was civil and set out best practice. According to Blumler and Coleman, such a space would be transformative of politics but not utopian, it would be genuinely listened to by the authorities, would win public respect by combining the virtues of amateurism (creativity and enthusiasm) with presentational professionalism, would be selectively inclusive and would be publicly funded but politically independent.

This suggestion is impractical for a number of reasons. In the first place, it is a monolithic idea—as likely to censor or suppress voices as allow them to be heard, let alone include them in decision-making. The authors recognise this criticism, and more recently reformulated their proposal in a Web 2.0 sort of way, though without changing form or function very much.[11] They now accept that publics in the UK are fragmented, so that the function of this privatised space should be 'to connect diverse social networks that could only hope to arrive at public judgments through the mediation of an impersonal institution committed to facilitating communication between people who do not necessarily know or understand one another'.[12]

But even this alteration does not make the forum appropriate for the Web 2.0 era. The fact that the proposal had to be altered from an integrative to a connective function within a few years of its initial flotation tells us that not only do fashions in technology change quickly, but that fashions in political theory do too. It is very likely that institutions built by well-meaning thinkers will be left behind by developments in both politics and technology. Furthermore, there are numerous democratic representative institutions, as well as elements of the mass media, that facilitate communication. It is unclear why someone who wished to communicate with diverse groups would not simply get on and take part in other political processes—for example, writing to newspapers, writing to representatives, joining pressure groups and so on. What extra functionality does a 'connecting' online space provide?

This is the sort of well-meaning exercise which would either die of neglect, or be monopolised by the type of small, loud, organised group which exploits unrepresentative platforms and committees to get its point across. Blumler and Coleman cite poll evidence that 79 per cent of British Internet users were in favour of creating a public space to debate policy issues.[13] Yet it seems a long step from there to the assumption that a large number of people would use such a space. Use gives institutions life, and there are institutions already in use which do much of this.

The second criticism of artificial civic commons is that their quasi-official status is hardly likely to be attractive to extremists. The literature reviewed in Part II strongly indicates that extremists receive important benefits from their irregular and disconnected social networks, and these would be lost if they began to take part in an online public sphere, just as if they took part in mainstream democratic processes. The somewhat paternalistic tone of the civic commons proposal wavers between state sponsorship and an arm's length relation with the state. This is a circle that is hard to square, and would almost certainly affect the number of groups willing to trust in such a space. An extremist or a radical may insist on absolute assurances of anonymity, but the 'light touch' agency that ran the show could hardly prove beyond all doubt that it was prepared to respect that insistence. Even if it genuinely respected anonymity, the fact that it was publicly supported would cause a great deal of suspicion; after Edward Snowden, who would believe it?

Blumler and Coleman want government involved at some level to provide legitimacy, and are concerned about genuinely privatised spaces—even those used by vast numbers of people. But this seems misguided. It is worth remembering that the original public sphere of the Enlightenment was similarly privately run, a long way from the state's influence, and of a very rambunctious nature that no doubt fell short of the ideals of well-mannered, deliberative debate. Yet it had an important role to play, and it endured. It even influenced Habermas.[14]

None of this is to say that governments cannot or should not try to understand, sample or even influence newly emerging online public spaces. For example, the EU project WeGov has developed a toolbox of software to engage with microbloggers and social networks.[15] The advantage of this idea over the civic commons is that social networking sites and Twitter are well accepted by citizens and are a familiar environment where discussions are already taking place. Hence they create the possibility of information retrieval and dissemination for policy-makers, and the beginning of a dialogue between policy-makers and citizens, as long as the tools are in place to sieve through multitudes of comments to get to the crux of a debate. In a similar vein, semantic analysis is being used on unstructured text; recent experiments have extracted a number of policy ideas from texts sent to particular numbers set up by the Obama administration.[16] This sort of analysis of and participation in already existing public discussion spaces will no doubt become an important factor in future political practice, but—remembering our own priorities in this book—still may not intersect with the extremists.

The third problem with the civic commons suggestion is that it misses the important point that online innovation not only happens very quickly, but that it also addresses demand. The fact that Blumler and Coleman failed to anticipate Web 2.0 and social networking is not a criticism—few did. However, the fact that, in the words of screenwriter William Goldman, nobody knows anything should have told them that their vision would be inaccurate.

Their argument suffers from the same problem as that of el-Nawawy and Khamis, which is that whether they are enthusiastic or dismissive of the Habermasian space, they take a very purist view of what it might entail. Some Habermasian things happen online, and very many non-Habermasian things happen too. There are also patterns of online discussion which emerge because individuals provide content from which wider phenomena can be observed. For example, on Twitter no individual tweet could possibly be regarded as a deep contribution to any discussion (the micro-blogger is allowed a mere 140 characters to get his point across), but sophisticated sentiment analysis of the language used about a particular topic allows millions of tweets to be mined for consensus—for example, whether events like Obama's re-election, the release of a new gadget by Apple, or a terrorist attack, are positively or negatively received. Indeed, Obama's finely calibrated election campaign of 2012 used this analysis in the key swing states.[17] When there are sufficient tweets to support large-scale analysis, the results can be extremely interesting.

This is not to say that this sort of objective and democratic aggregation function is always accurate, comprehensive or unbiased. But parts of the Web can still have an emergent Habermasian feel. They depend on scale and therefore need to be attractive to hundreds of millions of users. No single contribution to debate via microblog will be very profound, but at scale the total can provide an important addition to our understanding of trends in social thought. Moreover, as contributions are time-stamped, we can track changes on a day-to-day or even on an hour-to-hour basis. Sometimes the conclusions are too swift and facile—but this is a facility that we never had before. It will take us time to get used to it, but there is no need to think it will have a wholly negative effect.

It is likely that extremist discussion will appear as mere noise on Twitter or Facebook, although individual extremist sites or feeds may be discovered and isolated by concerned citizens, politicians or policemen.[18] The danger with 'outing' extremists in this way is that mainstream political actors paint themselves into a corner; it is hard to engage subsequently with people whose behaviour has been branded as intolerable. Suppression may then be the only realistic option available, but this will not challenge those whose identity includes a commitment to opposing the shibboleths of mainstream society.[19]

Contagion revisited

A key theme of this book is that any methods designed to prevent the misuse of the Internet to disseminate extremism must leave the basic infrastructure broadly intact. They must instead try to interfere with what is being said, or how it is being said, while guarding against suppressing debate in the public sphere. The metaphor of contagion for the adoption of messages through a network, explored in Chapter Nine, has provoked a number of ideas about how to prevent their spread. In particular, a common theme has been that unwelcome messages can be countered by preventing exposure to them.[20] This has never been a particularly effective strategy, but in a world with many channels for communication, a huge supply of low-cost information and particularly dense networks, it appears peculiarly irrelevant.

As the use of the Internet was growing, it was expected that it would be a tool for democracy, tolerance and liberalism, partly reflecting the values of its liberal founders and American sponsors. For instance, neo-conservative Mark Palmer, founder of the National Endowment for Democracy (funded by the US Congress) and member of the splendidly-named Committee on the Present Danger,[21] argued that the Internet was 'a force multiplier for democracy and an expense multiplier for dictators'.[22] Palmer's understanding was premised on the isolation-from-exposure method; he assumed that, if the friends of freedom and liberalism spread anti-totalitarian messages, then the dictators' response has to be to try to close them down and prevent their subjects from receiving them. If that is the totalitarians' only policy response, then clearly the Internet will make it much harder. The democrat finds it easier to spread his message, while the totalitarian finds it harder to suppress it.

However, this force multiplier model is a poor representation of the situation. As Yevgeny Morozov argues,[23] the blithe assumption that the Internet will foster messages supportive of pluralism and tolerance and crowd out the intolerant and illiberal is borne out by neither experience nor evidence. In many places pro-government messages hold sway online.[24] Many supposed cyber-criminals or hackers are actually motivated by a wish to defend their own governments or to attack the United States, rather than by criminal motivations as usually understood. Initiating a distributed denial-of-service attack against a critic of a government need not be the act of a government; such manoeuvres are often carried out by nationalistic private citizens (sometimes with tacit state support). It is a simple method for democratising repression.

The contagion model suggests twin strategies to prevent the spread of unwelcome messages and to flood the network with counterarguments. Neither can be totally successful, and the result is more likely to be a rough balance of availability of different messages, from which individuals select those they want to hear. As Caplan argues, 'the fundamental problem with persuasion is free entry. Opponents of terrorism can propagandize against the ideology of terrorism and hope the next generation changes its mind. But proponents of terrorism compete to radicalize the same audience.'[25] This of course is consistent with Sunstein's echo chamber argument, according to which people will naturally filter out what they are not interested in when armed with filtering technology. The reverse implication, however, is not true: it is quite possible that people are exposed to messages that they ignore. Rather more likely, in the general case, is that positions do get modified.[26] People are not passive receivers of messages with which they are injected.

The metaphor of injection suggests another policy variant, namely inoculation or vaccination. In medicine, a small dose of what you wish to resist can help you develop a resistance to it. In politics, conceding a small part of your opponents' demands can satisfy uncommitted voters without giving too much ground.[27] In regulating communications, can an inoculation strategy avoid the dangers (or temptations) of quackery?

The most important theory along these lines was developed by William McGuire, who argued that people exposed to a weakened form of an undesirable message, and maybe given a booster shot of counter-argument, would be more likely to develop and internalise a critique of the message.[28] Subsequent exposure to the message could then be resisted more easily. Inoculation theory has been shown to have positive effects in marketing and healthcare.

However, there are three reasons why this kind of idea will not prevent the spread of extremist messaging across the Internet. First, while most experiments to do with inoculation have taken place in relatively closed environments (e.g. volunteers are given specific messages by the experimenters), in the real world messages will be differentially spread, so that in any network some people will be exposed to the undesirable messages and others not, and some will be exposed to the vaccine and others not. Hence there will be subgroups and mini-networks within a network with different properties and structures, whose members have reacted to divergent stimuli in different ways. If there is a danger from echo chambers, inoculation over an open and distributed system such as the Internet is just as likely to create smaller but relatively tight-knit sub-networks of people who accept the undesirable message.

Secondly, the low barriers to entry on the Web mean that many tactics that were previously restricted to governments and large corporations can now be carried out by much smaller private organisations or even individuals. Hence a religious extremist group, or umbrella organisation, could just as easily mount an operation to inoculate people against the establishment messages which it defines as undesirable. Once again, the problem is free entry.

Thirdly, people are not empty vessels, and are swayed by many factors beyond the content of the message. The language used may be important, as may also be the means of communication and—perhaps most important of all—the identity of the messenger. Mere association with the government of the United States, for example, would prevent an organisation from making much political headway in Iran and vice versa. Indeed, the United States has pushed the Internet so strongly as an instrument of democracy that many private citizens in hostile countries, such as Russia, have assumed (a) that it is an instrument of US foreign policy, and (b) it is their duty to damage it if they can.[29]

The US counterterrorism programme called Viral Peace aims to disrupt al-Qaeda and extremist Islamist sites with trolling, or using 'logic, humor, satire, [and] religious arguments, not just to confront [extremists], but to undermine and demoralize them'.[30] As this policy is neither expensive nor violent, it should not be dismissed out of hand. But the purpose of many extremist sites is to harden views and cultivate group solidarity rather than recruit the uncommitted. The trolls with a moderate, liberal message on such sites will probably be outgunned by those who are even more extreme or outlandish. The former will be spotted and flamed immediately, even if the moderators do not take them down. Very few people on an extremist Islamist site will be receptive to even heavily disguised pro-American messages or messages that appear to emanate from someone with a Western background. For example, el-Nawawy and Khamis write that efforts to debate in the English-language forums of Islamonline 'were overshadowed by the assertiveness, dogmatism, and defensiveness expressed by many participants'. There were 'heated debates between Muslims and non-Muslims', while on the Arabic-language forum, where religious differences were much smaller, 'Muslim participants who tried to be somewhat reflexive in their discussion of highly sensitive issues ... were sometimes shunned by other Muslim participants, and even attacked and accused of being "traitors."'[31] Alternative extreme views are more likely to be effective for the purposes of trolling, but even then they will be of limited worth. As earlier chapters have argued at length, it is not ideas that play the explanatory part in the dissemination of extremism.

Belonging revisited

Recent research points to the significant influence a person's network exercises over their actions and beliefs. As network scientist James Fowler put it, 'If you're not looking at the friends, you're not looking at all the story. 80% of the total effect [studied in his experiment] was on the friends of those treated. We have to shift the way we evaluate interventions, from the individual to the network.'[32] This means that any attempt to shift the individual's behaviour will need to co-opt their social network. An important concern, though it is beyond the scope of this book, is that data about the network is often in private hands, and, worse, is often unavailable to the data subjects themselves. This is hardly democratically empowering.

The spread of religiosity in recent years is often seen as a self-defining response by individuals to a perceived crisis of secularisation with which they reject or resist social pressures. For instance, Olivier Roy argues that:

Common features of religiosity among born-again or 'true' believers include the crisis of the social authority of religion, the delinking of religious and cultural patterns, the constitution of religious communities on the basis of an individual self-definition of 'me as a believer', the explicit criticism of 'non-religious elements', and the will to return to the true tenets of the religion.[33]

Religiosity is a personal experience, and cultural, familial and religious legacies are featuring less as factors in deciding which religions to follow and what attitude to strike vis-à-vis the embedding society.[34] 'A personal and emotional experience leads directly to the truth.'[35] Yet work by network scientists also makes it clear that the individual's decision is likely to be influenced by his or her social network.[36]

Roy is concerned by the lack of a social substratum for the 'Muslim community',[37] which is often talked about but based neither on territory, social class nor culture. The community exists to the extent that people wish to join it, and it consists in whatever aspects they highlight (and hence there are as many *umma*s as there are groups claiming to embody it). But online networked technology allows the construction of groups linked by nothing other than faith, language and a certain level of facility with gadgets.

Hence democratic governments attempting to sway the opinions of extremists have two problems. First, the people whose behaviour or opinions they are attempting to alter are hostile, sometimes to the extent of defining their identities in opposition to them. Second, although they can 'get at' such people via their social networks, it may well be that the nearest friends in these networks are fellow extremists (identifying these key elements is an inexact art, but recent research suggests that it is the closest dozen or so friends that really count).[38]

There is clearly a Catch-22 here—to divert extremist A to the mainstream, we need to bring his social network to the mainstream too. However, if his social network is primarily made up of extremists, then the problem is now distributed across the network. On the other hand, if his social network is not primarily made up of extremists, then we might hope that the moderate network will help drag him to the mainstream, but it is not clear what extra interventions might facilitate that process.

Reframing revisited

The danger is that the issue is framed by democratic governments as part of a war on extremism which merely reinforces the extremists' own characterisation of the interaction, and sets up a 'virtual dialogue of the deaf' between the numerically overwhelming mainstream and the embattled extremists. A better form of engagement would emphasise and disaggregate the practical issues underlying support for extremist groups, and would transcend simple binary oppositions.

Political scientist Marc Lynch delineates three different conceptions of what he calls the 'war of ideas' in the specific context of the US response to Islamism and al-Qaeda.[39] First there is the explicit effort to delegitimise extremist ideas directly, favoured by the Bush administration. This has been something of a success in its own narrow terms, although the Americans made the mistake of assuming that marginalising al-Qaeda would necessarily help their own profile among Muslims (which is not the case).

Second, there is a wider campaign to spread liberal values across the Arab world—which may or may not be a worthwhile thing to do—but the United States is very badly placed to conduct such a campaign. As Lynch says, 'trying to do so is likely to discredit the approved carriers of the message and to ignite fierce opposition'. Morozov points out that 'when American diplomats call Facebook a tool of democracy promotion, it's safe to assume that the rest of the world believes that America is keen to exploit this tool to its fullest, rather than just stare at it in awe'.[40]

The third conception of the war of ideas is a broad-based engagement in debate. The key points are that engagement involves accepting the interlocutor as an equal, at least with respect to the dialogue, and that one needs to be prepared to engage with people and organisations that one might not be happy to deal with ordinarily. It may also need policy changes to give substance to the dialogue. One important advantage is that governments can then use private sector spaces, such as social network sites and microblogs, and also exploit tools such as the WeGov toolset to analyse responses. However, governments and the media also need to accept that this is a long-term process in which immediate success is unlikely, and that patience is a virtue.

The aim of such engagement is not necessarily to 'win'. It might be possible to neutralise extremist opinion in the way that al-Qaeda has been marginalised, but this will not necessarily bring extremists to the mainstream (it may merely set off another round of the Church–Sect Cycle). In the Middle East, Arab opinion has not moved in a pro-American direction,[41] even after the Arab Spring.[42] A better option would be to engage in such a way as to disaggregate the extremists' grievances, so as to undermine their straightforward Manichaean narrative.

However, ideas are not the key variables, as we have already seen. The main reason for engaging in this way is to include extremists in different overlapping social networks. The key variable in the growth of extremist groups, as we argued in Part II, is the sense of belonging. Disaggregating grievances should help to bring extremists into contact with a wider set of disaffected people. The net result—whether the many are dragged away to the extremes, or the few are pulled toward the mainstream—will be unpredictable, but our examination of the social forces governing the growth and diminution of religious groups implies it is the only way forward if extremism is to be countered.

What to do

With respect to the Internet, democratic governments' hands are not tied. There is a great deal they can do to address the problem of extremism online. Their freedom of action is only curtailed if:

• They want to preserve their democratic credentials.

- They want to preserve the utility of the Internet and the Web for the population at large and for specialist sectors such as academe and e-commerce.
- They want their citizens to retain trust in the Internet.
- They want the Internet to remain as secure as possible.
- They want to act effectively.

Governments can implement almost any policy, as long as they do not mind being undemocratic, curtailing liberty, slowing down the Internet and turning their citizens away from it, and wasting their time with measures that will not work. However, as governments are likely to want to uphold the five conditions outlined above, their hands will be tied quite tightly. This is not a bad thing. Mass surveillance, inserting cryptographical backdoors, acting for the sake of acting ('security theatre') and driving radical discussion underground are all counterproductive. There is no 'solution' to the problem of violent religious extremism—the violent are always with us—but equally governments can refrain from making the problem worse, and from having a negative effect on civil society and the Internet.

In this section, we will set out some of the positive attitudes and policies that we believe governments should pursue, on the basis of our review of the literature in computer science and the sociology of religion.

1. Be patient and realistic

The demands of the 24/7 media agenda—which ironically is made worse by analysis of the Twittersphere and the instantaneity of online comment—are inimical to good, reflective government and deliberative democracy. It is tempting to governments, in the face of violence which has a Web-based component, to clamp down on the technology as a means of appearing to do something, or even simply to announce something so that it can be reported.

The problem with doing so is that it maintains a vicious circle of problem–solution–problem. The media, including online media, thrive on immediacy and problems, with the result that governments are pressured into declaring immediate solutions. Violent extremism is not a problem that will go away quickly, and also not something, as Part II demonstrates, that can be dealt with through grand gestures.

Furthermore, it is nearly impossible to suppress negative attitudes in society; those who hold such attitudes need to work out the advantages of the mainstream for themselves. This may take time, and since it has to be a freely taken decision, it may not happen at all in some cases. At some point, we will have to agree to disagree, and respect the other's view.

Hence governments need to be patient in their approach. They need to understand the timescales that are involved in absorbing potentially large networks of people into mainstream society. If they judge any initiative by instant results, then it will fail.

We should also add that the media and commentariat need to understand the difficulties of finding single terrorists in a multitude. The fact that an atrocity occurred—even if the perpetrators were known to the intelligence services—does not necessarily indicate bad policing. Policing is resource-intensive, and it would be impossible and undesirable for police to follow up every lead. They have to prioritise, which means they will sometimes get it wrong. Some mistakes are avoidable, and sometimes there is outright negligence, but in general if it is assumed that the police should get it right all the time, then they will respond to that impossible dream the only way possible: by universal surveillance. And, of course, as Snowden has informed us, that is unfortunately what has happened.

2. Ideas are not the cause of terrorism: include those with hostile views of the mainstream in dialogue

As shown in Part II, theology is not the main variable in extremist violence. As a result, cracking down on people who are exploring a particular ideology, however inimical to mainstream thought and liberal tolerance, will not have much of an effect.

Counterterrorism is a policing operation, requiring all the usual skills of intelligence and evidence-gathering. Plots to kill or to damage property should be treated as what they are—threats to the safety of the public. Not all behaviour which is inspired by radical ideas—demonstrations, accessing jihadi literature, contributing to jihadi chatrooms—is a threat at the same level.

In this book, we leave it open as to whether radicalism in terms of ideas and extremism qua violence inspired by ideas are points on the same continuum. But spatial metaphors can mislead. In particular, placing radical ideologies on a one-dimensional spectrum with moderation in the middle gives rise to extensions of the metaphor—for instance, that radicalism is connected by a slippery slope to violent extremism. There is little evidence that this is the case and plenty of evidence that it is not.

This means that marginalising radical voices within a democratic polity, as for example when the UK government abandoned attempts to co-operate with Islamist radicals in the prevention of terrorism in 2011,[43] is not a good strategy. The signal is, in effect, that my deeply held views are acceptable, but yours are not because they will inevitably lead to violence. Part II of this book summarises the evidence which suggests that this is unlikely to be correct.

3. Consider the goods that extremist groups provide

As the club model predicts, extremism works because of the goods it provides. In the case of violent Islamist groups, these tend to be non-corrupt, effective and sensitive public services, and the group solidarity that many people seek. Furthermore, the sacrifices that groups demand to screen out free-riders are most likely to be of publicly provided goods.[44]

Hence an important aim for governments should be to ensure a range of goods provided by the state, non-governmental organisations and the commercial market that compete with the goods provided by extreme groups, to render the sacrifices pointless and the benefits nugatory.[45] Fostering religious competition is an important factor.[46]

4. If you smoke democratic ideals, inhale them too

The ideals of a democratic society are what good governments should stand for, whether they are socialist, social-democratic, conservative or free market liberal. Freedom of expression and tolerance for others; protection from the government and from fellow citizens; autonomy of the citizen; and the rule of law—these are the keystones of a democratic society. Sometimes they are inconvenient, but governments, and those who aspire to government, should emphasise their importance and be prepared to debate with anyone who explicitly or implicitly denies them.

If terrorists have a reasonable case, they will want to present it to the public. This is why the Internet is an important tool for extremists—they are denied the opportunity to make their point by other media. But democrats should not be shy of this—and after all, words are far less harmful than bombs. Moreover, if terrorists are embedded in democratic societies, their experience of making their case via social networks (and maybe even other tools of democracy, such as polls, focus groups and a strategy to deal with independent media) may even nudge them in a more tolerant and democratic direction, as well as supplying a battleground on which the forces of democracy are accustomed to operate.[47]

But in addition to defending them, governments and those who aspire to government should also maintain democratic ideals. If jihadis are to be persuaded to be tolerant, democrats should be even more so. The strategy of President George W. Bush, which led to the suspension of democratic protections against torture and arbitrary detention and the eclipse of civil liberties of all kinds in the face of the security operation, failed to win the war on terror, was a useful recruiting tool for radical Islamism, embarrassed the United States abroad and ceded the moral high ground while the administration was working to export democratic values to the Middle East.

As a reporter for the *Economist* magazine put it in 2006:

if much of the war against terrorism is a contest between values—in short, a PR war—America should be winning hands down. A brand that stands for life, liberty and the pursuit of happiness is an easier sell than a brand that stands for beheading unbelievers and reviving the Middle Ages. And yet America is not doing half as well as it should be. The annual Pew survey of global attitudes this week reports yet another fall in its standing almost everywhere. Why? In part, because actions speak louder than words, and America sometimes betrays its own values.[48]

It should also be noted that violent extremism is correlated with undemocratic, totalitarian dictatorships and intolerant societies. Although terrorist acts often take place in democratic societies, such attacks frequently result from the freedoms of those societies which make it easier to plan large operations. It is a fallacy to think that reducing those freedoms would reduce terrorism. It would be harder to plan an attack, but a lapsed democracy would also be more likely to foster terrorists.[49]

5. Respect nuance: do not be Manichaean

Extremist groups frame their conflict with the embedding society in apocalyptic terms. 'We fight the Great Satan.' By labelling such groups as part of an axis of evil, a democratic government is clearly accepting the extremists' analysis (though with differing views about who the enemies are). This is a dangerous option as it repels the large number of people who may be attracted to parts of the extremists' ideology. It nudges people who might be interested in some aspects of the extremists' agenda to accept and adopt all of their agenda.

Worse, if a government which has characterised the conflict as a Manichaean struggle slips below accepted standards of behaviour—as for example with American abuse of prisoners in Abu Ghraib—then it can hardly complain if others label it as the enemy, and by elimination accepts the extremists as the victims. The Manichaean view turns policing and intelligence into a zero-sum game—if you do not support us, then you must support our enemy.

Accepting the nuances of the situation—the extremists probably have a point somewhere along the line, and provide useful services for their associates—means that it will be much easier to retain the moral high ground and to restrict the core of support that the extremists receive.

6. Find consensus

Suppression of online content is always an option for governments; many types of material, such as images of child abuse, are banned in most if not all polities. Why is it hard, therefore, to suppress terrorist literature?

As Maura Conway argues, in the context of policing and censorship we can class online content into three rough categories. First, there is content where there is a global consensus about whether it should be controlled. Child abuse images fall into this category, and we can see a campaign of consensus-formation gathering momentum against so-called 'revenge porn'.[50] Second, there is material that is sensitive in particular cultures because of the values in that culture. Many international disputes are centred on such issues, such as the prohibition of sales of Nazi regalia in France, the banning of gambling in the United States and the suppression of pornography involving consenting adults in China. Third, there is politically and ideologically sensitive material. Again, there are specific measures in place in certain countries, such as Singapore.[51]

Being a democrat means respecting difference across nations. Where there is no strong consensus against a particular set of beliefs, or a particular type of action, then global action is unlikely to happen. Where democrats have demonstrably betrayed their own ideals, as often in the US war on terror, they will not be taken seriously internationally. For democrats, the moral high ground is vital for consensus-formation; betraying democratic principles, even for the purposes of security and counterterrorism, is self-defeating in the long run.

7. Do not blame the Web

It will be noted that recommendations 1–6 have little to do with the Internet or the Web. As we argued in Chapter Nine, it is a mistake to assume that the Web plays a causal role in extremism.

Yet this is a mistake that governments often make, despite the fact that they are committing themselves to a Sisyphean task of regulating or repressing a widely adopted and popular public good for no obvious purpose. The British government's musings about 'whether it would be right to stop people communicating via [social media] websites and services [specifically BlackBerry] when we know they are plotting violence, disorder and criminality'[52] in the wake of riots across the United Kingdom was perhaps intended for the sake of a good headline.[53] Certainly nothing came of it. A Chinese government crackdown on its lively microblogging scene in 2013 resulted in a decline of activity on Sina Weibo, but serious and satirical political discussion merely migrated to less public mobile messaging services such as WeChat.[54] The anti-democratic turn taken by the AK government in Turkey reached a climax in 2014 with a ban on Twitter, which it blamed for spreading reports of government corruption. It was widely flouted, not least by the Turkish president himself, and overturned by the country's courts within days.[55] But it may have served the purpose of suppressing dissent for a brief period before local elections.

This sort of policy is analogous to trying to prevent sectarian graffiti by banning brick walls; self-defeating and naïve in the extreme. Terrorists use all sorts of public goods, such as transport networks; we do not assume these goods have causal powers and try to restrict their use. We should certainly expect terrorists to use the Web, social media, email, smartphones and other such innovations as it makes sense for them to do so.

In an ideal world there would be some way to prevent terrorists from using these technologies. But this is not possible in reality. The only way to prevent terrorists using digital networked technologies is to prevent a vast number of other people from using them. This will cause a great deal of annoyance and frustration to the people in question (i.e. the false positives). If the false positives had something in common—an ethnic or religious identity, for example—so that all people of a certain type were prevented or hindered from using such technologies, then that would breed resentment against the authorities and foster the very attitudes that the ban was trying to repress.

8. Do not kill the Web

Governments may still want to regulate the Internet by an alternative route. This would involve regulating not the Internet itself or the people putting offensive or dangerous content online, but rather the private sector middlemen who furnish the infrastructure.[56] There are many such extra-state actors who have been corralled into the war on terror, however reluctantly. Internet Service Providers, which provide access to the Internet itself, are already required to monitor their users' activity and surrender the data to police or intelligence services upon request.[57] Search engines provide the most straightforward access to Web content, and they are often asked to censor their results, or they self-censor to avoid political pressure.[58] Undermining the Internet and the Web by such means should be a tactic used sparingly at best—non-state actors, especially in a commercial setting, should be required to obey the law, not police the Web.

As another example of this, Edward Snowden's revelations about industrial-scale surveillance have clearly undermined both users' trust in the Internet and governments' trust in lightweight international regulation. Knowing what everyone did over a certain period may help catch criminals and terrorists, or indeed prevent crimes. But we must balance this against the incredible intrusion into people's lives. Some may argue that this is purely an ideological point, but we can add the practical point that confidence in the Web has been undermined, and may result in diminished use of it.[59]

Tim Berners-Lee has argued that we need a Magna Carta for the Web.[60] Brazil has already imposed one in direct retaliation for US spying on President Dilma Rousseff's communications.[61] Companies are worried by this development—if many nations adopt similar measures (the

EU has mused about doing so), then they may have to cope with a bewildering variety of national laws, which will make it hard for them to provide global services.

9. Forget the needle: love your haystack

Finding terrorists is a needle-in-a-haystack problem. Surveillance is not the solution. As security expert Bruce Schneier points out, if you want to find the needle in the haystack, the last thing you need is more hay.[62] The hay, in this case, is the transactions of bona fide Internet users—VOIP calls, emails, newspaper reading, game playing, social networking, online dating, chatting, sharing.

Any kind of profiling to find a weak signal in noisy data will produce many more false positives than correct ones. Worse, the false positives might be of a particular group which could resent the attention—Muslim men, for instance. The Olympic gold medal-winning runner Mo Farah complained in an interview that 'I have to turn up to every flight early, three hours at least. I don't know what it's about, maybe I should change my name. Ever since 9/11 that name must have been on their radar.'[63] He had indeed been arrested not long before.[64]

It is precisely this kind of profiling that runs the risk of damaging relations with particular ethnic or religious groups, and which undermines trust in the government and police. Even sensitive profiling techniques inhibit our freedom.[65] In fact, policing requires trust in the police and the state, and confidence in the technology. The policing appropriate to the Internet age is closer to the intelligence-led policing of old, and the apparent gold mine of a vast quantity of data about our online activities will simply undermine relations between communities, individuals, technology providers, the police and the state. In other words, the terrorists would have succeeded in bringing chaos to their enemies.

Conclusion: saving cyberspace

The Internet, and the Web in particular, serve democracy by reducing the friction of the flow of information. That much is agreed by all sides. Yet democracy is an ambiguous concept. On the one hand, it signifies the attitudes of tolerance and inclusion that support the idea that everyone has a role to play in governance. On the other, it signifies the freedom of expression that enables everyone's voice to be heard. Let us call the first concept 'toleration' and the second 'libertarianism'. These are similar but not equivalent concepts—together they create the dilemma of whether to allow the voices of the intolerant to be heard. Extremists will often abuse the inclusion that toleration supports.

This is a familiar dilemma and we should not be surprised to find that it emerges with respect to the governance of the Internet. However, the Internet raises specific issues. It relies on the free flow of information as an engineering concept, which makes censorship, even of offensive or incorrect speech, hard. Compare the mass media, where information is filtered to the audience via a small number of professionals, such as journalists, editors, lawyers, media owners and media regulators, who act as a collective bottleneck, increasing the barriers to entry and filtering out alternative voices, both malign and benign. Any kind of centralised intervention of this kind would slow the Web down, hindering it from scaling up in volume, and ultimately causing it to grind to a halt.

It would seem to follow from these engineering considerations that the Web's contribution is to the libertarian conception of democracy. Even if it was desirable to prevent extremists from spreading propaganda and communicating between themselves, it would require fairly complex interventions. Any government is of course able to ban any type of utterance on the Web, but the onus would be on it, not the technology, to police online speech and prosecute and punish transgressors. This would be extremely difficult, especially when the content issued from another jurisdiction, but it would not be impossible. For example, two French groups concerned with anti-Semitism successfully prevented Yahoo! from selling Nazi memorabilia on its auction site in 2000 through the courts, and as a result other online auction houses such as eBay have followed suit in banning such sales. However, any such ban has to be policed automatically, leading to perverse examples where common sense seems to be thrown out of the window. In 2010, an Englishman was prevented from selling a board game of *Dad's Army* (based on a lighthearted British TV show) because it featured a swastika on the lid of the box.[66] Facebook bans images of women's nipples as part of its anti-pornography policy, which means that perfectly innocent images of breastfeeding mothers are removed, as well as a *New Yorker* cartoon featuring Adam and Eve.[67]

Attempting to ban, or curb the influence of, extremist discourse online will lead to similar dilemmas. Either a sensitive but complex editorial process will become a chokepoint and restrict everyone's access, or an automated process will end up removing perfectly sensible and liberal discussions, satirical works and spoofs.

It is also worth mentioning a third possibility, crowdsourcing censorship by getting individuals to report, screen, monitor and possibly edit extreme content. This has a number of advantages, being a relatively democratic mode of censorship which also will scale. Most sites that solicit content allow users to flag up material of concern, such as pornography or offensive language. As Morozov reminds us, the technologies that allow good people to filter the bad stuff out of the Web, and to take censorship decisions out of the hands of government, also allow bad people to filter the good stuff out of the Web, and to put censorship decisions into the hands of individuals or groups who may not be well disposed to the tolerance model of democracy. The Saudi Arabian Communications and Internet Technology Commission, for example, crowdsources suggestions for sites that should be blocked.[68] In short, crowdsourcing is a valuable tool for matters of taste and judgement (for example, in identifying pornographic content), but it may not be a useful tool to arbitrate on fundamental matters of free speech.

In Figure 1 in the Introduction we posed a number of questions about the links between radicalism, extremism and the Internet. These links seem tenuous at best. Some radicals become extremists, but relatively few. The Internet is a valuable tool for people whose views are not mainstream in the same way that cars, roads and credit cards are valuable. But such people and the organisations that represent them do not depend on the Internet, and it is a source of weakness as well as strength (for example, by facilitating surveillance and leaving records of discussions).

Our review of the literature in Part II shows that the social properties of extreme organisations, and the networks they facilitate, drive membership. The dynamics of the Church–Sect Cycle mean that extremist, or purist, elements of organisations will tend to shear off on a regular basis. Preferences, even towards violence and suicide, are primarily explained by earthly considerations, as shown in Chapters Six and Seven. Campaigns against extremism often play into extremists' hands by implicitly endorsing their black-and-white view of society, which implies that the extremist organisation is the only effective opposition to oppressive authorities.

In this context, we should also note the decline in religious authority, and the importance of the individual's views in the increase in religiosity, as noted by scholars such as Olivier Roy. Social networks, rather than religio-cultural organisations, have the greatest influence here. And from the extremists' view, mainstream political or religious authorities have very little leverage. Any sources charged with disseminating mainstream ideas into radical groups will simply lose whatever legitimacy they have, as a result of their association with authority.

In any case, extremists' ideas are less important than the structures of their networks. The online echo chambers that some worry about are sometimes detectable, sometimes not. The Internet also plays a part in breaking open such chambers, and exposing ideas to scrutiny. Furthermore, the nature of the political process in most countries (democratic or otherwise) involves engaging with a large range of heterogeneous actors with diverse preferences, and as with Todd Akin, unacceptable ideas are easily exposed as such. On rare occasions, it may well be that extremists 'engage' with the embedding society directly with acts of violence—but it is not clear how 'opening out' the Internet to make such people read opposite points of view could help, except at the cost of dramatically undermining its value for others.

For all these reasons, we must conclude that manipulating the infrastructure of the Internet itself will be counterproductive—even if extremism were reduced as a result, the costs would massively outweigh the benefits. Some interventions that leave the Internet 'untouched', such as surveillance, could still be pursued. Even then, the results may not be very useful—we do know that most ordinary users ignore worries about surveillance, but those who are concerned with hiding criminal or antisocial behaviour or communications do not find it very difficult to evade the snoopers.

Widespread and heavy-handed surveillance, such as the NSA's and the GCHQ's persistent attempts to gather information online, could become counterproductive if they start putting even 'legitimate' users off and reducing interactions online. If snoopers become more effective, extremist groups will migrate offline, just as Falun Gong did in China in the 1990s when its Internet presence was monitored by the government (it began to use the country's hard-to-trace payphone network).[69]

The hardest thing for a politician to do is 'nothing'. President F.D. Roosevelt is supposed to have told an underling 'don't just do something, stand there!' Even in the face of an outrage perpetrated by an extreme religious organisation, we should remember these lessons and resist the temptation to hobble a very valuable and liberating piece of technology for the uncertain gain of possibly reducing the potential for similar acts to occur in the future.

NOTES

INTRODUCTION

1. On the Reformation and the printing press, see, for example, Karen Armstrong, *The Case for God: What Religion Really Means*, London: The Bodley Head, 2009, pp. 168–70.
2. Cf. e.g. Christine L. Borgman, *From Gutenberg to the Global Information Infrastructure: Access to Information in the Networked World*, Cambridge, MA: MIT Press, 2000; Asa Briggs and Peter Burke, *A Social History of the Media: From Gutenberg to the Internet*, Cambridge: Polity Press, 2009; John Naughton, *From Gutenberg to Zuckerberg: What You Really Need to Know About the Internet*, London: Quercus, 2012. In 1971, Project Gutenberg, the first digital library, was founded to digitise and disseminate classic cultural texts. Gutenberg's position as a reference point had already been cemented by Marshall McLuhan, *The Gutenberg Galaxy*, Toronto: Toronto University Press, 1962.
3. Luke Harding, *The Snowden Files: The Inside Story of the World's Most Wanted Man*, London: Guardian Faber Publishing, 2014. See also Richard A. Clarke, Michael J. Morell, Geoffrey R. Stone, Cass R. Sunstein and Peter Swire, *The NSA Report: Liberty and Security in a Changing World*, Princeton, NJ: Princeton University Press, 2014; Glenn Greenwald, *No Place to Hide: Edward Snowdon, the NSA and the Surveillance State*, London: Hamish Hamilton, 2014.
4. Adam Smith, *An Inquiry into the Nature and Causes of the Wealth of Nations*, 2 vols, Indianapolis, IN: Liberty Fund, 1994. See also Gary M. Anderson, 'Mr Smith and the Preachers: The Economics of Religion in the *Wealth of Nations*', *Journal of Political Economy*, 96, 5 (1988), pp. 1066–87.
5. For instance, Eli Berman, *Radical, Religious, and Violent: The New Economics of Terrorism*, Cambridge, MA: MIT Press, 2009; Eli Berman and David

D. Laitin, 'Religion, Terrorism and Public Goods: Testing the Club Model', *Journal of Public Economics*, 92 (2008), pp. 1942–67; Robert B. Ekelund, Robert F. Hébert, Robert D. Tollison, Gary M. Anderson and Audrey B. Davidson, *Sacred Trust: The Medieval Church as an Economic Firm*, New York: Oxford University Press, 1996; Laurence Iannaccone, 'Sacrifice and Stigma: Reducing Free-Riding in Cults, Communes, and Other Collectives', *Journal of Political Economy*, 100 (1992), pp. 271–92; Laurence R. Iannaccone, 'Why Strict Churches are Strong', *American Journal of Sociology*, 99, 5 (1994), pp. 1180–211; Laurence Iannaccone, 'Risk, Rationality, and Religious Portfolios', *Economic Enquiry*, 33 (1995), pp. 285–95. Iannaccone is widely recognised as the modern originator of the religious economy and club model explanations.

6. For an example of a paper focusing on the properties of a group, see Clark McCauley, 'Group Desistance from Terrorism: The Dynamics of Actors, Actions and Outcomes', in Rik Coolsaet (ed.), *Jihadi Terrorism and the Radicalisation Challenge: European and American Experiences*, 2nd edn, Farnham: Ashgate, 2011, pp. 187–203.

7. Chris Anderson, *The Long Tail: How Endless Choice is Creating Unlimited Demand*, London: Random House, 2006.

8. Cf. e.g. Eileen Barker, 'Crossing the Boundary: New Challenges to Religious Authority and Control as a Consequence of Access to the Internet', in Morten T. Højsgaard and Margit Warburg (eds), *Religion and Cyberspace*, Abingdon: Routledge, 2005, pp. 67–85.

1. RELIGION AND THE INTERNET: SOME INITIAL CONCEPTS

1. Robert D. Putnam and David E. Campbell, *American Grace: How Religion Divides and Unites Us*, New York: Simon & Schuster, 2010, p. 161.

2. http://twitter.com/#!/lambethpalace. Sample tweet: '"Like" the Archbishop of Canterbury on Facebook for more pictures and links http://on.fb.me/kjMkfh' (25 May 2011).

3. http://twitter.com/#!/chiefrabbi. Sample tweet: 'Chief Rabbi wishes Prince William and Catherine "mazel tov" for the #royalwedding http://t.co/S8cEpJY #BBCroyalwedding #tftd' (29 Apr. 2011).

4. http://twitter.com/#!/RCWestminster. Sample tweet: 'Wow, over 1800 followers! Thanks everyone:)' (3 June 2011).

5. There are several Islamic commentators on Twitter, such as @IslamicThinking from Bradford, http://twitter.com/#!/islamicthinking, or @DailyHadiths, https://twitter.com/DailyHadiths. Twitter was used extensively during the Arab Spring, but not particularly by Islamists. Written Arabic, in which vowels are routinely omitted, is actually quite Twitter-friendly as tweets can only be 140 characters long, and is now the eighth most-used language on Twitter

with over 2 million public tweets per day ('Twtr', *The Economist*, 31 Mar. 2012).

6. https://twitter.com/Pontifex_ln. Sample tweet: 'Matrimonium incitat coniuges ut intime convivant, iugiter ament perpetuoque amorem dilatent' (8 Mar. 2014). In English, Pope Francis tweets on https://twitter.com/Pontifex

7. Lester Haines, 'Aussies Launch SMS Bible', The Register, 7 Oct. 2005, http://www.theregister.co.uk/2005/10/07/sms_bible/. The article refers to a translation of 31,173 verses produced by the Bible Society in Australia (http://www.biblesociety.com.au/), although the link to the translation has not been operative since around 2008 due to 'technical difficulties'. The developer no longer has a connection with the Society, so there are no plans to revive it (personal communication). It may be that, having been the subject of media interest, it had served its purpose.

8. Brenda E. Brasher, *Give Me That Online Religion*, New Brunswick: Rutgers University Press, 2004, p. 88.

9. http://www.google.com/trends/hottrends?q=*&sa=X&date=2011-5-19

10. For greater detail and a plethora of examples, see Gabriel Weimann, *Terror on the Internet: The New Arena, the New Challenges*, Washington, DC: United States Institute for Peace, 2006, pp. 49–145, or Michael S. O'Neil and David H. Gray, 'Islamic Terror Networks Implementation of Network Technology', *Global Security Studies*, 2, 3 (2011), pp. 41–51.

11. 'A World Wide Web of Terror', *The Economist*, 14 July 2007.

12. Brian Michael Jenkins, 'Is Al Qaeda's Internet Strategy Working?' Testimony presented before the House Homeland Security Committee, Subcommittee on Counterterrorism and Intelligence, 6 Dec. 2011, RAND Corporation, http://www.rand.org/content/dam/rand/pubs/testimonies/2011/RAND_CT371.pdf. For a rebuttal see Nur Aziemah Binte Azman, 'Al Qaeda Internet Strategy a Failure? Online Jihadists Disprove', *CTTA: Counter Terrorist Trends and Analysis*, 4, 2 (Feb. 2012), http://www.pvtr.org/pdf/CTTA/2012/CTTA-February12.pdf

13. Gabriel Weimann, 'Al Qaeda Has Sent You A Friend Request: Terrorists Using Online Social Networking', paper submitted to the Israeli Communication Association, 2011, http://www.pintrestalk.com/ddata/2175.pdf; Ethel Quayle and Max Taylor, 'Social Networking as a Nexus for Engagement and Exploitation of Young People', *Information Security Technical Report*, 16, 2 (2011), pp. 44–50.

14. Aaron Y. Zelin, 'Jihad's Social Media Trend', The Washington Institute: Policy Analysis, 5 Feb. 2013, http://www.washingtoninstitute.org/policy-analysis/view/jihads-social-media-trend

15. 'Norway Attacks: Utoya Gunman Boasted of Links to UK Far Right', *Guardian*, 23 July 2011.

16. For the psychological and social similarities between perpetrators of school shootings and suicide bombers, see Adam Lankford and Nayab Hakim, 'From Columbine to Palestine: A Comparative Analysis of Rampage Shooters in the United States and Volunteer Suicide Bombers in the Middle East', *Aggression and Violent Behavior*, 16 (2011), pp. 98–107.

17. Roger Boyes, 'The Cyber School for Killers', *The Times*, 10 Nov. 2007.

18. Weimann, 'Al Qaeda Has Sent You A Friend Request'.

19. Maura Conway and Lisa McInerney, 'Broadcast Yourself: A History and Categorisation of Terrorist Video Propaganda', Web 2.0: An International Conference, New Political Communication Unit, Royal Holloway, University of London, 17 Apr. 2008.

20. 'Woolwich Attack: The Terrorist's Rant', *Daily Telegraph*, 23 May 2013.

21. 'Lee Rigby Murder: Couple Jailed for Glorification Videos', BBC News, 14 Mar. 2014, http://www.bbc.co.uk/news/uk-england-london-26579717

22. Hugh Roberts, 'Logics of Jihadi Violence in North Africa', in Rik Coolsaet (ed.), *Jihadi Terrorism and the Radicalisation Challenge: European and American Experiences*, 2nd edn, Farnham: Ashgate, 2011, pp. 27–43, at p. 30, where he discusses the differences in kind between different types of radical Islamism.

23. e.g. Andy Bloxham and Martin Evans, 'British Tenerife Tourist Beheaded by "Prophet of God" Attacker', *Daily Telegraph*, 14 May 2011.

24. Boyes, 'The Cyber School for Killers'. Although quite why he should acquire this label as opposed to alternatives such as the 'gun killer', 'the killer who was bullied at school', 'the killer who was also an excellent student of history' or 'the SSRI-antidepressant-using killer' is not entirely clear.

25. Sam Harris, *The End of Faith: Religion, Terror and the Future of Reason*, London: Free Press, 2005, p. 18.

26. R v. Arthur Pendragon, 1997.

27. Carole M. Cusack, *Invented Religions: Imagination, Fiction and Faith*, Farnham: Ashgate, 2010.

28. Similar phenomena have occurred elsewhere—the Jedi Order would have been the second largest religion in New Zealand in its 2001 Census, except its bean counters refused to include it in the final statistical breakdown. See Alan Perrott, 'Jedi Order Lures 53,000 Disciples', *New Zealand Herald*, 31 Aug. 2002.

29. Ronald Dworkin, *Religion Without God*, London: Harvard University Press, 2013.

30. Legendary Liverpool manager Bill Shankly famously remarked 'Some people believe football is a matter of life and death, I am very disappointed with that attitude. I can assure you it is much, much more important than that.' One of his lesser-known *bons mots* was his quip to a Liverpool fan who had travelled from London, 'Well, laddie, what's it like to be in Heaven?'

31. Here our account follows that of Rodney Stark and Roger Finke, *Acts of Faith: Explaining the Human Side of Religion*, Berkeley: University of California Press, 2000.
32. J.G. Frazer, *The Golden Bough*, New York: Macmillan, 1922, p. 58, cited in Starke and Finke, *Acts of Faith*, p. 89.
33. Stark and Finke, *Acts of Faith*, p. 91. See also Dworkin, *Religion Without God*, for the distinction between the realm of 'science' (broadly speaking) and the realm of value in religion, as well as a discussion regarding the necessary link, or lack thereof, between the two.
34. Jonathan Haidt, *The Righteous Mind: Why Good People Are Divided by Politics and Religion*, London: Allen Lane, 2012, p. 248.
35. Emile Durkheim, *The Elementary Forms of Religious Life*, New York: Free Press, 1995, p. 62.
36. Putnam and Campbell, *American Grace*, pp. 281–2.
37. Richard Dawkins, *The God Delusion*, London: Bantam, 2006; Harris, *The End of Faith*; Daniel C. Dennett, *Breaking the Spell: Religion as a Natural Phenomenon*, New York: Penguin, 2006.
38. Nicholas Wade, *The Faith Instinct: How Religion Evolved and Why It Endures*, New York: Penguin, 2009, p. 15.
39. Emile Durkheim objected to this understanding of religion on the basis that Buddhism—undeniably one of the world's great religions—bucked the trend because it did not include belief in supernatural entities or beings in the way that, say, Christianity or Islam or Hinduism subscribes to belief in a deity or deities. Therefore, he concluded, such an understanding of religion as concerned with the supernatural is false. Where Durkheim erred—as is now widely understood—was in his misinterpretation of the core tenets of Buddhism (mistaking a small elitist cult for Buddhism generally) where supernatural beings are present in abundance. See Stark and Finke, *Acts of Faith*, pp. 89–90.
40. John Rawls, *Political Liberalism*, New York: Columbia University Press, 1996, p. 13.
41. Victor M. Pérez-Díaz, *The Return of Civil Society: The Emergence of Democratic Spain*, Cambridge, MA: Harvard University Press, 1993, pp. 110–11.
42. Ibid. p. 111.
43. Quoted and translated in Philipp Blom, *A Wicked Company: The Forgotten Radicalism of the European Enlightenment*, New York: Basic Books, 2010, p. 104.
44. Haidt, *The Righteous Mind*, pp. 264–7.
45. See, for example, Ronald Dworkin, *Is Democracy Possible Here? Principles for a New Political Debate*, Oxford: Princeton University Press, 2006, pp. 24–6.

46. Putnam and Campbell, *American Grace*, p. 162.

47. See Eli Berman, *Radical, Religious, and Violent: The New Economics of Terrorism*, Cambridge, MA: MIT Press, 2009; and also the papers and books cited in the Preface. While we appropriate this—not uncontroversial—model in this book, to our knowledge its application to online markets (in particular online religious markets) has not been studied before.

48. Brasher, *Give Me That Online Religion*, p. 43. See also Jay Kinney, 'Net Worth? Religion, Cyberspace and the Future', *Futures*, 27, 7 (1995), pp. 763–76, and Lorne L. Dawson, 'The Mediation of Religious Experience in Cyberspace', in Morten T. Højsgaard and Margit Warburg (eds), *Religion and Cyberspace*, Abingdon: Routledge, 2005, pp. 15–37, at pp. 18–20.

49. Putnam and Campbell, *American Grace*, pp. 463–71.

50. Ibid. p. 467. It is worth pointing out that both authors claim to be religious; these are not two sniping atheists.

51. Ibid. pp. 488–9.

52. Roberts, 'Logics of Jihadi Violence in North Africa'.

53. C.S. Lewis, *God in the Dock: Essays on Theology and Ethics*, Grand Rapids, MI: William B. Eerdmans, 1970, p. 150.

54. Michael Oakeshott, *On Human Conduct*, Oxford: Oxford University Press, 1975, pp. 83–4.

55. Montaigne, *The Complete Essays of Montaigne*, trans. Donald Frame, Stanford: Stanford University Press, 1943; Ann Hartle, *Michel de Montaigne: Accidental Philosopher*, Cambridge: Cambridge University Press, 2003, pp. 157–68.

56. Cf. Alex Pentland, *Honest Signals: How They Shape Our World*, Cambridge, MA: MIT Press, 2008; Wade, *The Faith Instinct*; and David Sloan Wilson, *Evolution for Everyone*, New York: Delacorte Press, 2007, p. 256.

57. William Irons, 'Religion as a Hard-to-Fake Sign of Commitment', in Randolph M. Nesse (ed.), *Evolution and the Capacity for Commitment*, New York: Russell Sage Foundation, 2001, pp. 292–309, at pp. 306–7.

58. It may even be argued, as does Wade in *The Faith Instinct*, that theology as we understand it today is a relatively late accretion to religious practice, and that the earliest religions, which developed alongside hunter-gatherer society, were indeed focused on practicalities. Initiation rites helped bind such groups, for example, while other rituals helped settle disputes and feuds (*The Faith Instinct*, pp. 101–2).

59. Haidt, *The Righteous Mind*, pp. 255–64, discusses theories of how religious systems support evolutionary group selection.

60. Kenneth D. Bailey, *Social Entropy Theory*, New York: State University of New York Press, 1989.

61. Barry M. Leiner, Vinton G. Cerf, David D. Clark, Robert E. Kahn, Leonard Kleinrock, Daniel C. Lynch, Jon Postel, Larry G. Roberts and Stephen

Wolff, 'Brief History of the Internet', the Internet Society, n.d., http://www.internetsociety.org/internet/what-internet/history-internet/brief-history-internet

62. Andrew Blum, *Tubes: Behind the Scenes at the Internet*, London: Viking, 2012.

63. Tim Berners-Lee, Wendy Hall, James A. Hendler, Kieron O'Hara, Nigel Shadbolt and Daniel J. Weitzner, 'A Framework for Web Science', *Foundations and Trends in Web Science*, 1, 1 (2006), pp. 1–130.

64. Nicholas Carr, *The Shallows: How the Internet is Changing the Way We Think, Read and Remember*, New York: W.W. Norton, 2010; Sherry Turkle, *Alone Together: Why We Expect More From Technology and Less From Each Other*, New York: Basic Books, 2011.

65. W. Richard Stevens, *TCP/IP Illustrated Volume 1: The Protocols*, New York: Addison-Wesley, 1994.

66. Tim Berners-Lee, *Weaving the Web: The Past, Present and Future of the World Wide Web by its Inventor*, London: Texere Publishing, 1999.

67. Search engines do, of course, and remarkable feats of engineering are required to keep their indexes up to date. But although search engines are enormously valuable resources, they are not required to keep the Web going. As it is, their indexes and caches approximate an astonishingly high proportion of the Web, but this task is becoming harder as the Web grows.

68. Tim Berners-Lee, 'Net Neutrality: This Is Serious', MIT Computer Science and Artificial Intelligence Laboratory blog, 21 June 2006, http://dig.csail.mit.edu/breadcrumbs/node/144

69. Dawn C. Nunziato, *Virtual Freedom: Net Neutrality and Free Speech in the Internet Age*, Stanford: Stanford University Press, 2009.

70. Jan Krämer, Lukas Wiewiorra and Christof Weinhardt, 'Net Neutrality: A Progress Report', *Telecommunications Policy*, 37, 9 (2013), pp. 794–813.

71. Larry Downes, 'Requiem for Failed UN Telecom Treaty: No One Mourns the WCIT', *Forbes Magazine*, 17 Dec. 2012, http://www.forbes.com/sites/larrydownes/2012/12/17/no-one-mourns-the-wcit/

72. Cf. e.g. http://eliotswasteland.tripod.com/

73. 'Sunny Skies or Stormy Weather—Monks Wrote it in their Diaries 500 Years Ago', *The Scotsman*, 17 Jan. 2011.

74. That is, no one is forbidden access by the technology of the Web itself. Certain individuals who have misused the Internet can be forbidden from using it by an injunction or antisocial behaviour order. See e.g. Chris Matyszczyk, 'Neighbor Banned From Web After Naked Man Shows Up At Woman's House', CNET, 14 Feb. 2014, http://news.cnet.com/8301–17852_3–57618908–71/neighbor-banned-from-web-after-naked-man-shows-up-at-womans-house/. All governments have powers which allow them to impose such constraints on people—but these are social or legal

constraints, not technical ones. The more open the society, the more difficult the job of enforcing such bans.

75. Kieron O'Hara, *The Enlightenment: A Beginner's Guide*, Oxford: Oneworld, 2010, pp. 207–9, and also Kieron O'Hara, *Plato and the Internet*, Duxford: Icon Books, 2004.

76. Keith Martin, *Everyday Cryptography: Fundamental Principles and Applications*, Oxford: Oxford University Press, 2012; Fred Piper and Sean Murphy, *Cryptography: A Very Short Introduction*, Oxford: Oxford University Press, 2002.

77. Nicole Perlroth, Jeff Larson and Scott Shane, 'N.S.A. Able to Foil Basic Safeguards of Privacy on Web', *New York Times*, 5 Sep. 2013, http://www.nytimes.com/2013/09/06/us/nsa-foils-much-internet-encryption.html?pagewanted=all&_r=2&

78. Antonio Regolado, 'Before Snowden, there was Huawei', *MIT Technology Review*, 18 Mar. 2014, http://www.technologyreview.com/news/525596/before-snowden-there-was-huawei/

79. Sergei Skorobogatov and Christopher Woods, 'Breakthrough Silicon Scanning Discovers Backdoor in Military Chip,' Cryptographic Hardware and Embedded Systems Workshop, Leuven, Belgium, 2012, http://www.cl.cam.ac.uk/~sps32/ches2012-backdoor.pdf

80. 'Cracked Credibility', *The Economist*, 14 Sep. 2013; Matt Blaze, 'How Worried Should We Be About the Alleged RSA–NSA Scheming?' *Wired*, 27 Dec. 2013, http://www.wired.com/opinion/2013/12/what-we-really-lost-with-the-rsa-nsa-revelations/

81. But for the record, in the opinion of the authors, it is very likely.

82. For the NSA in the 1990s, see Steven Levy, *Crypto: How the Code Rebels Beat the Government—Saving Privacy in the Digital Age*, New York: Viking Penguin, 2001. For a hint at Chinese attitudes towards the Internet, see Ying Liu, Jianping Wu, Qian Wu and Ke Xu, 'Recent Progress in the Study of the Next Generation Internet in China', *Philosophical Transactions of the Royal Society A: Mathematical, Physical and Engineering Sciences*, 371(1987) (2013), http://dx.doi.org/10.1098/rsta.2012.0387, which argues that it is important to track the sources of all data packets to help 'network operators in diagnosing and locating failures and charge users, and to prevent or trace-back malicious attacks or misbehaving hosts, etc.' The 'etc.' might also include knowing who was interested in what information, and who was broadcasting it.

83. These four axioms need to be supplemented by two more. In perfect competition, firms are supposed to have a single aim, to maximise profit, and the goods produced are absolutely homogenous, i.e. no one sells anything any different from anyone else. Clearly these axioms, which have nothing to do with information, are unaffected in their realism (or lack thereof) by the shift from offline to online transactions.

84. Michael D. Smith, 'The Impact of Shopbots on Electronic Markets', *Journal of the Academy of Marketing Science*, 30, 4 (2002), pp. 442–50.

85. Spencer Ackerman and James Ball, 'Optic Nerve: Millions of Yahoo Webcam Images Intercepted by GCHQ', *The Guardian*, 28 Feb. 2014.

86. Steven Johnson, *Future Perfect: The Case For Progress in a Networked Age*, London: Allen Lane, 2012.

87. https://www.mturk.com/mturk/welcome

88. http://www.galaxyzoo.org

89. http://www.galaxyzoo.org/#/papers lists over two dozen of them.

90. http://ushahidi.com

91. Ory Okolloh, 'Ushahidi, or "Testimony": Web 2.0 Tools for Crowdsourcing Crisis Information', *Participatory Learning and Action*, 59, 1 (2009), pp. 65–70.

92. Berners-Lee, *Weaving the Web*, p. 172, Berners-Lee's emphasis. See also James Hendler and Tim Berners-Lee, 'From Semantic Web to Social Machines: A Research Challenge for AI on the World Wide Web', *Artificial Intelligence*, 174, 2 (2010), pp. 156–61; David Robertson and Fausto Giunchiglia, 'Programming the Social Computer', *Philosophical Transactions of the Royal Society A: Mathematical Physical and Engineering Sciences*, 371(1987) (2013); Kieron O'Hara, Noshir S. Contractor, Wendy Hall, James A. Hendler and Nigel Shadbolt, 'Web Science: Understanding the Emergence of Macro-Level Features on the World Wide Web', *Foundations and Trends in Web Science*, 4, 2/3 (2013), pp. 103–267; and Paul R. Smart and Nigel R. Shadbolt, 'Social Machines', in Mehdi Khosrow-Pour (ed.), *Encyclopedia of Information Science and Technology*, Hershey PA: IGI Global, 2014.

93. There are a number of illustrative websites used in this book. Of course, a perennial risk with the dynamic Web is that sites will close down, cease to be maintained, change their addresses or change their purposes. The sites mentioned in this book were checked in 2014. Most are indicative of types of site, rather than crucial to the argument.

94. For an account of the controversy surrounding the Mosque, reported on a Channel 4 *Dispatches* documentary 'Undercover Mosque' in 2007, see the broadcasting regulator Ofcom's exoneration of the programme in Ofcom Broadcasting Bulletin, 97 (19 Nov. 2007), pp. 9–20, http://stakeholders. ofcom.org.uk/binaries/enforcement/broadcast-bulletins/obb97/issue97.pdf

95. One of the authors of this book was somewhat surprised to find a shrine devoted to a friend of his, broadcaster Aleks Krotoski. This shrine has since disappeared.

96. 'Church Leaders Launch Online Pilgrimage for Lent', *Christian Today*, 13 Feb. 2009, http://www.christiantoday.co.uk/article/church.leaders. launch.online.pilgrimage.for.lent/22518.htm

97. Oliver Krüger, 'The Internet as Distributor and Mirror of Religious and Ritual Knowledge', *Asian Journal of Social Sciences*, 32, 2 (2004), pp. 183–97.

98. For this distinction, see Anastasia Karaflogka, 'Religious Discourse and Cyberspace', *Religion*, 32 (2002), pp. 279–91, and Morten T. Højsgaard, 'Cyber-Religion: On the Cutting Edge between the Virtual and the Real', in Højsgaard and Warburg, *Religion and Cyberspace*, pp. 50–63, at 50–1.

99. M.A. Kellner, 'Losing Our Souls in Cyberspace', *Christianity Today*, Sep. 1997, pp. 54–5, and cf. Cusack, *Invented Religions*.

100. Brasher, *Give Me That Online Religion*, pp. 4–5.

101. Though Steve Jobs has been the object of cult-like devotion. Robert Zaller, 'On Worshipping Steve Jobs', *Broad Street Review*, 13 Dec. 2011, http://www.broadstreetreview.com/index.php/main/article/on_worshipping_steve_jobs/

102. Don Slater, 'Social Relationships and Identity Online and Offline', in Leah Lievrouw and Sonia Livingstone (eds), *Handbook of New Media: Social Shaping and Consequences of ICTs*, London: Sage, 2002, pp. 533–46; 'Future Identities: Changing Identities in the UK: The Next 10 Years', Government Office for Science, 2013, http://www.bis.gov.uk/assets/foresight/docs/identity/13–523-future-identities-changing-identities-report.pdf

103. At the time of writing, Lee Pashley, http://leepashley.com/, was taking bookings in the UK a year in advance. The Scott Jordan live entertainment agency listed four other acts as well as Mr Pashley, http://www.scottjordan.co.uk/categories/robbie-williams-tribute-acts.html

104. Richard Dawkins, 'Diary', *New Statesman*, 30 Jan. 2006.

105. Mohammed el-Nawawy and Sahar Khamis, *Islam Dot Com: Contemporary Islamic Discourses in Cyberspace*, New York: Palgrave Macmillan, 2009, p. 210.

106. Anthony Giddens, *The Consequences of Modernity*, Cambridge: Polity Press, 1990, p. 21.

107. El-Nawawy and Khamis, *Islam Dot Com*, pp. 67–73.

108. Eileen Barker, 'Crossing the Boundary: New Challenges to Religious Authority and Control as a Consequence of Access to the Internet', in Højsgaard and Warburg, *Religion and Cyberspace*, pp. 67–85.

109. Lorne L. Dawson and Douglas E. Cowan, 'Introduction', in Lorne L. Dawson and Douglas E. Cowan (eds), *Religion Online: Finding Faith on the Internet*, New York: Routledge, 2004, pp. 1–16, at p. 2. The quote does not include Dawson and Cowan's references. See also Dawson, 'The Mediation of Religious Experience in Cyberspace'.

110. Harris, *The End of Faith*.

111. Christopher Goffard, 'Harold Camping is at the Heart of a Mediapocalypse', *Los Angeles Times*, 21 May 2011.

112. '"Rapture": Believers Perplexed after Prediction Fails', BBC Online, 22 May 2011, http://www.bbc.co.uk/news/world-us-canada-13489641

2. THE POLARISATION OF ONLINE DEBATE

1. Will Self, 'Worldwide Web Morality', in *Two Boys*, London: English National Opera, 2011, pp. 27–30, at pp. 28, 30.
2. Jonathan Kay, *Among the Truthers: A Journey Through America's Growing Conspiracist Underground*, New York: HarperCollins, 2011, p. 239.
3. Friedrich Engels, *The Condition of the Working-Class in England in 1844*, trans. Florence Kelley Wischnewetzky, London: George Allen & Unwin, 1892 edn, pp. 45–8.
4. Jaron Lanier, *You Are Not a Gadget: A Manifesto*, London: Penguin, 2011.
5. Sherry Turkle, *Alone Together: Why We Expect More From Technology and Less From Each Other*, New York: Basic Books, 2011.
6. Ibid. pp. 8–9.
7. 'Better Than People', *The Economist*, 20 Dec. 2005.
8. Turkle, *Alone Together*, pp. 23–147.
9. Ibid. p. 4.
10. David L. Levy, *Love and Sex with Robots*, New York: HarperCollins, 2007.
11. Turkle, *Alone Together*, pp. 300–2.
12. Ibid. p. 4.
13. Ibid. p. 156.
14. Susan Sontag, *On Photography*, New York: Dell, 1978, p. 9.
15. The *locus classicus* is Alan Turing's 'Computing Machinery and Intelligence', *Mind*, 59 (1950), pp. 433–60, reprinted in many anthologies.
16. Turkle, *Alone Together*, p. 179.
17. Ibid. p. 177.
18. Ibid. p. 187.
19. Slavoj Žižek, *The Plague of Fantasies*, London: Verso, 1997, pp. 137–8. Cf. Turkle, *Alone Together*, pp. 179–86.
20. Turkle, *Alone Together*, p. 156.
21. Eileen Barker, 'Crossing the Boundary: New Challenges to Religious Authority and Control as a Consequence of Access to the Internet', in Morten T. Højsgaard and Margit Warburg (eds), *Religion and Cyberspace*, Abingdon: Routledge, 2005, pp. 67–85, at p. 69.
22. Cass Sunstein, *Republic.com*, Princeton: Princeton University Press, 2001.
23. Cass Sunstein, *Republic.com 2.0*, Princeton: Princeton University Press, 2007.
24. Lanier, *You Are Not a Gadget*, p. 62.
25. Greg Linden, Brent Smith and Jeremy York, 'Amazon.com Recommendations: Item-to-Item Collaborative Filtering', *IEEE Internet Computing*, 7, 1 (2003), pp. 76–80.

26. Ian Ayres, *Super Crunchers: How Anything Can Be Predicted*, London: John Murray, 2007.

27. Viktor Mayer-Schönberger and Kenneth Cukier, *Big Data: A Revolution That Will Transform How We Live, Work and Think*, New York: Houghton Mifflin, p. 51.

28. A term coined by Eli Pariser, *The Filter Bubble: What the Internet is Hiding From You*, London: Viking, 2011.

29. Nicholas Negroponte, *Being Digital*, London: Coronet Books, 1996.

30. Pariser, *The Filter Bubble*.

31. Boris Johnson, 'Newspapers are Worth Fighting For—Even When They're Wrong', *Daily Telegraph*, 29 Oct. 2012.

32. Sunstein, *Republic.com 2.0*, pp. 5–6.

33. Ibid. pp. 44–5.

34. Kieron O'Hara, *Aldous Huxley: A Beginner's Guide*, Oxford: Oneworld, esp. pp. 71–7.

35. Sunstein, *Republic.com 2.0*, pp. 22–9.

36. Ibid. pp. 32–7.

37. Ibid. p. 38.

38. Ibid. pp. 54–5.

39. Lada A. Adamic and Natalie Glance, 'The Political Blogosphere and the 2004 U.S. Election: Divided they Blog', 2nd Annual Workshop on the Weblogging Ecosystem: Aggregation, Analysis and Dynamics, WWW05, 2005, http://www.hpl.hp.com/research/idl/papers/politicalblogs/Adamic GlanceBlogWWW.pdf. See also Cass R. Sunstein, *Infotopia: How Many Minds Produce Knowledge*, Oxford: Oxford University Press, 2006, pp. 190–1, and Eszter Hargittai, Jason Gallo and Matthew Kane, 'Cross-Ideological Discussions among Conservative and Liberal Bloggers', *Public Choice*, 134 (2008), pp. 67–86.

40. Sunstein, *Republic.com 2.0*, p. 59.

41. Kay, *Among the Truthers*, pp. 227–59.

42. Sunstein, *Infotopia*, p. 191.

43. Thomas C. Davenport and John C. Beck, *The Attention Economy: Understanding the New Currency of Business*, Cambridge, MA: Harvard Business School Press, 2001.

44. Stuart Sim, *Fundamentalist World: The New Dark Age of Dogma*, Duxford: Icon, 2004.

45. Peter Mandaville, 'Reimagining the *Ummah*? Information Technology and the Changing Boundaries of Political Islam', in Ali Mohammadi (ed.), *Islam Encountering Globalization*, London: Routledge Curzon, 2002, pp. 61–90, at p. 70.

46. Commentators such as Roger Scruton, *The West and the Rest: Globalization and the Terrorist Threat*, London: Continuum, 2002, Olivier Roy, *Globalized*

Islam: The Search for a New Ummah, New York: Columbia University Press, 2004, Sam Harris, *The End of Faith: Religion, Terror and the Future of Reason*, London: Free Press, 2005.

47. Sunstein, *Republic.com 2.0*, pp. 60–4.

48. Ibid. pp. 64–7.

49. Ibid. p. 67.

50. A list cribbed from James Gordon Finlayson, *Habermas: A Very Short Introduction*, Oxford: Oxford University Press, 2005, p. 76.

51. Jürgen Habermas, *The Structural Transformation of the Public Sphere*, trans. Thomas Burger and Frederick Lawrence, Cambridge: Polity Press, 1989.

52. Even though Habermas's account is biased toward its roots in the European Enlightenment, Mohammed el-Nawawy and Sahar Khamis find that his notion of the public sphere is potentially applicable to online Islamic discourse as well. See their *Islam Dot Com: Contemporary Islamic Discourses in Cyberspace*, New York: Palgrave Macmillan, 2009, pp. 23–54. They ultimately reject its applicability; we discuss this judgement in Chapter Ten.

53. Jürgen Habermas, *Between Naturalism and Religion*, trans. Ciaran Cronin, Cambridge: Polity Press, 2008, p. 50.

54. Cass R. Sunstein, 'Neither Hayek nor Habermas', *Public Choice*, 134 (2008), pp. 87–95, at p. 87. See also Sunstein, *Infotopia*, pp. 147–96.

55. Sunstein, 'Neither Hayek nor Habermas', p. 94.

56. Matthew Hindman, *The Myth of Digital Democracy*, Princeton: Princeton University Press, 2009, at p. 128.

57. Ibid. pp. 38–57.

58. El-Nawawy and Khamis, *Islam Dot Com*, p. 127. They also argue, reasonably, that the Habermasian requirements are too idealistic to apply in detail to the forums they study (ibid. p. 211), but it is surely true that if we succumb to the temptation to be purist about Habermasian doctrine, then there will be no public sphere anywhere. Much better to consider the extent to which real forums approach the Habermasian ideal.

59. Gary Bunt, *iMuslims: Rewiring the House of Islam*, London: Hurst, 2009, at p. 133.

60. Sunstein, *Republic.com 2.0*, p. 150.

61. Sunstein, *Infotopia*, p. 186.

62. See, for instance, James Surowiecki, *The Wisdom of Crowds: Why the Many Are Smarter than the Few*, London: Little, Brown, 2004; Don Tapscott and Anthony D. Williams, *Wikinomics: How Mass Collaboration Changes Everything*, London: Atlantic Books, 2007; and Charles Leadbeater, *We-Think: Mass Innovation, Not Mass Production*, London: Profile Books, 2008.

63. Leadbeater, *We-Think*, p. 33. With tongue somewhat in cheek, we might point out that Leadbeater's thesis about collaboration would be more con-

vincing if, in his book (which was produced in collaboration with 257 other people according to the title page), he had not spelt the names of Mark Zuckerberg (p. 35) and danah boyd (pp. 213–14) wrong.

64. Chris J. Lintott, Kevin Schawinski, Anže Slosar, Kate Land, Steven Bamford, Daniel Thomas, M. Jordan Raddick, Robert C. Nichol, Alex Szalay, Dan Andreescu, Phil Murray and Jan Vandenberg, 'Galaxy Zoo: Morphologies Derived from Visual Inspection of Galaxies from the Sloan Digital Sky Survey', *Monthly Notices of the Royal Astronomical Society*, 389, 3 (2008), pp. 1179–89.

65. Ory Okolloh, 'Ushahidi, or "Testimony": Web 2.0 Tools for Crowdsourcing Crisis Information', *Participatory Learning and Action*, 59, 1 (2009), pp. 65–70.

66. Nathan Morrow, Nancy Mock, Adam Papendieck and Nicholas Kocmich, 'Independent Evaluation of the Ushahidi Haiti Project', Development Information Systems International, 2011, http://ggs684.pbworks.com/w/file/fetch/60819963/1282.pdf

67. Even if ultimately the hype began to take over. In 2006, the *Time* magazine person of the year was 'You—Yes, You!' (http://www.time.com/time/magazine/article/0,9171,1570810,00.html).

68. According, naturally, to http://en.wikipedia.org/wiki/Wikipedia_community when accessed in 2014.

69. See Sunstein, *Infotopia*, pp. 148–64, for a summary and discussion of wikis.

70. See Bunt, *iMuslims*, p. 136, regarding this feature of the Islamic blogosphere.

71. Leadbeater, *We-Think*, p. 86.

72. Ibid. p. 68.

73. Sunstein, *Republic.com 2.0*, p. 192.

74. Ibid. pp. 193–5.

75. Ibid. pp. 202–4.

76. Ibid. p. 12.

77. John Perry Barlow, 'A Declaration of the Independence of Cyberspace', Electronic Frontier Foundation, 1996, https://projects.eff.org/~barlow/Declaration-Final.html

78. Sunstein, *Republic.com 2.0*, 160–2.

79. We argued this point against Sunstein's first edition of *Republic.com* in Kieron O'Hara and David Stevens, *Inequality.com: Power, Poverty and the Digital Divide*, Oxford: Oneworld, 2006, pp. 181–9, and Kieron O'Hara, 'The Internet: A Tool for Democratic Pluralism?' *Science and Culture*, 11, 2 (2002), pp. 287–98. We also revisit it in Chapter Ten.

80. Robert Nozick, 'The Characteristic Features of Extremism', in *Socratic Puzzles*, Cambridge, MA: Harvard University Press, 1997, pp. 296–9.

81. Karen Mossberger, Caroline J. Tolbert and Ramona S. McNeal, *Digital*

Citizenship: The Internet, Society and Participation, Cambridge, MA: MIT Press, 2008, p. 77.

82. Sarah Kliff, 'Rep. Todd Akin is Wrong About Rape and Pregnancy But He's Not Alone', *Washington Post* blog, 20 Aug. 2012, http://www.washington-post.com/blogs/wonkblog/wp/2012/08/20/rep-todd-akin-is-wrong-about-rape-and-pregnancy-but-hes-not-alone/

83. Barker, 'Crossing the Boundary', p. 74.

84. Gordon W. Allport, *The Nature of Prejudice*, Cambridge, MA: Perseus Books, 1979.

3. INTERVENTIONIST POLICY STRATEGIES

1. John Horgan and Max Taylor, 'Disengagement, De-Radicalization and the Arc of Terrorism: Future Directions for Research', in Rik Coolsaet (ed.), *Jihadi Terrorism and the Radicalisation Challenge: European and American Experiences*, 2nd edn, Farnham: Ashgate, 2011, pp. 173–86, esp. p. 186.

2. Rik Coolsaet, 'Counterterrorism and Counter-Radicalisation in Europe: How Much Unity in Diversity?' in Coolsaet, *Jihadi Terrorism and the Radicalisation Challenge*, pp. 227–46, at p. 228.

3. Ibid. pp. 230–1.

4. A later amended version can be found in 'CONTEST: The United Kingdom's Strategy for Countering Terrorism', London: National Archives, 2011, https://www.gov.uk/government/uploads/system/uploads/attachment_data/file/97994/contest-summary.pdf

5. Coolsaet, 'Counterterrorism and Counter-Radicalisation in Europe', p. 238.

6. There is a significant degree of terminological slippage in the Prevent language and discussions of it, and in much of the 'radicalisation' literature. In particular, the boundaries and differences between 'radical' and 'extremist' or 'violent extremist' tend to shift. Throughout, we are at pains to stress the distinctness of these phenomena, such as they exist. Radical thoughts and positions—religious or otherwise—are a natural part of a decent, well-ordered society and often play an important social function. Violent extremism—though it may depend upon radical ideas—is not the inevitable outcome of radicalism, as argued on the basis of a study of North African groups in Hugh Roberts, 'Logics of Jihadi Violence in North Africa', in Coolsaet, *Jihadi Terrorism and the Radicalisation Challenge*, pp. 27–43, at p. 30. Seeking to prevent radicalism as a method of preventing violent extremism is, we argue, both impossible and misguided. We elaborate on this in Part II, and especially Chapter Seven.

7. Cabinet Office, 'The National Security of the United Kingdom: Security in an Interdependent World', London: HMSO, 2008, §4.8, also §§4.4 and 4.9.

8. In an interview on *BBC Breakfast*, 16 Apr. 2008.
9. See Y. Haddad and M. Balz, 'Taming the Imams: European Governments and Islamic Preachers since 9/11', *Islam and Christian–Muslim Relations*, 19, 2 (2008), pp. 215–35; and Y. Haddad and T. Golson, 'Overhauling Islam: Representation, Construction, and Co-Option of "Moderate Islam" in Western Europe', *Journal of Church and State*, 49, 3 (2007), pp. 487–516.
10. Cabinet Office, 'The National Security of the United Kingdom'.
11. www.radicalmiddleway.co.uk.
12. 'Blair in Moderate Muslims Appeal', BBC News, 4 June 2007, http://news.bbc.co.uk/1/hi/uk_politics/6718235.stm
13. Paul Thomas, 'Failed and Friendless: The UK's "Preventing Violent Extremism" Programme', *British Journal of Politics and International Relations*, 12, 3 (2010), pp. 442–58, at p. 444.
14. Department for Communities and Local Government, 'Preventing Violent Extremism: Winning Hearts and Minds', London: DCLG, 2007.
15. F. Reeves, T. Abbas and D. Pedroso, 'The "Dudley Mosque Project": A Case of Islamophobia and Local Politics', *The Political Quarterly*, 80 (2009), pp. 502–16.
16. www.quilliamfoundation.org/images/stories/pdfs/us-senate-submission-09–2008.pdf; www.quilliamfoundations.org/images/stories/pdfs/pulling-together-to-defeat-terrorism.pdf
17. Douglas Murray, 'The Prevent Strategy: A Textbook Example of How to Alienate Just About Everybody', *The Daily Telegraph*, Mar. 2010. Quoted in The International Centre for the Study of Radicalisation and Political Violence (ICSR), 'Countering Radicalization in Europe', London: Kings College, 2010, p. 14.
18. 'Polarisation and Radicalisation Action Plan 2007–2011', Ministry of the Interior and Kingdom Relations, 2006.
19. ICSR, 'Countering Radicalization in Europe', p. 30.
20. 'National Counterterrorism Strategy 2011–2015', June 2011, p. 71. Quoted in ICSR, 'Countering Radicalisation in Europe', pp. 30–1.
21. ICSR, 'Countering Radicalization in Europe', p. 47.
22. See 'Terrorists to be De-Radicalised in NSW Supermax', ABC News, 25 Feb. 2010, http://www.abc.net.au/news/2010–02–25/terrorists-to-be-de-radicalised-in-nsw-supermax/342376, and Sam Mullins, 'Australian Jihad: Radicalisation and Counter-Terrorism (ARI)', Real Instituto Elcano, http://www.realinstitutoelcano.org/wps/wcm/connect/0dff410048b9dec58ad1b
a9437ec6e7e/ARI140–2011_Mullins_Australian_Jihad_Radicalisation_
Counter-Terrorism.pdf?MOD=AJPERES&CACHEID=0dff410048b9de
c58ad1ba9437ec6e7e
23. Coolsaet, 'Counterterrorism and Counter-Radicalisation in Europe', p. 230.
24. Samuel Rascoff, 'Establishing Official Islam? The Law and Strategy of Counter-Radicalization', *Stanford Law Review*, 64 (Jan. 2012), pp. 153–4.

25. Ibid. p. 154.
26. Ibid. p. 160.
27. Center for Security Policy, 'Shariah, the Threat to America: An Exercise in Competitive Analysis—Report of Team "B" II', Washington, DC: Center for Security Policy, 2010, http://www.centerforsecuritypolicy.org/upload/wysiwyg/article%20pdfs/Shariah%20-%20The%20Threat%20to%20America%20(Team%20B%20Report)%2009142010.pdf
28. Lorenzo Vidino, 'Counter-Radicalization in the United States', in Coolsaet, *Jihadi Terrorism and the Radicalisation Challenge*, pp. 247–58.
29. Jon Cole and Benjamin Cole, *Martyrdom: Radicalisation and Terrorist Violence among British Muslims*, London: Pennant Books, 2009, p. 269.
30. Bipartisan Policy Center, 'Countering Online Radicalization in America', p. 34.
31. http://www.newamerica.org/
32. Reported in Bipartisan Policy Centre, 'Countering Online Radicalization in America', p. 34.
33. A point often overlooked in the focus on the dangers of modern terrorist, but emphasised in Bryan Caplan, 'Terrorism: The Relevance of the Rational Choice Model', *Public Choice*, 128 (2006), pp. 91–107, at p. 97.
34. See Tim Stevens and Peter R. Neumann, *Countering Online Radicalisation: A Strategy for Action*, London: ICSR, King's College, 2011, pp. 43–5.
35. Bipartisan Policy Centre, 'Countering Online Radicalization in America', p. 35. Footnotes omitted. The idea of a 'grass-roots fund' for counter-radicalisation messages is also prominent in Stevens and Neumann, *Countering Online Radicalisation*, Chapter Seven.
36. Coolsaet, 'Counterterrorism and Counter-Radicalisation in Europe', pp. 232–4.
37. Robert Lambert, formerly of the Muslim Contact Unit at Scotland Yard, argues that these have been important propaganda gifts for al-Qaeda. Robert Lambert, 'Competing Counter-Radicalisation Models in the UK', in Coolsaet, *Jihadi Terrorism and the Radicalisation Challenge*, pp. 215–25, at p. 221.
38. Coolsaet, 'Counterterrorism and Counter-Radicalisation in Europe', p. 240.
39. Paul Thomas, 'Between Two Stools? The Government's "Preventing Violent Extremism" Agenda', *The Political Quarterly*, 80, 2 (2009), pp. 282–91; and Thomas, 'Failed and Friendless'.
40. Thomas, 'Failed and Friendless', pp. 445–6.
41. Lee Jarvis and Michael Lister, 'Disconnected Citizenship? The Impacts of Anti-Terrorism Policy on Citizenship in the UK', *Political Studies*, 61 (2013), pp. 656–75.
42. Ibid. p. 668.
43. Ibid. p. 670.

44. Lambert, 'Competing Counter-Radicalisation Models in the UK', p. 224.
45. Yahya Birt, 'Promoting Virulent Envy: Reconsidering the UK's Terrorist Prevention Strategy', *Royal United Services Institute (RUSI) Journal*, 154, 4 (2009), pp. 52–8.
46. See also Lambert, 'Competing Counter-Radicalisation Models in the UK'.
47. Birt, 'Promoting Virulent Envy'.
48. Olivier Roy, 'Islamic Terrorist Radicalisation in Europe', in S. Amghhar, A. Boubekeur and M. Emerson (eds), *European Islam—Challenges for Society and Public Policy*, Brussels: Centre for European Policy Studies, 2007, at p. 53.
49. Ibid. As Roy also points out, the geographically based community mismatch can be pushed further. Those who volunteer for jihad rarely return to the country of their forebears to fight. Even those British Pakistanis who returned to Pakistan did not fight against the regime of Musharraf, but joined the 'global terrorist hub' based there and went on to fight in the peripheral jihads of Afghanistan, Bosnia and Chechnya.
50. See Robert A. Pape, 'The Strategic Logic of Suicide Terrorism', *American Political Science Review*, 97, 3 (2003), pp. 343–61, at p. 344.
51. Roy, 'Islamic Terrorist Radicalisation in Europe', p. 55. See also Alan B. Krueger, 'What Makes a Homegrown Terrorist? Human Capital and Participation in Domestic Islamic Terrorist Groups in the USA', *Economic Letters*, 101 (2008), pp. 293–6, for similar conclusions on the case of homegrown terrorism in the United States.
52. Diego Gambetta, 'Epilogue to the Paperback Edition', in Diego Gambetta (ed.), *Making Sense of Suicide Missions*, Oxford: Oxford University Press, 2005, pp. 301–33, at p. 317.
53. Roy, 'Islamic Terrorist Radicalisation in Europe', p. 55. See also Olivier Roy, 'Al-Qaeda: A True Global Movement', in Coolsaet, *Jihadi Terrorism and the Radicalisation Challenge*, pp. 19–25, at p. 23.
54. Cole and Cole, *Martyrdom*, p. 146.
55. Vidino, 'Counter-Radicalization in the United States', p. 258.
56. A relatively recent and much-publicised example of the former sort was seen in the case of the reaction to the publication of *The Satanic Verses* in the UK in the 1990s. The episode raised questions of free speech, but these overlapped with complaints about the state's protection of religion. A serious criticism was that the British state was premised upon a commitment to the superiority of the Christian (specifically Anglican) faith. This was evidenced in its willingness to protect Christian beliefs from ridicule, and Christians from offence, via the law of blasphemy, which had been used successfully as recently as 1979 in the case of *R v. Lemon*, but which was not extended (when requested) to Islam.
57. For recent views and debate on the criteria and importance of the legiti-

macy condition in liberal thought, see, for example, John Rawls, *Political Liberalism*, New York: Columbia University Press, 1993; Brian Barry, *Justice as Impartiality*, Oxford: Oxford University Press, 2001.

58. Theresa May, 'Foreword', in 'Secretary of State for the Home Office, Prevent Strategy', June 2011, Lambert, 'Competing Counter-Radicalisation Models in the UK'.

59. Prevent Strategy, June 2011. Quoted in Rascoff, 'Establishing Official Islam?' p. 125.

4. RELIGION AS A MARKETPLACE

1. Of course, in Romney's second bid in 2012 he gained the Republican nomination, and came a very close second in the popular vote (though he failed to appeal to non-whites or females). At the time of writing, academic analysis of the results has not yet reached a settled consensus; however, it is a plausible hypothesis that Romney himself was an acceptable candidate to many voters (his poll figures surged after his first debate with President Obama), but was held back by a dysfunctional Republican Party.

2. This was not actually true, as a number of the other candidates only had one wife too. The joke was a primarily a dig at much-married Rudy Giuliani.

3. Lydia Saad, 'Percentage Unwilling to Vote for a Mormon Holds Steady', 11 Dec. 2007, http://www.gallup.com/poll/103150/Percentage-Unwilling-Vote-Mormon-Holds-Steady.aspx. The figures, according to Robert D. Putnam and David E. Campbell, *American Grace: How Religion Divides and Unites Us*, New York: Simon & Schuster, 2010, pp. 501–2, were more or less similar to those pertaining to people who were unwilling to vote for a Catholic in 1960, the year of John F. Kennedy's election, or who were unwilling to vote for a Mormon in 1967 when George Romney made his bid.

4. Official figures from the Church of Jesus Christ of Latter Day Saints.

5. That said, surveys by Putnam and Campbell, *American Grace*, pp. 507–9, 511, show that Mormons are still relatively unpopular compared to Christian groups in the United States, though more popular than Muslims or Buddhists.

6. Admittedly, Smith also believed in 'continuous revelation', the idea that God will constantly drip-feed revelation to the leaders of the Church of Jesus Christ of Latter Day Saints. This notion has served the Mormons well in their journey from exclusion to ultra-respectability, and for example justified changes in beliefs about polygamy and race. Yet this idea is a meta-level construct; if we want to see who today shares Smith's actual beliefs about society and conduct, it is hard to argue that the fundamentalists are not more in tune with the Church's founder. And, of course, Rulon Allred, Joel LeBaron, Ervil LeBaron and others such as Warren Jeffs all thought they had been in receipt of new revelations as well.

7. Christianity has undergone a similar set of transformations from a small transgressive cult to a giant global religion, has split on theological lines, has sponsored extraordinary violence and has never been able to rid itself of a vocal fundamentalist minority that treats the letter of theology as more important than the welfare of humankind or individual people. The development of Mormonism happens to be a short story of less than two centuries, but violence, extremism and cultism is rife in Christianity, Islam, Hinduism, Buddhism and so on and so on. On the rise and progress of Christianity along these lines see Rodney Stark, *The Rise of Christianity: How the Obscure, Marginal Jesus Movement became the Dominant Religious Force in the Western World in a Few Centuries*, San Francisco: HarperSanFrancisco, 1997; Rodney Stark, *The Triumph of Christianity: How the Jesus Movement became the World's Largest Religion*, New York: HarperOne, 2011.

8. Excerpted in Isaac Kramnick (ed.), *The Portable Enlightenment Reader*, New York: Penguin, 1995, pp. 90–6, at p. 94.

9. Quoted in Adam Smith, *An Enquiry into the Nature and Causes of the Wealth of Nations*, 2 vols, Indianapolis, IN: Liberty Fund, 1994, p. 377.

10. Rodney Stark, Laurence Iannaccone and Roger Finke, 'Rationality and the "Religious Mind"', *Economic Enquiry*, 36, 3 (2007), pp. 373–89.

11. Victor M. Pérez-Díaz, *The Return of Civil Society: The Emergence of Democratic Spain*, Cambridge, MA: Harvard University Press, 1993, p. 111.

12. Ronald Dworkin, *Religion Without God*, London: Harvard University Press, 2013, at p. 23.

13. Karen Armstrong, *The Case for God*, London: The Bodley Head, 2009, p. 279.

14. Israel Finkelstein and Neil Asher Silberman, *The Bible Unearthed*, New York: Simon & Schuster, 2001.

15. Jonathan Haidt, *The Righteous Mind: Why Good People Are Divided by Politics and Religion*, London: Allen Lane, 2012, pp. 246–73.

16. Cf. Putnam and Campbell, *American Grace*, p. 472.

17. A statistic that is initially surprising, though less so when one considers the advantages of belonging and social networking, is that almost 5 per cent of Americans who attend church once a month or more are not sure they believe in God. Ibid. p. 473.

18. Roger Scruton, *The West and the Rest: Globalization and the Terrorist Threat*, London: Continuum, 2002, p. 69.

19. A point emphasised by Emile Durkheim, *The Elementary Forms of the Religious Life*, Oxford: Oxford University Press, 2001, and also a central part of the functionalist thesis from genetic theory that drives Nicholas Wade, *The Faith Instinct: How Religion Evolved and Why It Endures*, New York: Penguin, 2009.

20. Maybe not just extremists. Putnam and Campbell found that religious

Americans, though not as a whole intolerant, are significantly less tolerant of dissent and less supportive of civil liberties than their secular fellow citizens. Putnam and Campbell, *American Grace*, pp. 479–89.

21. Those who describe a social capital view of trust often appear to argue that trust should simply be increased. Cf. Francis Fukuyama, *Trust: The Social Virtues and the Creation of Prosperity*, New York: Basic Books, 1995, or Robert D. Putnam, *Bowling Alone: The Collapse and Revival of American Community*, New York: Simon & Schuster, 2000.

22. Martin Hollis, *Trust Within Reason*, Cambridge: Cambridge University Press, 1998, is in this vein.

23. Cf. Kieron O'Hara, 'A General Definition of Trust', Southampton: University of Southampton, http://eprints.soton.ac.uk/341800/, or Russell Hardin, 'Trustworthiness', *Ethics*, 107 (1996), pp. 26–42.

24. For a much more detailed treatment, see O'Hara, 'A General Definition of Trust'.

25. Ibid.

26. Paul Seabright, *The Company of Strangers: A Natural History of Economic Life*, Princeton: Princeton University Press, 2004, and Alexander Pentland, *Honest Signals: How They Shape Our World*, Cambridge, MA: MIT Press, 2008.

27. Haidt, *The Righteous Mind*.

28. Russell Hardin, *Trust*, Cambridge: Polity Press, 2006, p. 122.

29. Putnam and Campbell, *American Grace*, p. 468.

30. Russell Hardin, 'The Crippled Epistemology of Extremism', in Albert Breton, Gianluigi Galeotti, Pierre Salmon and Ronald Wintrobe (eds), *Political Extremism and Rationality*, Cambridge: Cambridge University Press, 2002, pp. 3–22.

31. See Hardin, *Trust*, and Annette C. Baier, 'Trust and Antitrust', in *Moral Prejudices: Essays on Ethics*, Cambridge, MA: Harvard University Press, 1994, pp. 95–129 for more on this.

32. Smith, *The Wealth of Nations*, p. 380.

33. Ibid. pp. 380–1.

34. Note that our argument is about the religious marketplace and its effect on extremism, not the different idea that a pluralistic religious marketplace will tend to produce highly religious societies. The latter, advanced by Roger Finke and Rodney Stark, *The Churching of America 1776–2005: Winners and Losers in Our Religious Economy*, London: Rutgers University Press, 2006, is countered by Pippa Norris and Ronald Inglehart, *Sacred and Secular*, Cambridge: Cambridge University Press, 2004, who argue that highly religious societies are inversely correlated with the level of security that people in those societies feel. It is important to note that we are not commenting on the latter dispute.

35. Smith, *The Wealth of Nations*, p. 377.

36. Gary Bunt, 'The Islamic Internet Souq', Q-News, 2000, p. 325, no longer extant online, but quoted in Mohammed el-Nawawy and Sahar Khamis, *Islam Dot Com: Contemporary Islamic Discourses in Cyberspace*, New York: Palgrave Macmillan, 2009, p. 2.

37. Gary Bunt, *iMuslims: Rewiring the House of Islam*, London: Hurst, 2009, pp. 178–82.

38. Robert Graves, *Claudius the God*, Harmondsworth: Penguin, 1943, p. 292.

39. Mark Chaves, *Congregations in America*, Cambridge, MA: Harvard University Press, 2004.

40. Putnam and Campbell, *American Grace*, pp. 136–7.

41. Ibid. p. 148.

42. And as a matter of fact, in the United States at least, religious competition is less divisive than political competition, in that people have lower opinions of those with different political convictions than those with different religious convictions. Ibid. pp. 509–10.

43. Harold Hotelling, 'Stability in Competition', *Economic Journal*, 39 (1929), p. 54.

44. 'A Traditionalist Avant-Garde', *The Economist*, 15 Dec. 2012.

45. Putnam and Campbell, *American Grace*, pp. 519–26, 550.

46. Finke and Stark, *The Churching of America*, p. 23.

47. See David B. Barrett, *World Christian Encyclopaedia: Comparative Survey of Churches and Religions in the Modern World*, Oxford: Oxford University Press, 1982. This figure is even more pronounced when it is taken into account that Barrett does not distinguish between the many different sects within the Catholic Church, but treats them all as one single Church for the purpose of aggregation.

48. Massimo Introvigne, 'Niches in the Islamic Religious Market and Fundamentalism: Examples from Turkey and Other Countries', *Interdisciplinary Journal of Research on Religion*, 1, 1 (2005), pp. 13–16.

49. Smith, *The Wealth of Nations*, 2, V,i,g,12, p. 795. Footnote omitted.

50. Smith, *The Wealth of Nations*, 2, V.i.g.12, pp. 795–6.

51. Adam Smith, *The Theory of Moral Sentiments*, Indianapolis: Liberty Fund, 1984, III.i.5., p. 112.

52. Benjamin Grant Purzycki and Richard Sosis, 'The Religious System as Adaptive: Cognitive Flexibility, Public Displays and Acceptance', in Eckart Voland and Wulf Shiefenhövel (eds), *The Biological Evolution of Religious Mind and Behavior*, New York: Springer, 2009, pp. 243–56.

53. See Rodney Stark, *America's Blessings: How Religion Benefits Everyone, Including Atheists*, West Conshohocken, PA: Templeton Press, 2012, for the claim that the benefits of religious beliefs to religious adherents along a number of dimensions—mental health, marital and sexual happiness, less

criminal behaviour—also benefit wider society in terms of knock-on consequences.

54. Azim F. Shariff and Ara Norenzayan, 'God is Watching You: Priming God Concepts Increases Prosocial Behavior in an Anonymous Economic Game', *Psychological Science*, 18, 9 (2007), pp. 803–9.

55. James Dow, 'Is Religion an Evolutionary Adaptation?' *Journal of Artificial Societies and Social Simulation*, 11, 2 (2008), http://jasss.soc.surrey.ac.uk/11/2/2.html

56. See Nancy L. Rosenblum, *Membership and Morals: The Personal Uses of Pluralism in America*, Princeton: Princeton University Press, 2000.

57. Thus Smith writes: 'In free countries, where the safety of government depends very much upon the favourable judgement which the people may form of its conduct, it must surely be of the highest importance that they should not be disposed to judge rashly or capriciously of it.' (*The Wealth of Nations*, 2, V.i.f.61, p. 788).

58. Finke and Stark, *The Churching of America*.

59. Gary M. Anderson, 'Mr Smith and the Preachers: The Economics of Religion in the *Wealth of Nations*', *Journal of Political Economy*, 96, 5 (1988), pp. 1066–87.

60. See Finke and Stark, *The Churching of America*; Laurence Iannaccone, 'The Consequences of Religious Market Structure', *Rationality and Society*, 3, 2 (1991), pp. 156–77.

61. Chaves, *Congregations of America*.

62. Scruton, *The West and the Rest*, p. 59.

63. Eileen Barker, 'Crossing the Boundary: New Challenges to Religious Authority and Control as a Consequence of Access to the Internet', in Morten T. Højsgaard and Margit Warburg (eds), *Religion and Cyberspace*, Abingdon: Routledge, 2005, pp. 67–85, at p. 68.

64. Putnam and Campbell, *American Grace*, pp. 542–7.

65. Ibid. p. 145.

66. Sextus Empiricus, *Outlines of Scepticism*, ed. Julia Annas and Jonathan Barnes, Cambridge: Cambridge University Press, 2000, I.23–4 (p. 9).

67. Putnam and Campbell, *American Grace*, p. 174.

68. Ibid. p. 389.

69. Gabriel A. Almond, R. Scott Appleby and Emmanuel Sivan, *Strong Religion: The Rise of Fundamentalisms around the World*, Chicago: University of Chicago Press, 2003, pp. 185–7.

70. Laurence R. Iannaccone, 'Why Strict Churches are Strong', *American Journal of Sociology*, 99, 5 (1994), pp. 1180–211, at p. 1192; Stark and Finke, *The Churching of America*, p. 142.

71. Benton Johnson, 'On Church and Sect', *American Sociological Review*, 28 (1963), pp. 539–49, at p. 544.

72. Charles Leadbeater, *We-Think: Mass Innovation, Not Mass Production*, London: Profile Books, 2008, pp. 68–75.

73. Understandably Howell changed his name; the likelihood of anyone following a Messiah named Vernon is slim. His choice of name reflected his own understanding of his God-given role on earth. David signified his antitype role as King David—the future temporal king of the new Jerusalem; Koresh—a Hebrew translation of 'Branch'—the name attributed to Jesus Christ on his second coming, the spiritual ruler of God's coming kingdom on earth. Howell was both David and Christ—temporal and spiritual king of God's coming kingdom.

74. See Wade, *The Faith Instinct*, p. 147, where it is argued that '[r]eligions are composite cultural creations in that they generally consist of a core of beliefs or rituals derived from a preceding religion, combined with new material'. He argues that no religion can be entirely 'new' because of the way they are learned in the adherent's formative years. Even if Wade's theory of a genetic aetiology is unconvincing, the outcome he is trying to explain is commonly observed.

75. See Jon Cole and Benjamin Cole, *Martyrdom: Radicalisation and Terrorist Violence among British Muslims*, London: Pennant Books, 2009, pp. 152–3, for discussion of the Saviour Sect (or Saved Sect) and Al-Gurabaa, including their use of the Internet to attack mainstream British values.

76. Hugh Roberts, 'Logics of Jihadi Violence in North Africa', in Rik Coolsaet (ed.), *Jihadi Terrorism and the Radicalisation Challenge: European and American Experiences*, 2nd edn, Farnham: Ashgate, 2011, pp. 27–43, at pp. 37–43; Clark McCauley, 'Group Desistence from Terrorism: The Dynamics of Actors, Actions and Outcomes', in Coolsaet, *Jihadi Terrorism and the Radicalisation Challenge*, pp. 187–203, at p. 191.

77. As a variant on this dynamic, sometimes groups continue with only their opposition to mainstream society holding them together, as criminal organisations devoid of serious ideological content, but retaining the slogans of resistance together with the protection rackets and drug-dealing that financed them during a more committed phase, as for example with the FARC in Columbia, some paramilitary groups in Northern Ireland, and arguably some of the groups in North Africa. See Roberts, 'Logics of Jihadi Violence in North Africa', p. 43. No doubt the borderline between a committed group pursuing political ends and financing them by criminal means, and a criminal gang, is extremely nuanced and hard to draw.

78. Quintan Wiktorowicz, *Radical Islam Rising: Muslim Extremism in the West*, Oxford: Rowan & Littlefield, 2005, p. 57.

79. See also Wade, *The Faith Instinct*, pp. 58–62 for more on this from the point of evolutionary psychology.

80. Cf. Putnam and Campbell, *American Grace*, p. 282, where they talk of African Americans 'seeking solace' in the biblical stories of the exile.

81. Olivier Roy, *Globalized Islam: The Search for a New Ummah*, New York: Columbia University Press, 2004.

82. Iannaccone, 'The Consequences of Religious Market Structure', p. 160.

83. Gordon Tullock, 'The Welfare Costs of Tariffs, Monopolies, and Theft', *Western Economic Journal*, 5, 3 (1967), pp. 224–32, at p. 231.

84. Finke and Stark, *The Churching of America*, pp. 72–87.

85. Rodney Stark and Laurence R. Iannaccone, 'A Supply-Side Reinterpretation of the "Secularization" of Europe', *Journal for the Scientific Study of Religion*, 33, 3 (1994), pp. 230–52. See also Steve Bruce, *Choice and Religion: A Critique of Rational Choice Theory*, Oxford: Oxford University Press, 1999, pp. 90–2; Iannaccone, 'The Consequences of Religious Market Structure', pp. 164–5; Barrett, *World Christian Encyclopedia*. The figures in this and the following paragraph are drawn from these pieces.

86. Introvigne, 'Niches in the Islamic Religious Market and Fundamentalism', pp. 6–7.

87. Ibid. p. 6.

88. Mark Chaves, Peter J. Schraeder and Mario Sprindys, 'State Regulation of Religion and Muslim Religious Vitality in the Industrial West', *The Journal of Politics*, 56, 4 (1994), pp. 1087–97, at p. 1094. Emphasis in original.

89. Ibid. p. 1095.

90. Wiktorowicz, *Radical Islam Rising*, pp. 135–57.

91. Introvigne, 'Niches in the Islamic Religious Market and Fundamentalism', p. 10.

5. THE SUPPLY SIDE: FRAMING AND THE CONSTRUCTION OF THE CENTRE GROUND

1. Andrew Hindmoor, *New Labour at the Centre: Constructing Political Space*, Oxford: Oxford University Press, 2004, p. 127. Hindmoor's analysis of New Labour's electoral struggle is a pioneering work in its study of framing effects in the context of spatial analysis, and we draw on it extensively in this chapter.

2. Thomas E. Nelson and Zoe M. Oxley, 'Issue Framing Effects on Belief Importance and Opinion', *The Journal of Politics*, 61 (1999), pp. 1040–67, at p. 1061. For a review, see Dennis Chong and James N. Druckman, 'Framing Theory', *Annual Review of Political Science*, 10 (2007), pp. 103–26.

3. Gabriel A. Almond, R. Scott Appleby and Emmanuel Sivan, *Strong Religion: the Rise of Fundamentalisms Around the World*, London: University of Chicago Press, 2003, p. 125.

4. Andrew Sullivan, 'The Revolution Will Be Twittered', The Daily Dish, *The Atlantic*, 13 June 2009, http://www.theatlantic.com/daily-dish/archive/2009/06/the-revolution-will-be-twittered/200478/

5. Mark Pfeifle, 'A Nobel Peace Prize for Twitter?' *Christian Science Monitor*, 6 July 2009, http://www.csmonitor.com/Commentary/Opinion/2009/0706/p09s02-coop.html

6. Cf. Evgeny Morozov, *The Net Delusion: How Not to Liberate the World*, London: Allen Lane, 2011, pp. 1–31.

7. The frame also has a long history. As Morozov points out, *Newsweek* had been predicting the imminent fall of the Iranian Islamic regime under pressure from the Internet since 1995. Ibid. p. 18.

8. Nelson and Oxley, 'Issue Framing Effects on Belief Importance and Opinion', p. 1041. References omitted. See also Hindmoor, *New Labour at the Centre*, pp. 130–5.

9. William A. Gamson and Andre Modigliani, 'The Changing Culture of Affirmative Action', in Richard G. Braungart and Margaret M. Braungart (eds), *Research in Political Sociology*, vol. 3, Greenwich, CT: JAI Press, 1987, pp. 137–77, at p. 143. See also Hindmoor, *New Labour at the Centre*, p. 130; Nelson and Oxley, 'Issue Framing Effects on Belief Importance and Opinion', pp. 1041–1042.

10. Pierre Bourdieu, *Outline of a Theory of Practice*, Cambridge: Cambridge University Press, 1977, at p. 40.

11. Hindmoor, *New Labour at the Centre*, p. 129.

12. James N. Druckman 'On the Limits of Framing Effects: Who Can Frame?' *The Journal of Politics*, 63, 4 (2001), pp. 1041–66, at p. 1042.

13. Thomas E. Nelson, Rosalee A. Clawson and Zoe M. Oxley, 'Media Framing of a Civil Liberties Conflict and its Effect on Tolerance', *American Political Science Review*, 91 (1997), pp. 567–83.

14. Hindmoor, *New Labour at the Centre*, p. 133, Chong and Druckman, 'Framing Theory'.

15. The reader can try such tests at http://www.projectimplicit.org/index.html

16. Jonathan Haidt, *The Righteous Mind: Why Good People Are Divided by Politics and Religion*, London: Allen Lane, 2012, pp. 57–9.

17. Nelson and Oxley, 'Issue Framing Effects on Belief Importance and Opinion', p. 1042.

18. Nelson et al., 'Media Framing of a Civil Liberties Conflict and its Effect on Tolerance'. See also Hindmoor, *New Labour at the Centre*, pp. 133–4.

19. Nelson and Oxley, 'Issue Framing Effects on Belief Importance and Opinion', p. 1043.

20. Ibid. p. 1043. Emphasis in original.

21. See Hindmoor, *New Labour at the Centre*, Chapters Seven and Eight, and for the original model, Anthony Downs, *An Economic Theory of Democracy*, London: Prentice Hall, 1997.

22. Downs, *An Economic Theory of Democracy*, p. 115, as cited in Hindmoor, *New Labour at the Centre*, p. 136.

23. Hindmoor, *New Labour at the Centre*, p. 136.

24. Ibid. p. 138.

25. William Riker, *The Art of Political Manipulation*, London: Yale University Press, 1986.

26. For a comprehensive overview and analysis of the Palestinian case, see Luca Ricolfi, 'Palestinians, 1981–2003', in Diego Gambetta (ed.), *Making Sense of Suicide Missions*, Oxford: Oxford University Press, 2005, pp. 77–129. Details on levels of support can be found at pp. 108–10. We follow Ricolfi's analysis here.

27. See Beverley Milton-Edwards, 'Hamas: Victory with Ballots and Bullets', *Global Change, Peace, and Security*, 19, 3 (2007), pp. 301–16.

28. See Bader Araj, 'Harsh State Repression as a Cause of Suicide Bombing: The Case of the Palestinian–Israeli Conflict', *Studies in Conflict and Terrorism*, 31, 4 (2008), pp. 284–303.

29. Ricolfi, 'Palestinians, 1981–2003', p. 111.

30. Ibid. p. 115.

31. Stathis Kalyvas and Ignacio Sánchez-Cuenca, 'Killing Without Dying: The Absence of Suicide Missions', in Gambetta, *Making Sense of Suicide Missions*, pp. 209–32, at p. 228.

32. See Mohammed Hafez, 'Rationality, Culture, and Structure in the Making of Suicide Bombers: A Preliminary Theoretical Synthesis and Illustrative Case Study', *Studies in Conflict and Terrorism*, 29, 2 (2006), pp. 163–85; Mark Tessler and Michael D.H. Robbins, 'What Leads Some Ordinary Arab Men and Women to Approve of Terrorist Acts against the United States?' *Journal of Conflict Resolution*, 51, 2 (2007), pp. 305–28; Eran Zaidise, Daphna Canetti-Nisim and Ami Pedahzur, 'Politics of God or Politics of Man? The Role of Religion and Deprivation in Predicting Support for Violence in Israel', *Political Studies*, 55, 3 (2007), pp. 499–521; Mohammed M. Hafez, *Suicide Bombers in Iraq: The Strategy and Ideology of Martyrdom*, Washington, DC: United States Institute of Peace Press, 2007.

33. Fathali M. Moghaddam, *From the Terrorists' Point of View: What They Experience and Why They Come to Destroy*, Westport, CT: Praeger Security International, 2006, especially pp. 59–126.

34. Ricolfi, 'Palestinians, 1981–2003', p. 115.

35. Quintan Wiktorowicz, 'Framing Jihad: Intramovement Framing Contests and al-Qaeda's Struggle for Sacred Authority', *International Review of Social History*, 49 (2004), pp. 159–77.

36. Ibid. p. 162.

37. Ibid. p. 171.

38. Matthew Hindman, *The Myth of Digital Democracy*, Princeton: Princeton University Press, 2009, makes the case for the United States.

39. Mohammed el-Nawawy and Sahar Khamis, *Islam Dot Com: Contemporary Islamic Discourses in Cyberspace*, New York: Palgrave Macmillan, 2009.

40. Ibid. p. 169.

41. Hafez, *Suicide Bombers in Iraq*, p. 224.

42. Samuel P. Huntington, *The Clash of Civilizations and the Remaking of World Order*, London: Simon & Schuster, 1997, p. 29.

43. Dale F. Eickelman and James Piscatori, *Muslim Politics*, Princeton: Princeton University Press, 2004, p. 162.

44. Muzafer Sherif, 'Superordinate Goals in the Reduction of Intergroup Conflicts', *American Journal of Sociology*, 63 (1958), pp. 349–56.

45. Marc Lynch, 'Dialogue in an Age of Terror', in M.A. Muqtedar Khan (ed.), *Islamic Democratic Discourse: Theory, Debates, and Philosophical Perspectives*, Lanham, MD: Lexington Books, 2006, pp. 193–225, at p. 206.

46. Marc Lynch, 'Taking Arabs Seriously', *Foreign Affairs*, Sep./Oct. 2003.

47. Ibid.

48. Olivier Roy, *Globalized Islam: The Search for a New Ummah*, New York: Columbia University Press, 2004, p. 20.

49. Douglas J. Swanson, 'The Framing of Contemporary Christian Apostasy on the World Wide Web', *Journal of Media and Religion*, 3, 1 (2004), pp. 1–20.

50. Ibid. p. 15.

51. Albert Bandura, 'The Role of Selective Moral Disengagement in Terrorism and Counterterrorism', in Fathali M. Moghaddam and Anthony J. Marsella (eds), *Understanding Terrorism: Psychological Roots, Consequences and Interventions*, Washington, DC: American Psychological Association, 2004, pp. 121–50.

52. Gabriel Weimann, *Terror on the Internet: The New Arena, the New Challenges*, Washington, DC: United States Institute of Peace Press, 2006, pp. 54–61.

53. Kacy Capobres, 'Election 2012: President Obama, Twitter, Break Records', Fox News, 7 Nov. 2012, http://latino.foxnews.com/latino/news/2012/11/07/election-2012-president-obama-twitter-break-records/

54. Andrew Kirell, 'Bill Maher Rips Obama's Performance Via Twitter: "Looks Like He Does Need a Teleprompter"', Mediaite, 4 Oct. 2012, http://www.mediaite.com/tv/bill-maher-rips-obamas-performance-via-twitter-looks-like-he-does-need-a-teleprompter/

6. THE DEMAND SIDE: THE CLUB MODEL

1. See http://news.bbc.co.uk/1/hi/world/asia-pacific/641588.stm. The proper name of the 'Moonies' (so-called after its founder the Reverend Sun Myung Moon) is The Unification Church.

2. See H. Paul Douglas and Edmund deS Brunner, *The Protestant Church as a Social Institution*, New York: Harper and Bros, 1935, for an example of this. See also Rodney Stark and Roger Finke, *Acts of Faith: Explaining the Human Side of Religion*, Berkeley: University of California Press, 2000, p. 44 for a discussion of Douglas and Brunner.

3. See, for example, Stark and Finke, *Acts of Faith*, pp. 52–4; Elaine Howard Ecklund and Christopher P. Scheitle, 'Religion among Academic Scientists: Distinctions, Disciplines, and Demographics', *Social Problems*, 54, 2 (2007), pp. 289–307. Although science faculty exhibit a lower level of religious belief than the general population (around 50 per cent compared with over 80 per cent), the fact that almost half the science faculty population retain religious beliefs is significant. The type of religious view held by faculty is much more likely to be a moderate, liberal variant of their faith than among the general population.

4. In a recent Gallup Poll (June 2012), 46 per cent of Americans affirmed their acceptance of some kind of creationism or intelligent design. http://www.gallup.com/poll/155003/Hold-Creationist-View-Human-Origins.aspx

5. Roger Scruton, *The West and the Rest: Globalization and the Terrorist Threat*, London: Continuum, 2002, p. 43.

6. Eileen Barker, *The Making of a Moonie: Choice or Brainwashing*, Oxford: Blackwell, 1984.

7. For reasons of recruitment failure, see Laurence Iannaccone, 'The Market for Martyrs', *Interdisciplinary Journal for Research on Religion*, 2 (2006). Apparently, because of this extremely high defection rate, the Moonies introduced a revision to their membership structure to include lay members—essentially part-timers who did not have to give up their personal possessions and dedicate themselves totally to the group. For the dwindling hard core, this most likely diluted the benefits of membership and contributed to the demise of the cult.

8. On the cost–benefit decision-making of potential cult members see, in addition to Barker and Iannaccone, Rodney Stark, Laurence Iannaccone and Roger Finke, 'Rationality and the "Religious Mind"', *Economic Enquiry*, 36, 3 (2007), pp. 373–89.

9. Stark et al., 'Rationality and the Religious Mind', p. 12. See also Roger Finke and Rodney Stark, *The Churching of America 1776–2005: Winners and Losers in Our Religious Economy*, London: Rutgers University Press, 2006, p. 46; and Rodney Stark, 'The Basis of Mormon Success: A Theoretical Application', in J.T. Duke (ed.), *Latter Day Saint Social Life: Social Research on the LDS Church and its Members*, Provo, UT: Religious Studies Center, Brigham Young University, 1998, pp. 29–70.

10. Ronald Wintrobe, *Rational Extremism: The Political Economy of Radicalism*, Cambridge: Cambridge University Press, 2007; Eli Berman, *Radical,*

Religious, and Violent: The New Economics of Terrorism, London: MIT Press, 2009, pp. 95–116.

11. See John Lofland and Rodney Stark, 'Becoming a World-Saver: A Theory of Conversion to a Deviant Perspective', *American Sociological* Review, 30, 6 (1965), pp. 862–75; Willem Kox, Wim Meeus and Harm't Hart, 'Religious Conversion of Adolescents: Testing the Lofland and Hart Model of Religious Conversion', *Sociological Analysis*, 52, 3 (1991), pp. 227–40.

12. Iannaccone, 'The Market for Martyrs', p. 7.

13. Stephen Holmes, 'Al-Qaeda, September 11, 2001', in Diego Gambetta (ed.), *Making Sense of Suicide Missions*, Oxford: Oxford University Press, 2006, pp. 131–72, at pp. 132–3.

14. Ed Husain, *The Islamist: Why I Joined Radical Islam in Britain, What I Saw Inside, and Why I Left*, London: Penguin, 2007.

15. Ibid. pp. 156–8.

16. Berman, *Radical, Religious, and Violent*; Richard Cornes and Todd Sandler, *The Theory of Externalities, Public Goods and Club Goods*, New York: Cambridge University Press, 1986, and see n.7 of the Introduction for further references. Our exposition draws on these and other leading writers within the paradigm.

17. Finke and Stark, *The Churching of America*, p. 40.

18. Quintan Wiktorowicz, *Radical Islam Rising: Muslim Extremism in the West*, Oxford: Rowan & Littlefield, 2005, p. 57.

19. See Laurence R. Iannaccone, 'Why Strict Churches are Strong', *American Journal of Sociology*, 99, 5 (1994), pp. 1180–211, at p. 1183.

20. Ibid. p. 1188.

21. Bradley J. Ruffle and Richard Sosis, 'Does it Pay to Pray? Costly Ritual and Co-Operation', *The B.E. Journal of Economic Analysis and Policy*, 7, 1 (2003), pp. 1–37.

22. Berman, *Radical, Religious, and Violent*, pp. 85–8.

23. Stark and Finke, *The Churching of America*, p. 148.

24. See Laurence R. Iannaccone and Eli Berman, 'Religious Extremism: The Good, the Bad, and the Deadly', *Public Choice*, 128, 1 (2006), pp. 109–29, at pp. 116–17; Berman, *Radical, Religious, and Violent*, pp. 89–91.

25. See Stark and Finke, *The Churching of America*, pp. 14–50; Stark, 'The Basis of Mormon Success'; Berman, *Radical, Religious, and Violent*, pp. 81–8. Stark and Finke, *The Churching of America*, pp. 152–3 gives a fuller set of statistics on membership and commitment across a number of Christian sects and churches. For details applicable to Judaism and Islam, see Berman, *Radical, Religious, and Violent*, pp. 61–93, and Massimo Introvigne, 'Niches in the Islamic Religious Market and Fundamentalism: Examples from Turkey and Other Countries', *Interdisciplinary Journal of Research on Religion*, 1, 1 (2005).

26. This is a stronger and less plausible definition than the one we gave in Chapter Four, where the trustee claims that she will pursue the trustor's interests while subordinating her own where necessary (see Kieron O'Hara, 'A General Definition of Trust', University of Southampton, 2012, http://eprints.soton.ac.uk/341800/). Whether Hardin's definition is in dispute is not the point, however. At this stage, our aim is to show how close trust and coercion can seem to be.

27. Russell Hardin, *Trust*, Cambridge: Polity Press, p. 19, Hardin's emphasis.

28. F.A. Hayek, *The Constitution of Liberty*, London: Routledge & Kegan Paul, 1960, p. 133. Again it is not necessary for our purposes to endorse Hayek's definition here, only to accept that there are circumstances where coercion may look pretty much like this.

29. Laurence R. Iannaccone, 'Rational Choice: Framework for the Scientific Study of Religion', in Lawrence A. Young (ed.), *Rational Choice Theory and Religion: Summary and Assessment*, New York: Routledge, 1997, pp. 25–44, at p. 26.

30. Amartya Sen, 'Behaviour and the Concept of Preference', *Economica*, 40, 159 (1973), pp. 241–59, at p. 241.

31. Jon Elster, *Sour Grapes: Studies in the Subversion of Rationality*, Cambridge: Cambridge University Press, 1983.

32. Dean R. Hoge, Benton Johnson and Donald A. Luidens, 'Determinants of Church Involvement of Young Adults who Grew Up in Presbyterian Churches', *Journal for the Scientific Study of Religion*, 32 (1993), pp. 242–55; Bruce Hunsberger and L.B. Brown, 'Religious Socialization, Apostasy, and the Impact of Family Background', *Journal for the Scientific Study of Religion*, 23 (1984), pp. 239–51; Ecklund and Scheitle, 'Religion among Academic Scientists'.

33. About a third of Americans choose their church rather than inheriting it. Robert D. Putnam and David E. Campbell, *American Grace: How Religion Divides and Unites Us*, New York: Simon & Schuster, 2010, p. 148.

34. Darren E. Sherkat and John Wilson, 'Preferences, Constraints, and Choices in Religious Markets: An Examination of Religious Switching and Apostasy', *Social Forces*, 73, 3 (1995), pp. 993–1026, at p. 998.

35. Amartya Sen, 'Rational Fools: A Critique of the Behavioral Foundations of Economic Theory', *Philosophy and Public Affairs*, 6, 4 (1977), pp. 317–44, at p. 324.

36. Introvigne, 'Niches in the Islamic Religious Market and Fundamentalism'. Introvigne's labelling system is perhaps not quite intuitive. The 'liberal' niche might better be characterised as moderate, while moderate-conservatives sound quite conservative to us. However, the labels count for rather less than the clusters. See Introvigne's paper for more detail on where various Islamic sects fit into the framework.

37. Stark and Finke, *Acts of Faith*, p. 212.
38. Melanie Phillips, *Londonistan: How Britain Created a Terror State Within*, New York: Encounter Books, 2006.

7. THE DEMAND SIDE: THE MOTIVATIONS OF SUICIDE BOMBERS

1. Joseph Conrad, *The Secret Agent*, Cambridge: Cambridge University Press, 1990, p. 38.
2. We will make an analogous case for the crowded, but virtual, public space of the Internet in Part III.
3. Ulrich Beck, *World at Risk*, Cambridge: Polity Press, p. 155.
4. Bryan Caplan, 'Terrorism: The Relevance of the Rational Choice Model', *Public Choice*, 128 (2006), pp. 91–107, at p. 101.
5. Ibid. p. 101.
6. Ibid. p. 97.
7. Robert Nozick, 'The Characteristic Features of Extremism', in *Socratic Puzzles*, Cambridge, MA: Harvard University Press, 1997, pp. 296–9.
8. Brenda E. Brasher, *Give Me That Online Religion*, New Brunswick: Rutgers University Press, 2004, pp. 161–2.
9. See Hugh Barlow, *Dead For Good: Martyrdom and the Rise of the Suicide Bomber*, London: Paradigm, 2007, p. 186.
10. Ronald Wintrobe, *Rational Extremism: The Political Economy of Radicalism*, Cambridge: Cambridge University Press, 2006, p. 106.
11. Caplan, 'Terrorism', pp. 103–5.
12. Cf. Stathis Kalyvas and Ignacio Sánchez-Cuenca, 'Killing Without Dying: The Absence of Suicide Missions', in Diego Gambetta (ed.) *Making Sense of Suicide Missions*, Oxford: Oxford University Press, 2005, pp. 209–32.
13. Some imprisoned members of the IRA did, of course, embark on fatal hunger strikes as a form of protest. Dying without killing, and killing without dying (within certain confines such as aiming away from civilians) were acceptable means, but dying and killing together appeared to be taboo. One important factor was that the IRA needed to maintain support within Catholic communities in Northern Ireland. Al-Qaeda has often been indifferent to the suffering even of sympathetic members of the embedding community.
14. Kalyvas and Sánchez-Cuenca, 'Killing Without Dying', p. 220.
15. See Christof Reuter, *My Life is a Weapon: A Modern History of Suicide Bombing*, Princeton: Princeton University Press, 2004, pp. 79–114 for a fuller historical treatment of suicide missions in the Israeli–Palestinian conflict.
16. Robert A. Pape, 'The Strategic Logic of Suicide Terrorism', *American Political*

Science Review, 97, 3 (2003), pp. 343–61, at p. 343. Pape points out that 'The LTTE alone accounts for 75 of the 186 suicide terrorist attacks from 1980 to 2001. Even among Islamic suicide attacks, groups with secular orientations account for about a third of these attacks.' For a fuller historical account of the LTTE's suicide tactics, see Barlow, *Dead For Good*, pp. 133–46. For a rebuttal of Pape's thesis, see Stephen Hopgood, 'Tamil Tigers, 1987–2002', in Gambetta, *Making Sense of Suicide Missions*, pp. 43–76, at p. 45, which argues that the role of Marxist–Leninist ideology should not be exaggerated, and that there was a religious dimension to the struggle.

17. Gabriel A. Almond, R. Scott Appleby and Emmanuel Sivan, *Strong Religion: The Rise of Fundamentalisms Around the World*, London: University of Chicago Press, 2003, p. 3.

18. Roger Scruton, *The West and the Rest: Globalization and the Terrorist Threat*, London: Continuum, 2002, p. 39.

19. This has been a great source of inspiration for those fighting for freedom, including the powerful blues *If I Had My Way I Would Tear This Building Down*. Blind Willie Johnson was famously arrested by an over-zealous policeman for singing it while busking outside a Louisiana courtroom.

20. See Rodney Stark, *The Rise of Christianity: How the Obscure, Marginal Jesus Movement became the Dominant Religious Force in the Western World in a Few Centuries*, San Francisco: HarperSanFrancisco, 1997, pp. 179–84.

21. Quoted in Almond et al., *Strong Religion*, pp. 2–3.

22. With some support in the Koran and clearer statements in the Hadith.

23. Mohammed M. Hafez, *Suicide Bombers in Iraq: The Strategy and Ideology of Martyrdom*, Washington, DC: United States Institute of Peace, 2007, p. 129.

24. Barlow, *Dead For Good*, pp. 52–9.

25. Ibid. p. 53.

26. Ibid. pp. 64–7

27. *The Song of Roland*, trans. Glyn Burgess, London: Penguin, 1990, verse 89, 65.

28. Norman Cohn, *The Pursuit of the Millennium: Revolutionary Millenarians and Mystical Anarchists of the Middle Ages*, London: Secker & Warburg, 1957, pp. 61–2.

29. Scruton, *The West and the Rest*, pp. 120–3. See also Hafez, *Suicide Bombers in Iraq*, pp. 129–31 for examples of Koranic links to suicide and martyrdom.

30. Jon Elster, 'Motivations and Beliefs in Suicide Missions', in Gambetta, *Making Sense of Suicide Missions*, pp. 233–58, at p. 243, emphasis in original. See also Stark, *The Rise of Christianity*, pp. 179–80 for a discussion of whether the number of early Christian martyrs is as high as is often claimed.

31. Gaetano Mosca, *The Ruling Class*, New York: McGraw-Hill, 1939, pp. 181–

2, quoted in Bryan Caplan, *The Myth of the Rational Voter: Why Democracies Choose Bad Policies*, Oxford: Princeton University press, 2007, at p. 127.

32. Caplan, *The Myth of the Rational Voter*, p. 128. Emphasis in original.

33. Caplan, 'Terrorism', p. 100.

34. Caplan, *The Myth of the Rational Voter*, p. 128. Footnote omitted.

35. And see also Stephen Holmes, 'Al-Qaeda, September 11, 2001', in Gambetta, *Making Sense of Suicide Missions*, pp. 131–72.

36. V.G. Julie Rajan, *Women Suicide Bombers: Narratives of Violence*, Abingdon: Routledge, 2011. Rajan makes the point that while Western narratives of male suicide bombers tend to focus on the ideological reasons, they often assume that female bombers are motivated by personal reasons. *Women Suicide Bombers*, p. 78.

37. Hopgood, 'Tamil Tigers, 1987–2002', p. 45.

38. Kalyvas and Sánchez-Cuenca, 'Killing Without Dying', p. 226.

39. Olivier Roy, *Globalized Islam: The Search for a New Ummah*, New York: Columbia University Press, 2004, p. 43. See also Scruton, *The West and the Rest*, and John Gray, *Al Qaeda and What It Means to be Modern*, London: Faber & Faber, 2003.

40. Kalyvas and Sánchez-Cuenca, 'Killing Without Dying', p. 226.

41. Gray, *Al Qaeda and What It Means To Be Modern*.

42. Stark, *The Rise of Christianity*, pp. 176–88; and Rodney Stark, *The Triumph of Christianity: How the Jesus Movement became the World's Largest Religion*, New York: HarperOne, 2011, pp. 137–52.

43. Scruton, *The West and the Rest*, pp. 103–4.

44. Conrad, *The Secret Agent*, p. 57.

45. It can also occur because of strategic reasons, such as the fear of harsher reprisals by the enemy (see Kalyvas and Sánchez-Cuenca, 'Killing Without Dying', p. 219). However, in the case of Palestine, harsh reprisals by Israeli forces galvanised Palestinian resistance and pushed supporters closer to the radical position of Hamas. See also Reuter, *My Life is a Weapon*, pp. 79–114.

46. Kalyvas and Sánchez-Cuenca, 'Killing Without Dying', pp. 218–23.

47. Cerwyn Moore and Paul Tumelty, 'Foreign Fighters and the Case of Chechnya: A Critical Assessment', *Studies in Conflict and Terrorism*, 31, 5 (2008), pp. 412–33, at pp. 426–9.

48. Kalyvas and Sánchez-Cuenca, 'Killing Without Dying', p. 219.

49. Ibid. pp. 220–1.

50. 'The Politics of Fear', *The Economist*, 5 Apr. 2005.

51. Eli Berman and David Laitin, 'Hard Targets: Theory and Evidence on Suicide Attacks', NBER Working Paper Series, 2005, http://www.nber.org/papers/w11740.pdf

52. Eli Berman, *Radical, Religious, and Violent: The New Economics of Terrorism*, Cambridge, MA: MIT Press, 2009, especially Chapter Six.

53. Kalyvas and Sánchez-Cuenca, 'Killing Without Dying', p. 223.

54. Pape, 'The Strategic Logic of Suicide Terrorism', p. 344. See also Hafez, *Suicide Bombers in Iraq*, p. 121, for such an instrumental justification given in a speech by Abu Musab al-Zarqawi, the leader of al-Qaeda in Iraq.

55. Berman, *Radical, Religious, and Violent*, pp. 7–13; Ronald Horst, 'Does Theology Matter? A Theoretical Look at Religious Terrorists and their Organisations', ASREC Annual Meeting, 2010, http://horst.umd.edu/Conferences/Portland/HorstASREC2010.pdf

56. See, for instance, Laurence Iannaccone, 'A Formal Model of Church and Sect', *American Journal of Sociology*, 94 (1988), pp. 241–68; Laurence Iannaccone, 'Sacrifice and Stigma: Reducing Free-Riding in Cults, Communes, and Other Collectives', *Journal of Political Economy*, 100 (1992), pp. 271–92; Laurence Iannaccone, 'Why Strict Churches are Strong', *American Journal of Sociology*, 99 (1994), pp. 1180–211; Laurence Iannaccone, 'Risk, Rationality, and Religious Portfolios', *Economic Enquiry*, 33 (1995), pp. 285–95; Jerrold M. Post, 'Terrorist Psycho-Logic: Terrorist Behaviour as a Product of Psychological Forces', in Walter Reich (ed.), *Origins of Terrorism: Psychologies, Ideologies, Theologies, States of Mind*, Cambridge: Cambridge University Press, 1990, pp. 25–40.

57. See Wintrobe, *Rational Extremism*, p. 26. Solidarity is to be distinguished from (though it may overlap and operate in concert with) other aspects of social cohesion/interaction, including: social interdependencies (what I do depends on what others do); social capital or trust (what I do depends on the level of confidence I have in others doing their share); emotions (what I do depends upon how I feel about others).

58. For a discussion of honour, see Jon Elster, *Alchemies of the Mind: Rationality and the Emotions*, Cambridge: Cambridge University Press, 1999, pp. 203ff.

59. Caplan, 'Terrorism', p. 96, points out that compensation to family members does play a role in promoting suicide missions, but usually by making volunteers feel less guilty about the families they leave behind, rather than as a positive inducement.

60. Barlow, *Dead For Good*.

61. Berman, *Radical, Religious, and Violent*, p. 12.

62. Jon Cole and Benjamin Cole, *Martyrdom: Radicalisation and Terrorist Violence Amongst British Muslims*, London: Pennant, 2009, pp. 267–8.

63. Ibid. p. 268.

64. George Bernard Shaw, *The Devil's Disciple*, in his *Three Plays for Puritans: The Devil's Disciple, Caesar and Cleopatra, Captain Brassbound's Conversation*, London: Penguin, 1946. Though he might have added reality TV shows to the list, had he lived to see them.

65. Luca Ricolfi, 'Palestinians, 1981–2003', in Gambetta, *Making Sense of Suicide Missions*, pp. 77–129, at p. 113.

66. Ricolfi, 'Palestinians, 1981–2003', p. 114.
67. Stark, *The Rise of Christianity*, p. 188. Stark also stresses the way in which the Christian credo of equality in the eyes of God mitigated social divisions between rich and poor, and ensured that widows and orphans were cared for by the community.

8. THE LONG TAIL

1. Cf. e.g. 'Gateshead Celebrates Worlds [*sic*] First Online Shopper', Gateshead Council press release, 13 May 2009, http://www.gateshead.gov.uk/ Council%20and%20Democracy/news/News%20Articles/Gateshead%20 celebrates%20worlds%20first%20online%20shopper.aspx. The pioneering Mrs Snowball, surprisingly, was seventy-two years old at the time of her historic purchase.
2. Chris Anderson, *The Long Tail: How Endless Choice is Creating Unlimited Demand*, London: Random House, 2006.
3. Ibid. p. 53.
4. Nassim Nicholas Taleb, *The Black Swan: The Impact of the Highly Improbable*, London: Allen Lane, 2007.
5. Ibid. p. 11.
6. Cass Sunstein, *Republic.com 2.0*, Princeton: Princeton University Press, 2007, p. 213.
7. Ibid. p. 111.
8. Anderson, *The Long Tail*, p. 53. Paragraphs in italics are direct quotes from Anderson, emphases his. He capitalises 'long tail' throughout, and we have anglicised the spelling and corrected a grammatical error.
9. It is also worthy of note that the figures of Barrett et al. treat Catholicism as a monolith, rather than a denomination with many sub-denominations (unlike the treatment of Protestantism).
10. David B. Barrett, Todd M. Johnson and Peter F. Crossing, 'Analyzing the Megacensus of Religions 1900–2008', in Karen Sparks (ed.), *Encyclopaedia Britannica Book of the Year 2009*, Chicago: Encyclopaedia Britannica, 2009, pp. 302–3.
11. Source: Barrett et al., 'Analyzing the Megacensus of Religions 1900– 2008'.
12. I.e. followers of components of the complex of Chinese thought, including the yin/yang cosmology, ancestor worship, divination, household gods and local deities, shamans and elements of Taoism and Buddhism.
13. I.e. followers of local, tribal, animistic or shamanistic religions.
14. I.e. followers of Asian twentieth-century neo-religions, neo-religious movements, radical new crisis religions and non-Christian syncretic mass religions.

15. Non-Christian spiritualists, etc.

16. The average rate through the second half of the first decade of the twenty-first century. Figures in this paragraph also taken from Barrett et al.

17. See, for instance, George M. Marsden, *Understanding Fundamentalism and Evangelicalism*, Michigan: Eerdmans, 1991; Steve Bruce, *Fundamentalism*, Cambridge: Polity Press, 2008.

18. Lorne L. Dawson and Jenna Hennebry, 'New Religions and the Internet: Recruiting in a New Public Space', in Lorne L. Dawson and Douglas E. Cowan (eds), *Religion Online: Finding Faith on the Internet*, New York: Routledge, 2004, pp. 151–73, at p. 151.

19. http://forums.myspace.com/t/4637624.aspx?fuseaction=forums. viewthread, sadly defunct ever since forums were removed from MySpace, which may make Sean's proselytising task harder. Several dozen responses to the creed appeared in short order, featuring a relatively deep theological discussion about the merits or otherwise of virginity. At the time of writing, Sean's Sexastrian contribution to the Web is limited to a series of Yahoo! answers from 2009, such as https://answers.yahoo.com/question/index?qid= 20091007060045AA8mU9s

20. Elena Larsen, 'CyberFaith: How Americans Pursue Religion Online', in Dawson and Cowan, *Religion Online*, pp. 17–20.

21. Jane's Intelligence Review, 'Al-Qaeda Online: Understanding Jihadist Internet Infrastructure', 2 Dec. 2005, p. 5, http://www.mil.no/multimedia/archive/00075/Al-Qaeda_online__und_75416a.pdf

22. Joseph A. Schafer, 'Spinning the Web of Hate: Web-Based Hate Propagation by Extremist Organizations', *Journal of Criminal Justice and Popular Culture*, 9, 2 (2002), pp. 69–88.

23. Jane's Intelligence Review, 'Al-Qaeda Online', p. 6.

24. Indeed, one of the main limitations on terrorist groups is the probability of defection of its members. Those groups who are more 'successful' are the ones that manage to overcome the threat of defection. See Eli Berman, *Radical Religious and Violent: The New Economics of Terrorism*, Cambridge, MA: MIT Press, 2009, Chapter Two, for a discussion of the defection constraint.

25. Dawson and Hennebry, 'New Religions and the Internet', p. 153.

26. Ibid. p. 164.

27. Ibid. p. 161.

28. Peter R. Monge and Noshir S. Contractor, *Theories of Communication Networks*, Oxford: Oxford University Press, 2003, pp. 233–5.

29. Anthony Giddens, *Runaway World*, London: Profile Books, 2002.

30. Berman, *Radical, Religious, and Violent*, pp. 61–119.

31. Michael D. Makowsky, 'A Computational Model of Religious Extremism', 2007, http://mason.gmu.edu/~mmakowsk/ReligiousExtremism.pdf

32. Nicole B. Ellison and danah m. boyd, 'Sociality through Social Network Sites', in William H. Dutton (ed.), *The Oxford Handbook of Internet Studies*, Oxford: Oxford University Press, 2013, pp. 151–72.

33. See John Palfrey and Urs Gasser, *Born Digital: Understanding the First Generation of Digital Natives*, New York: Basic Books, 2008.

34. Anderson, *The Long Tail*, pp. 53–7.

35. For a partisan discussion of folksonomies, see Clay Shirky, 'Ontology is Overrated: Categories, Links and Tags', 2005, http://www.shirky.com/writings/ontology_overrated.html

36. Originally named by sociologist Robert K. Merton who noted that awards and citations go disproportionately to famous scientists. Robert K. Merton, 'The Matthew Effect in Science: The Reward and Communication Systems of Science are Considered', *Science*, 159, 3810 (5 Jan. 1968), pp. 56–63. It has nothing to do with Matthew Hindman, but nevertheless see Matthew Hindman, *The Myth of Digital Democracy*, Princeton: Princeton University Press, 2009, for an interesting discussion of how a small number of not very diverse bloggers dominate the political blogosphere in the United States.

9. ECHO CHAMBERS AND LONG TAILS: A CRITICAL EXAMINATION

1. Anita Elberse, 'Should You Invest in the Long Tail?' *Harvard Business Review* (July–Aug. 2008); Anita Elberse, *Blockbusters: Why Big Hits—and Big Risks—Are the Future of the Entertainment Business*, London: Faber & Faber, 2014.

2. R. Alexander Bentley, Mark E. Madsen and Paul Ormerod, 'Physical Space and Long-Tail Markets', *Physica A: Statistical Mechanics and its Applications*, 388, 5 (2009), pp. 691–6.

3. Telco 2.0, 'Exclusive Interview: The Long Tail Interrogated (Part 2)', 12 Nov. 2008, http://www.telco2.net/blog/2008/11/exclusive_interview_will_page.html

4. Matthew J. Salganik, Peter Sheridan Dodds and Duncan J. Watts, 'Experimental Study of Inequality and Unpredictability in an Artificial Cultural Market', *Science*, 311, 5762 (10 Feb. 2006), pp. 854–6.

5. Actually, seen in context, the notorious 'Dean scream' had at least an element of playing to the crowd and self-spoofing (the video can be found on YouTube, and his supporters can be heard laughing). American elections create a space in which no politician can ever take himself or herself less than seriously. A comment of Romney's in 2012 about why aeroplane windows do not open looked like a little off-the-cuff quip, but was taken as symptomatic of incredible ignorance about airline safety. It is of course possible that Dean is demented and Romney is a cretin, but perhaps a more likely hypoth-

esis is that clever people are unable to keep themselves buttoned up permanently.

6. Lexington, 'A Useful Piece of Scream Therapy', *The Economist*, 12 Feb. 2004.

7. David Weinberger, 'Is There an Echo in Here?' *Salon*, 20 Feb. 2004, http://www.salon.com/technology/feature/2004/02/20/echo_chamber/

8. Eszter Hargittai, Jason Gallo and Matthew Kane, 'Cross-Ideological Discussions among Conservative and Liberal Bloggers', *Public Choice*, 134 (2008), pp. 67–86, at 76–7.

9. Ibid. pp. 78–80.

10. Karen Mossberger, Caroline J. Tolbert and Ramona S. McNeal, *Digital Citizenship: The Internet, Society and Participation*, Cambridge, MA: MIT Press, 2008, pp. 67–93.

11. Hargittai et al., 'Cross-Ideological Discussions among Conservative and Liberal Bloggers', pp. 81–4.

12. In the printed version of the paper, this figure is incorrectly given as 36 per cent. Our thanks to the paper's authors for providing the correct figure.

13. Aaron Smith, 'The Internet and Campaign 2010', The Pew Internet and American Life Project, 17 Mar. 2011.

14. Nassim Nicholas Taleb, *The Black Swan: The Impact of the Highly Improbable*, London: Allen Lane, 2007.

15. Douglas Carswell, *The End of Politics: And the Birth of iDemocracy*, London: Biteback, 2012, pp. 158–9.

16. 'Google à la Française', *The Economist*, 31 Mar. 2005.

17. David Piff and Margit Warburg, 'Seeking for Truth: Plausibility Assignment on a Baha'i Email List', in Morten T. Højsgaard and Margit Warburg (eds), *Religion and Cyberspace*, Abingdon: Routledge, 2005, pp. 86–101. The site was eventually closed down by the group's elders. We do not wish to imply that this will always be the result of such an exercise, only that not every discussion between like-minded individuals turns into an echo chamber.

18. Massimo Introvigne, 'A Symbolic Universe: Information Terrorism and New Religions in Cyberspace', in Højsgaard and Warburg, *Religion and Cyberspace*, pp. 102–17, at p. 113.

19. E.g. Roger Scruton, *The West and the Rest: Globalization and the Terrorist Threat*, London: Continuum, 2002, Olivier Roy, *Globalized Islam: The Search for a New Ummah*, New York: Columbia University Press, 2004.

20. Peter Mandaville, *Transnational Muslim Politics: Reimagining the Umma*, Abingdon: Routledge, 2001.

21. Anthony Giddens, *A Contemporary Critique of Historical Materialism Volume 1: Power, Property and the State*, London: Macmillan, 1980, pp. 90–108, Manuel Castells, *The Information Age: Economy, Society and Culture Volume 1: The Rise of the Network Society*, 2nd edn, Malden, MA: Blackwell, 2000, pp. 460–99.

22. Mohammed el-Nawawy and Sahar Khamis, *Islam Dot Com: Contemporary Islamic Discourses in Cyberspace*, New York: Palgrave Macmillan, 2009, pp. 113–16.

23. Mandaville, *Transnational Muslim Politics*, p. 119.

24. El-Nawawy and Khamis, *Islam Dot Com*, pp. 119–20.

25. Cf. Barry Wellman and Caroline Haythornthwaite (eds), *The Internet in Everyday Life*, Malden, MA: Blackwell, 2002, Hua Wang and Barry Wellman, 'Social Connectivity in America: Changes in Adult Friendship Network Size from 2002 to 2007', *American Behavioral Scientist*, 53, 8 (2010), pp. 1148–69, and also see the Pew Internet and American Life project, http://pewinternet.org/

26. Lee Raimie and Barry Wellman, *Networked: the New Social Operating System*, Cambridge, MA: MIT Press, 2012.

27. Wang and Wellman, 'Social Connectivity in America'.

28. Tracy Kennedy and Barry Wellman, 'The Networked Household', *Information, Communication and Society*, 10, 5 (2007), pp. 647–70.

29. As shown in the Telus Canadians and Technology survey, with some of the results reported in Barry Wellman, Amanda Garofalo and Vanessa Garofalo, 'The Internet, Technology and Connectedness', *Transition* (Winter 2009), pp. 5–7.

30. Raimie and Wellman, *Networked*.

31. John B. Horrigan, 'Home Broadband Adoption 2006: Home Broadband Adoption is Going Mainstream and that Means User-Generated Content is Coming From All Kinds of Internet Users', Pew Internet and American Life Project, 2006, http://www.pewinternet.org/~/media//Files/Reports/2006/PIP_Broadband_trends2006.pdf.pdf, Mossberger et al., *Digital Citizenship*, pp. 123–37.

32. John Horrigan, Kelly Garrett and Paul Resnick, 'The Internet and Democratic Debate: Wired Americans Hear More Points of View About Candidates and Key Issues Than Other Citizens. They Are Not Using the Internet to Screen Out Ideas With Which They Disagree', Pew Internet and American Life Project, 2004, http://www.pewinternet.org/~/media//Files/Reports/2004/PIP_Political_Info_Report.pdf.pdf

33. Diana Mok, Barry Wellman and Juan-Antonio Carrasco, 'Does Distance Still Matter in Connected Lives? A Pre- and Post-Internet Comparison', *Urban Studies*, 47, 3 (2010), pp. 2747–84.

34. Robert D. Putnam and David E. Campbell, *American Grace: How Religion Divides and Unites Us*, New York: Simon & Schuster, 2010, p. 436.

35. Ibid. p. 441.

36. Peter R. Monge and Noshir S. Contractor, *Theories of Communication Networks*, New York: Oxford University Press, 2003, pp. 21–5.

37. In this context, it is interesting to find that religious Americans are very

much more likely to volunteer for, and to give money to, good causes both religious and secular, to do community work and to take part in community politics. Putnam and Campbell, *American Grace*, pp. 444–58. However, they are also joiners—they are more likely to be members of several groups than secular Americans, on Putnam and Campbell's figures. Hence it is also prudent to note that they are relatively less likely to be 'captured' by a particular organisation or narrow radical religious creed.

38. Norbert L. Kerr, 'Efficacy as a Causal and Moderating Variable in Social Dilemmas', in Wim Liebrand, David Messick and Henk Wilke (eds), *Social Dilemmas: Theoretical Issues and Research Findings*, Oxford: Pergamon Press, 1992, pp. 59–80.

39. Cf. Gerald Marwell and Pamela Oliver, *The Critical Mass in Collective Action: A Micro-Social Theory*, Cambridge: Cambridge University Press, 1993.

40. Although this is not a work in which we wish to use technical, quantitative or abstract methods to describe and address social phenomena, the idea of a 'clique' actually does have a technical meaning. In graph theory and social network theory, a clique is a sub-network of a network in which every node is connected by an edge to every other node, as defined by R. Duncan Luce and Albert D. Perry, 'A Method of Matrix Analysis of Group Structure', *Psychometrika*, 14 (1949), pp. 95–116. The broader, intuitive meaning which we wish to use is a subgroup of a wider group which is very interconnected, in that everyone in the subgroup knows everyone, or virtually everyone else in the subgroup.

41. John R. Schermerhorn Jr, 'Information Sharing as an Interorganizational Activity', *Academy of Management Journal*, 20 (1977), pp. 148–53, Joseph Galaskiewicz, *Exchange Networks and Community Politics*, Newbury Park, CA: Sage, 1979, Robert D. McPhee and Steven R. Corman, 'An Activity-Based Theory of Communication Networks in Organizations, Applied to the Case of a Local Church', *Communications Monographs*, 62 (1995), pp. 132–51.

42. Matthew Day, 'German Quits "Unhygienic, Drug-Using" Taliban', *Daily Telegraph*, 2 Nov. 2012.

43. El-Nawawy and Khamis, *Islam Dot Com*, p. 122.

44. Monge and Contractor, *Theories of Communication Networks*, pp. 231–3, Ronald E. Rice, 'Network Analysis and Computer-Mediated Communications Systems', in Stanley Wasserman and Joseph Galaskiewicz (eds), *Advances in Social Network Analysis: Research in the Social and Behavioral Sciences*, Thousand Oaks, CA: Sage, 1994, pp. 167–206, Siobhan O'Mahony and Stephen R. Barley, 'Do Digital Telecommunications Affect Work and Organization? The State of Our Knowledge', in Robert I. Sutton and Barry M. Staw (eds), *Research in Organizational Behavior Vol. 21*, Stamford, CT: JAI Press, 1999, pp. 125–62.

45. Claude S. Fischer, *America Calling: A Social History of the Telephone to 1940*, Berkeley: University of California Press, 1992.

46. Majid Tehranian, *Technologies of Power: Information Machines and Democratic Prospects*, Norwood, NJ: Ablex, 1990.

47. Monge and Contractor, *Theories of Communication Networks*, pp. 173–86.

48. David Krackhardt and Daniel J. Brass, 'Intraorganizational Networks: The Micro Side', in Wasserman and Galaskiewicz, *Advances in Social Network Analysis*, pp. 207–29, at p. 219.

49. Mark Granovetter, 'Threshold Models of Diffusion and Collective Behavior', *Journal of Mathematical Sociology*, 9 (1978), pp. 165–79.

50. Kenneth D. Wald, Dennis E. Owen and Samuel S. Hill, 'Churches as Political Communities', *American Political Science Review*, 82 (1988), pp. 531–48.

51. Putnam and Campbell, *American Grace*, p. 439.

52. Monge and Contractor, *Theories of Communication Networks*, pp. 184–5.

10. THE HARDEST THING

1. John Horgan and Max Taylor, 'Disengagement, De-Radicalisation and the Arc of Terrorism: Future Directions for Research', in Rik Coolsaet (ed.), *Jihadi Terrorism and the Radicalisation Challenge: European and American Experiences*, 2nd edn, Farnham: Ashgate Publishing, 2011, pp. 173–86.

2. David C. Rapoport, 'The Four Waves of Modern Terrorism', in Audrey Kurth Cronin and James M. Ludes (eds), *Attacking Terrorism: Elements of a Grand Strategy*, Washington, DC: Georgetown University Press, 2004, pp. 46–73.

3. Indeed, as one example, the UK's absurdly drafted libel laws prior to the Defamation Act 2013 allowed people to be sued for alleged libels committed in other countries (so-called 'libel tourism'). In 2004, a Saudi billionaire, accused by an Israeli-American writer of funding terrorism, sued in the UK, despite the fact that only twenty-three copies of her book had been sold from UK websites. Excerpts from the book were available online, but only on the ABC news website in the United States. The judge, who found for the billionaire, was unable to determine how many hits the ABC website received from the UK, but decided it was probably a large number.

4. John G. Wirtz, Prisca S. Ngondo and Philip Poe, 'Talking *With* Us or *At* Us: How U.S. Religious Denominations use Organizational Web Sites to Communicate with their Constituents', *Journal of Media and Religion*, 12 (2013), pp. 165–80. Justin Farrell, 'The Divine Online: Civic Organizing, Identity Building, and Internet Fluency among Different Religious Groups', *Journal of Media and Religion*, 10, 2 (2011), pp. 73–90 argues that more established churches with older members cleave to the brochure model, while evangelical churches encourage interaction.

5. Pauline Hope Cheong, Jessie P.H. Poon, Shirlena Huang and Irene Casas,

'The Internet Highway and Religious Communities: Mapping and Contesting Spaces in Religion-Online', *The Information Society*, 25 (2009), pp. 291–302.

6. Mohammed el-Nawawy and Sahar Khamis, *Islam Dot Com: Contemporary Islamic Discourses in Cyberspace*, New York: Palgrave Macmillan, 2009, p. 214.

7. Ibid.

8. Steven Knowles, '*Rapture Ready* and the World Wide Web: Religious Authority on the Internet', *Journal of Media and Religion*, 12 (2013), pp. 128–43, gives an example of a restrictive religious website.

9. El-Nawawy and Khamis, *Islam Dot Com*, p. 215.

10. Jay G. Blumler and Stephen Coleman, *Realising Democracy Online: A Civic Commons in Cyberspace*, London: Institute of Public Policy Research, 2001. Their aim, it is fair to point out, is not to integrate extremists into mainstream politics, but to reinvigorate Britain's moribund political life. But it is not unreasonable to consider their proposal in the light of our own concerns, given that the phenomena of moribund politics and extremism are often linked by commentators, such as Anthony Painter, *Democratic Stress, the Populist Signal and Extremist Threat: A Call For a New Mainstream Statecraft and Contact Democracy*, London: Policy Network, 2013.

11. Stephen Coleman and Jay G. Blumler, *The Internet and Democratic Citizenship: Theory, Practice and Policy*, Cambridge: Cambridge University Press, 2009, pp. 166–97.

12. Ibid. p. 179.

13. Ibid. p. 188.

14. Jürgen Habermas, *The Structural Transformation of the Public Sphere*, trans. Thomas Burger and Frederick Lawrence, Cambridge: Polity Press, 1989.

15. Timo Wandhöfer, Steve Taylor, Harith Alani, Somya Joshi, Sergej Sizov, Paul Walland, Mark Thamm, Arnim Bleier and Peter Mutschke, 'Engaging Politicians with Citizens on Social Networking Sites: The WeGov Toolbox', *International Journal of Electronic Government Research*, 8, 3 (2012), pp. 22–43.

16. Nicholas Evangelopoulos and Lucian Visinescu, 'Text-Mining the Voice of the People', *Communications of the ACM*, 55, 2 (Feb. 2012), pp. 62–9.

17. Kieron O'Hara, 'Social Machine Politics are Here to Stay', *IEEE Internet Computing*, 17, 2 (2013), pp. 87–90.

18. As a typical example of how a racist Facebook group simply disappears under scrutiny, see the fate of a page called Aboriginal Memes in 2012. Cf. e.g. Andrew Colley, 'Racist Page Denigrating Aborigines Disappears Overnight', *The Australian*, 9 Aug. 2012, Paul Wallis, '"Aboriginal Memes" FB Racist Content Gone, but Page Still Exists', Digital Journal, 9 Aug. 2012, http://digitaljournal.com/article/330418

19. For a discussion of the dialectic between freedom, engagement and suppression, see Erik Bleich, *The Freedom to be Racist? How the United States and Europe Struggle to Preserve Freedom and Combat Racism*, New York: Oxford University Press, 2011.

20. Cf. Peter R. Monge and Noshir S. Contractor, *Theories of Communication Networks*, New York: Oxford University Press, 2003, pp. 185–6.

21. http://www.committeeonthepresentdanger.org/

22. Mark Palmer, *Breaking the Real Axis of Evil: How to Oust the World's Last Dictators by 2025*, Lanham, MD: Rowman & Littlefield, 2003, p. 78.

23. Evgeny Morozov, *The Net Delusion: How Not to Liberate the World*, London: Allen Lane, 2011.

24. Since Morozov wrote his book, one of his main exhibits, Ukraine, underwent a grass-roots revolution, leading to the toppling of the pro-Russian leader and a serious international crisis. This undercut his argument to some extent, although at the time of writing the academic analysis of the use of the Internet to foment the revolution has still to be performed.

25. Bryan Caplan, 'Terrorism: The Relevance of the Rational Choice Model', *Public Choice*, 128 (2006), pp. 91–107, at p. 103.

26. Monge and Contractor, *Theories of Communication Networks*, p. 185.

27. Kieron O'Hara, *Conservatism*, London: Reaktion Books, 2011, pp. 201–5.

28. William J. McGuire, 'Attitudes and Opinions', *Annual Review of Psychology*, 17 (1966), pp. 475–514.

29. Morozov, *The Net Delusion*.

30. Spencer Ackerman, 'Newest US Counterterrorism Strategy: Trolling', *Wired*, 18 June 2012, http://www.wired.com/dangerroom/2012/07/counterterrorism-trolls/all/

31. El-Nawawy and Khamis, *Islam Dot Com*, p. 213.

32. Quoted in O'Hara, 'Social Machine Politics are Here to Stay', p. 88.

33. Olivier Roy, *Globalized Islam: The Search for a New Ummah*, New York: Columbia University Press, 2004, p. 27.

34. Compare Putnam and Campbell on religious 'churn' in their study of the United States. Robert D. Putnam and David E. Campbell, *American Grace: How Religion Divides and Unites Us*, New York: Simon & Schuster, 2010, pp. 134–60.

35. Roy, *Globalized Islam*, p. 29.

36. For a survey of recent studies of influence, see Kieron O'Hara, Noshir S. Contractor, Wendy Hall, James A. Hendler and Nigel Shadbolt, 'Web Science: Understanding the Emergence of Macro-Level Features on the World Wide Web', *Foundations and Trends in Web Science*, 4, 2/3 (2013), pp. 103–267, at pp. 162–91.

37. Roy, *Globalized Islam*, pp. 197–200.

38. e.g. Robert M. Bond, Christopher J. Farris, Jason J. Jones, Adam D.I. Kramer,

Cameron Marlow, Jaime E. Settle and James H. Fowler, 'A 61-Million-Person Experiment in Social Influence and Political Mobilization', *Nature*, 489 (13 Sep. 2012), pp. 295–8.

39. Marc Lynch, 'Engaging the Muslim World beyond al Qaeda', 2011, http://www.marclynch.com/wp-content/uploads/2011/04/Ruger09_Lynch.pdf

40. Morozov, *The Net Delusion*, p. 25.

41. By 2011, the US's ratings across the Arab world were lower than they were in the last year of the Bush administration. 'Arab Attitudes: 2011', Arab American Institute, 2011, http://www.aaiusa.org/reports/arab-attitudes-2011

42. A poll of Egyptians in 2013 produced a remarkable confidence rating in President Obama of 3 per cent (96 per cent not confident), and in the United States 1 per cent (98 per cent not confident). 'Egyptian Attitudes in the Post-Tamarrud, Post-Morsi Era', Arab American Institute, 2013, http://www.aaiusa.org/reports/egyptian-attitudes-in-the-post-tamarrud-post-morsi-era

43. Robert Lambert, 'Competing Counter-Radicalisation Models in the UK', in Coolsaet, *Jihadi Terrorism and the Radicalisation Challenge*, pp. 215–25.

44. Eli Berman and David D. Laitin, 'Religion, Terrorism and Public Goods: Testing the Club Model', *Journal of Public Economics*, 92 (2008), pp. 1942–67.

45. Michael D. Makowsky, 'Emergent Extremism in a Multi-Agent Model of Religious Clubs', *Economic Inquiry*, 50, 2 (2012), pp. 327–47.

46. Laurence R. Iannaccone and Eli Berman, 'Religious Extremism: The Good, the Bad and the Deadly', *Public Choice* 128, 1/2 (2006), pp. 109–29.

47. Clark McCauley, 'Group Desistance from Terrorism', in Coolsaet, *Jihadi Terrorism and the Radicalisation Challenge*, pp. 187–203, at p. 203.

48. 'Mind Your Language', *The Economist*, 15 June 2006.

49. Alan B. Krueger, *What Makes a Terrorist: Economics and the Roots of Terrorism*, Princeton: Princeton University Press, 2007.

50. Carole Cadwalladr, 'Charlotte Laws' Fight with the Internet's Revenge Porn King', *The Observer*, 30 Mar. 2014.

51. Maura Conway, 'Terrorism and Internet Governance: Core Issues', *Disarmament Forum 2007*, 3 (2007), pp. 23–34.

52. David Cameron in Hansard, 11 Aug. 2011, col. 1053, http://www.publications.parliament.uk/pa/cm201011/cmhansrd/cm110811/debtext/110811–0001.htm

53. Tim Shipman, 'Unmask the Thugs! Looters will no Longer be Able to Cover up, Says PM as he also Promises Cash for the Rioters' Victims AND a Crackdown on Social Media', *Daily Mail*, 12 Aug. 2011. Or bad headlines. Josh Halliday and Juliette Garside, 'Rioting Leads to Cameron Call for Social Media Clampdown', *Guardian*, 11 Aug. 2011.

54. 'From Weibo to WeChat', *The Economist*, 18 Jan. 2014.

55. 'Court in Turkey Moves to Suspend Ban on Twitter', BBC, 26 Mar. 2014, http://www.bbc.co.uk/news/technology-26749374

56. Conway, 'Terrorism and Internet Governance'.

57. Majid Yar, *Cybercrime and Society*, 2nd edn, London: Sage, 2013, p. 164.

58. As an example, see Daniel Foster, 'Why Vince Cable is Wrong about Content Policing', Huffington Post, 13 June 2013, http://www.huffington-post.co.uk/daniel-foster/vince-cable-wrong-content-policing_b_3435081.html

59. It should also be pointed out that there has been research focusing surveillance efforts specifically on extremist sites and forums. Of course, this is not guaranteed to find everything, and much depends on how effectively extremist forums are identified in the first place. See for instance Yilu Zhou, Jialun Qin, Guanpi Lai and Hsinchun Chen, 'Collection of U.S. Extremist Online Forums: A Web Mining Approach', in *Proceedings of the 40th Hawaii International Conference on System Sciences*, and for work on the use of social media, see for instance Joseph A. Carter, Shiraz Maher and Peter R. Neumann, *#Greenbirds: Measuring Importance and Influence in Syrian Foreign Fighter Networks*, London: International Centre for the Study of Radicalisation and Political Violence, 2014. It remains to be shown that the total surveillance of the intelligence services adds any value to these more targeted efforts, and even if that is demonstrated, it would still have to be shown that the added value makes up for the dramatic loss of confidence that total surveillance has caused. Clarke et. al., *The NSA Report: Liberty and Security in a Changing World*, argues that 'there is no instance in which NSA could say with confidence that the outcome would have been different without the section 215 [bulk] telephony metadata program', p. 71, n. 119.

60. Jemima Kiss, 'An Online Magna Carta: Berners-Lee Calls for Bill of Rights for the Web', *Guardian*, 12 Mar. 2014. See also https://webwewant.org/

61. 'The Net Closes', *The Economist*, 29 Mar. 2014.

62. Bruce Schneier, 'Intelligence Analysis and the Connect-the-Dots Metaphor', Schneier on Security blog, 7 May 2013, https://www.schneier.com/blog/archives/2013/05/intelligence_an.html

63. Tim Jonze, 'Mo Farah: "I Could Walk around Naked and Nobody would Recognise Me"', *The Guardian*, 16 Oct. 2013.

64. David Knowles, 'Olympic Gold Medalist Mo Farah Mistaken for a Potential Terrorist by U.S. Customs Agents in Portland, Ore.', *New York Daily News*, 31 Dec. 2012.

65. David Lyon, *Surveillance After September 11*, Cambridge: Policy Press, 2003; Mireille Hildebrandt, 'The Dawn of a Critical Transparency Right for the Profiling Era', in Jacques Bus, Malcolm Crompton, Mireille Hildebrandt and George Metakides (eds), *The Digital Enlightenment Yearbook 2012*, Amsterdam: IOS Press, 2012, pp. 41–56.

66. Nick Britten, 'eBay Bans Sale of Dad's Army Board Game for Promoting "Hatred and Racial Intolerance"', *Daily Telegraph*, 28 Jan. 2010.

67. Robert Mankoff, 'Nipplegate', *New Yorker Online*, 10 Sep. 2012, http://www.newyorker.com/online/blogs/cartoonists/2012/09/nipplegate-why-the-new-yorker-cartoon-department-is-about-to-be-banned-from-facebook.html

68. http://www.internet.gov.sa/resources/block-unblock-request/view?set_language=en. The Internet Services Unit, the organisation which previously had responsibility for censoring the Web, claimed to receive 'hundreds of requests per day from concerned citizens for the blocking of new objectionable sites'. Its Frequently Asked Questions can still be read at the time of writing, at http://www.isu.net.sa/saudi-internet/contenet-filtring/filtring.htm (the spelling mistakes are in the URI); bizarrely it cites both Cass Sunstein and the Qur'an in the same section. For some quantification of crowdsourced censorship from 2004, see the OpenNet Initiative's report on 'Internet Filtering in Saudi Arabia', http://opennet.net/studies/saudi

69. 'Caught in the Net', *The Economist*, 23 Jan. 2003.

INDEX

INDEX

INDEX